IMAGES
of America

ROCHESTER
LABOR AND LEISURE

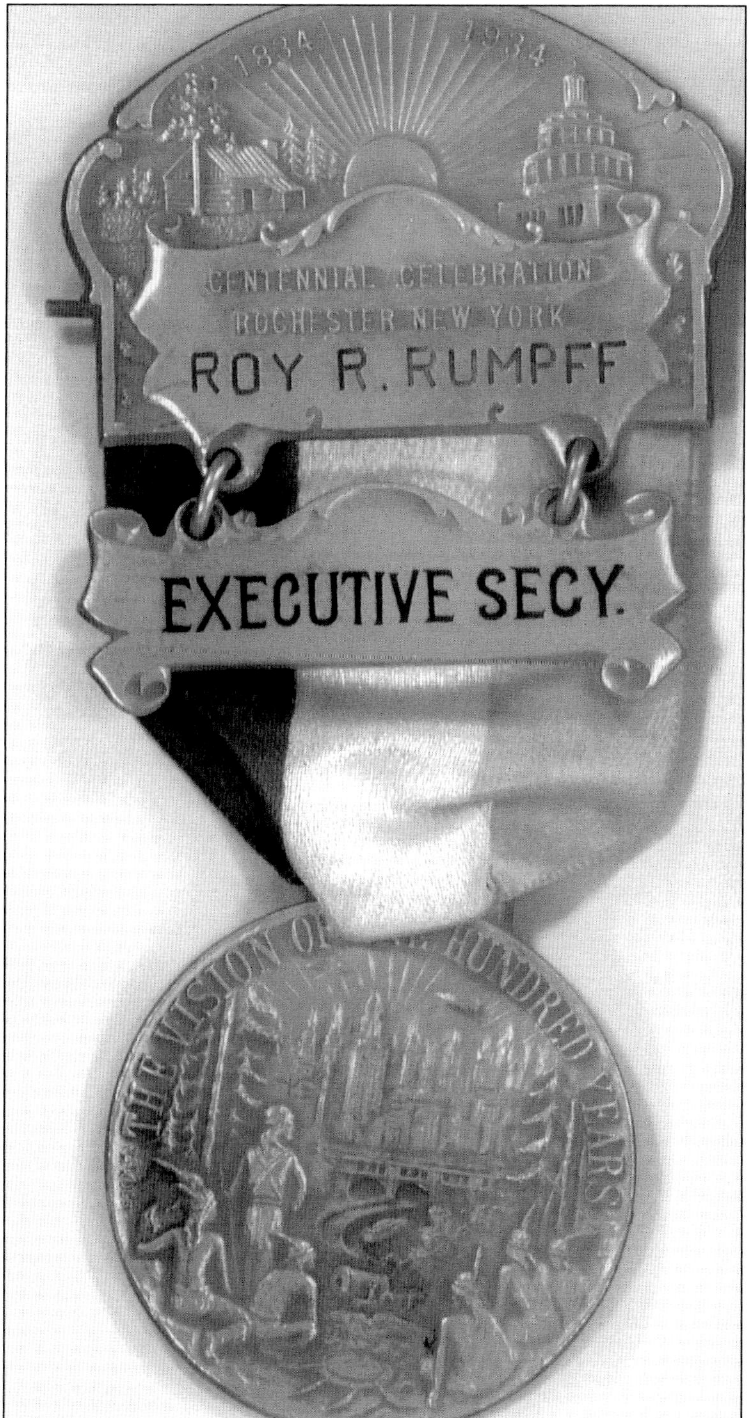

Among the rarest artifacts of Rochester's centennial celebration are the showy badges worn by the members of the executive committee. This closeup shows the elaborate work done by the Bastian Brothers, the Rochester firm that produced the badge and medal.

IMAGES
of America

ROCHESTER
LABOR AND LEISURE

Donovan A. Shilling

ARCADIA
PUBLISHING

ISBN 978-0-7385-1042-4

Published by Arcadia Publishing
Charleston, South Carolina

Printed in the United States of America

Library of Congress Catalog Card Number: 2002103802

For all general information contact Arcadia Publishing at:
Telephone 843-853-2070
Fax 843-853-0044
E-mail sales@arcadiapublishing.com
For customer service and orders:
Toll-Free 1-888-313-2665

Visit us on the Internet at www.arcadiapublishing.com

Acknowledgments

Among those who deserve credit for their much appreciated assistance in helping me with the book are Jim Faesel; Ann Salter of the Rochester Historical Society; Gerry Muhl, for his patient examination of the photographs; the staff of the Rochester Public Library History Division; George Brown, for his photographs; and my wife, Yolanda Shilling, for providing the support and patience needed in helping me to complete the volume.

—Donovan A. Shilling

Contents

Acknowledgments		4
Introduction		7
1.	Only Yesterday	9
2.	"Rochester-Made Means Quality"	31
3.	Industries on the Genesee	51
4.	Exposition Park	69
5.	Edgerton Park	79
6.	Night Life in the Gay 1890s	95
7.	Downtown's Entertainment Centers	105
8.	Pride in Rochester's Past	121

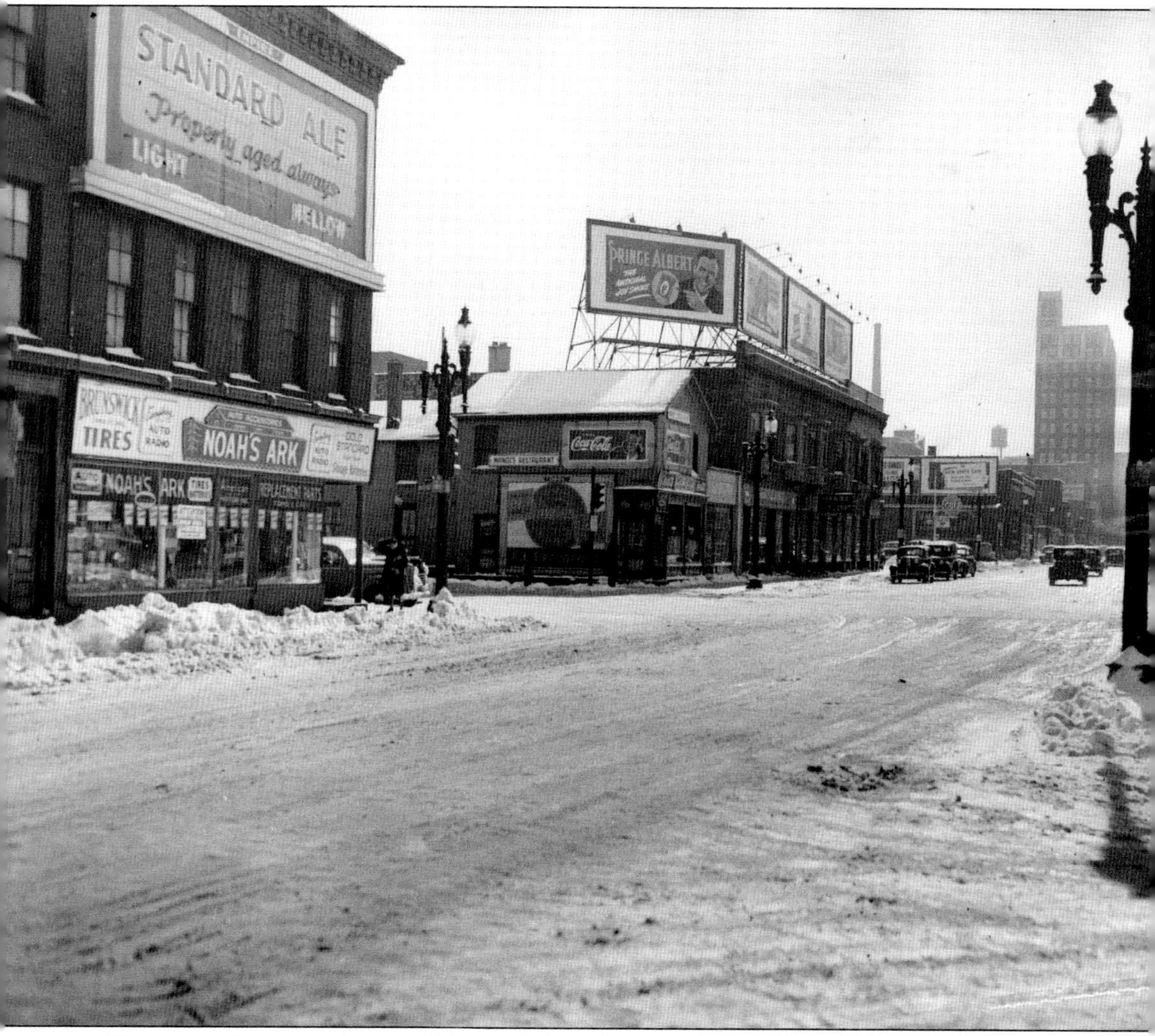

The snows of a wintry day in 1934 are piled up along the curbs of North Street at the corner of Cumberland Street, on the right. So deep was the economic depression years of 1932 to 1935 that the city of Rochester turned off a third of its streetlights—6,000 out of 18,000 remained unlit. The street lamps seen up and down North Street were part of that effort to conserve the city's resources. University Avenue intersects with North Street, on the left, just beyond the Noah's Ark emporium.

INTRODUCTION

Rochester: Labor and Leisure is a unique opportunity to see the city through a visual time capsule. Revealed in these pages are street scenes, homes, school and church groups, bygone entertainment centers, hot night spots, the old playhouses, and vaudeville and burlesque theaters that abounded in Rochester. Here, too, are photographs of the musicians, actors, and actresses that brightened Rochester's lively nightlife.

Remember Front Street? It was a mecca for both the less fortunate and the many who frequented its lively meat, poultry, and clothing shops. It was a hangout and eating place for the denizens of the third estate for the nearby news offices. It bred characters like showman Rattlesnake Pete as well as compassionate souls like Albert F. Hines, who started the People's Rescue Mission.

The development of Rochester's Exposition Park is also recorded in a series of unusual mementos, clippings, and photographs. They depict its early start as the venerable Western House of Refuge. Its grounds were later converted into the site for the public library, a museum, a concert band pavilion, and an expansive exhibition center. Also featured is Hiram H. Edgerton, the popular visionary who served as mayor for more than 14 years.

One cannot document the outstanding moments of the city's leisure days without mentioning the 1934 Rochester Centennial Exhibition. For thousands of locals, the spectacular exhibition was a benchmark in local pride and showmanship. It was the place to go during the summer of 1934. A huge historical pageant, Pathways of Progress, was presented. A record attendance was set during the elaborate 30-day affair.

Of course, it was mostly labor not leisure that many Rochesterians remember. A visual record has been assembled of rarely seen photographs to bring back the lives and labors of the men and women who worked in the massive flour mills, the steaming foundries, the great optical and photographic firms, the button works, and Rochester's nationally noted garment and shoe factories. It was the superior labor by so many that went into Rochester products that earned the city its slogan, "Rochester-made means quality."

It was along the banks of the mighty Genesee River that so many industries flourished. The great entrepreneurs included millionaire Hiram Bond Everest, the harness-oil tycoon and lubricating-oil baron; William Smith Kimball, who ran the nation's largest cigarette factory; H.H. Warner, who created a brown bottle empire with his patent medicines; William Bausch and Henry Lomb of optical fame; and George Eastman, who founded the city's outstanding industry, employing thousands.

Finally, there are the city's proud civic projects, such as the remarkable Erie Canal Aqueduct over the Genesee River and the transformation of that famous water bridge to a subway route and, finally, to an automobile expressway. The statue of Mercury that dominates the city skyline is another famous landmark featured in a series of rare photographs. Do enjoy Rochester's historical legacy from the horse-and-trolley days to the near present. All of this is woven into a chapter-by-chapter look at Rochester's labor and leisure.

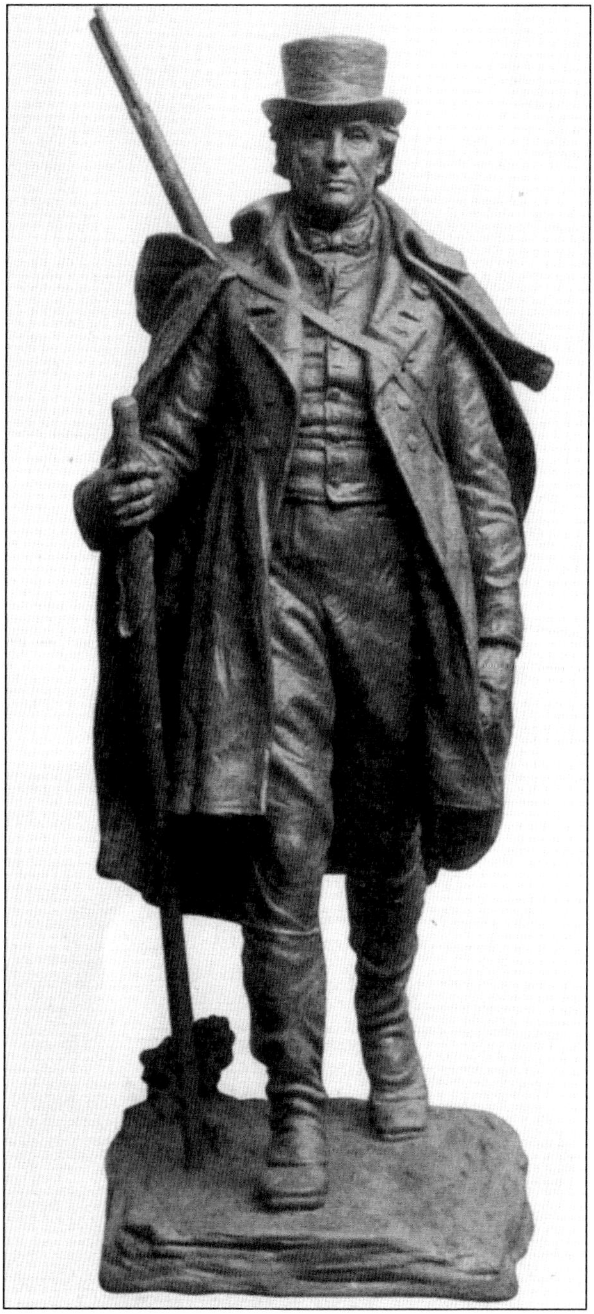

Rare is the city that has no statue of its founder. In 1934, when Rochester celebrated its 100th birthday, many citizens were in favor of a statue in tribute to Col. Nathaniel Rochester. Bryant Baker, a noted artist, designed this model. Colonel Rochester is sculpted as he appeared at age 48 on his first trek to Genesee Country in 1800. The plan was to erect a nine-foot bronze statue atop a seven-foot granite base. A joint committee of the Society of the Genesee and the Rochester Historical Society was to determine an appropriate site for the statue. Unfortunately, the Great Depression drained the resources for such an undertaking. Perhaps the fair city itself is honor enough for the founder.

One

ONLY YESTERDAY

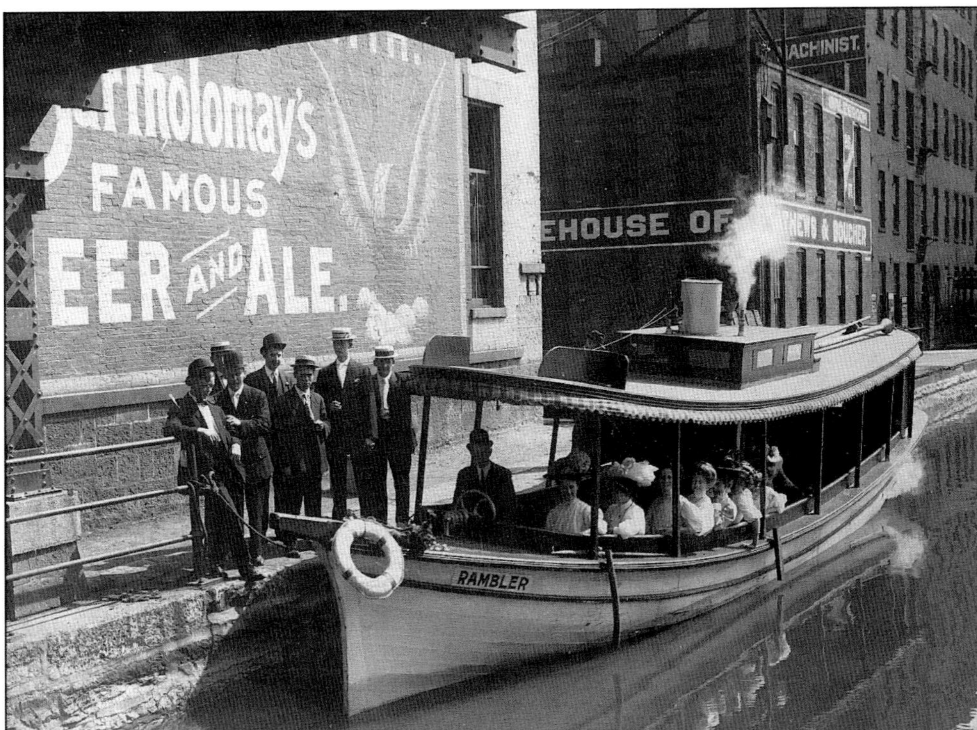

This nostalgic photograph harkens back to 1908, when the good ship *Rambler* navigated through downtown Rochester on the Erie Canal. It berthed just beyond the Mathews & Boucher warehouse (hardware and house furnishings) where the canal passed under Exchange Street. Aboard the vessel, in the front seats, are Janie and Robert Zimmerli. Robert was the brother of Charles Zimmerli, owner of the Zimmerli Business Furniture Company on South Avenue. Floyd L. Crellin provided this photograph, which identifies his mother-in-law and father-in-law aboard the vessel.

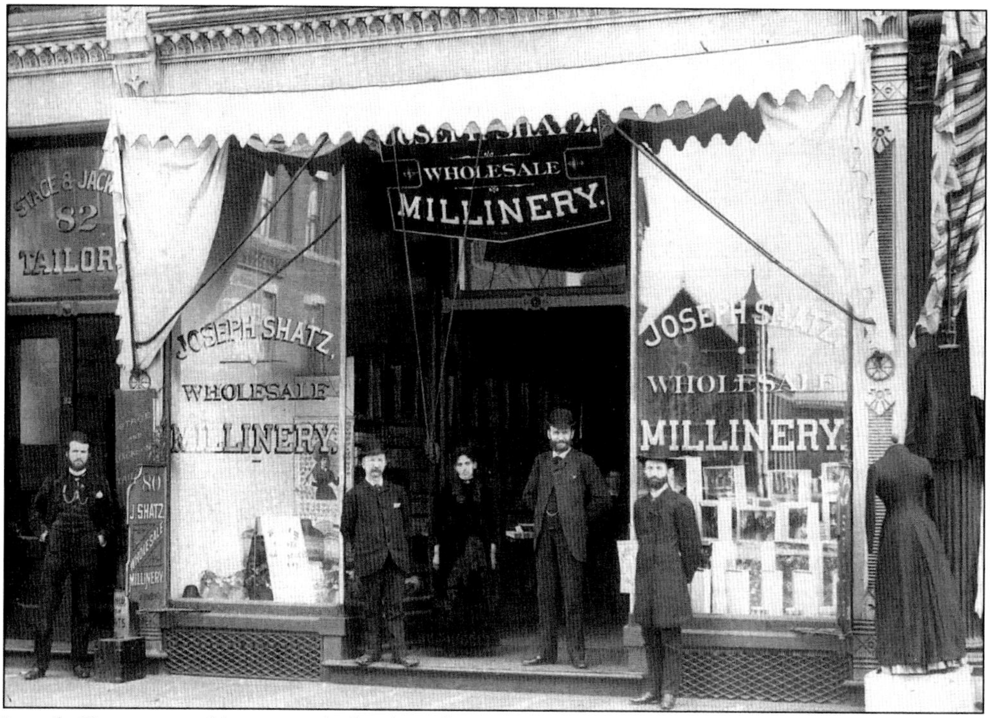

Joseph Shatz opened his new wholesale millinery emporium at 80 State Street *c.* 1880. Stage & Jackson, next-door, was available to transform fancy dry goods from Shatz into wearing apparel.

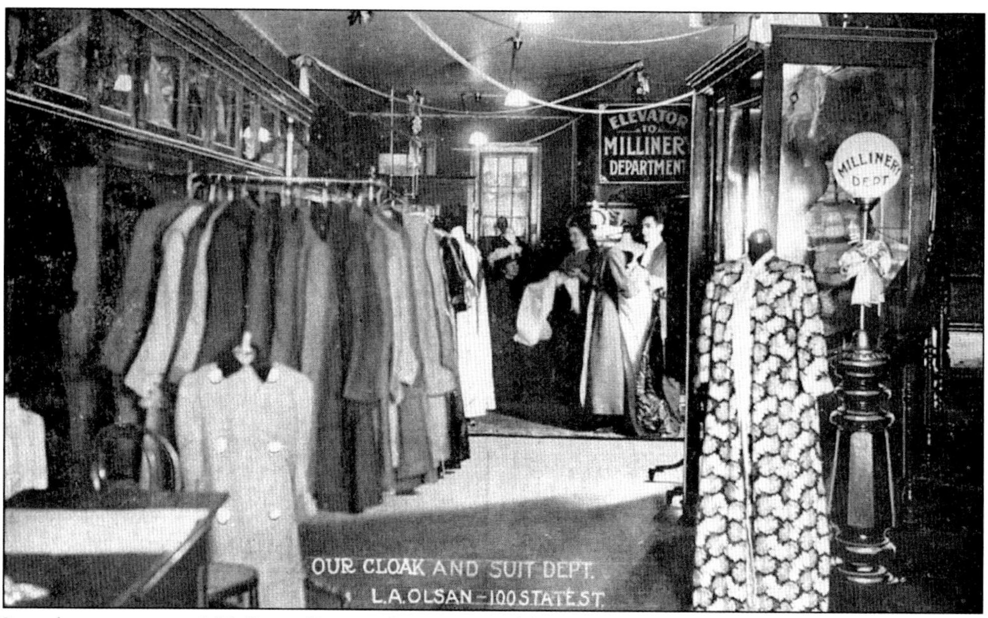

Just doors away at 100 State Street, shoppers could stop at another new store. The interior of L.A. Olsan's first floor reveals "Our Cloak and Suit Department." The newel post, on the right, holds a sign directing patrons upstairs to the millinery department.

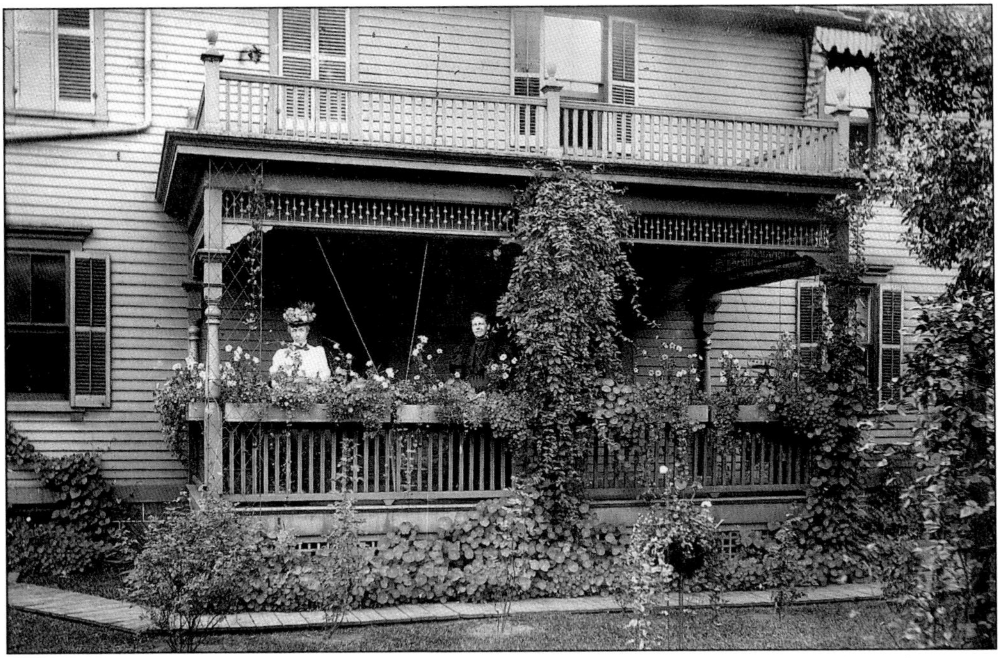

This is the Caldwell home at 209 North Clinton Avenue, a house typical of those that once graced the street. Lucy and Sarah Caldwell are on the porch. In the early 1900s, William H. Caldwell, their father and president of the Caldwell Manufacturing Company, made sash balances for windows. The nasturtiums blooming below the ornate Victorian porch were the sisters' favorite flowers.

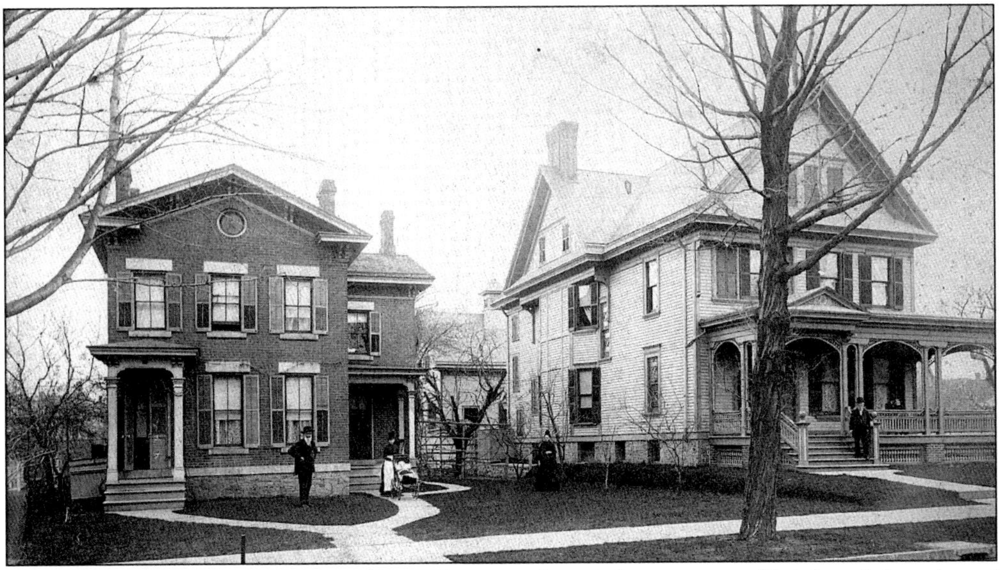

At 36 Tremont Street, in Corn Hill, stood a pair of sturdy homes, one of brick and the other of clapboard. On the left is the John B. Loomis home. Loomis, who was in real estate, is standing in the yard. His wife, Marthinetta Loomis, is at the right on the lawn. Next to the baby carriage is Carrie Loomis, the wife of Alvin I. Loomis. Next-door, on the steps at No. 32 is Daniel W. Fish, who was an author. His wife, Angelina Fish, is on the porch. The photograph was taken c. 1893.

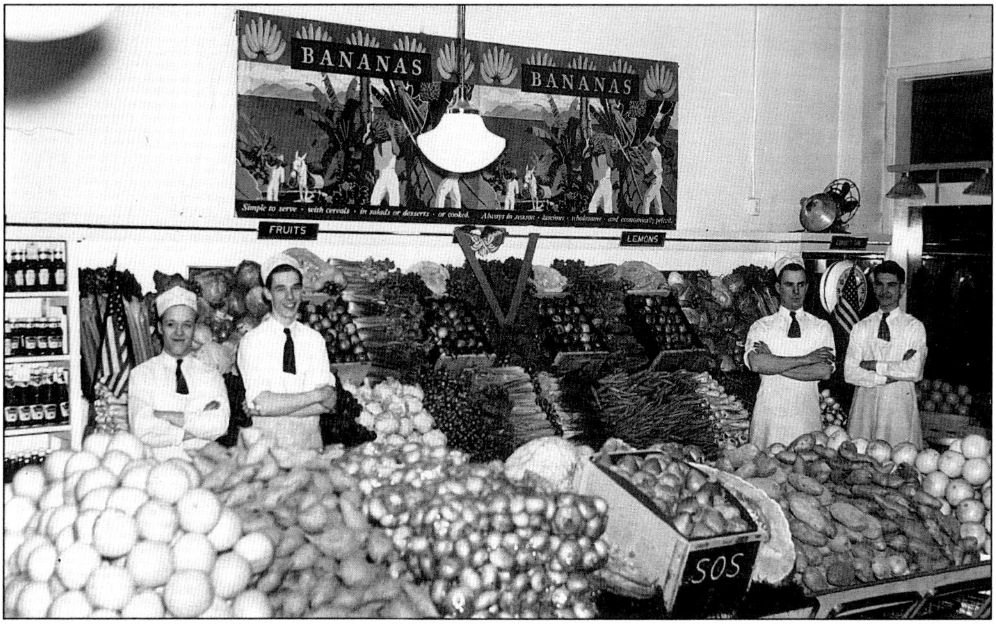

This photograph, taken in 1944 or 1945, shows the produce section of Loblaw's Grocery Store at 1880 East Avenue. The Canadian-based chain had 13 stores in Rochester. The manager and his young assistants seem pleased with their efforts. The display includes a lot of local fruits and vegetables, but no bananas. A letter V for victory is seen above the stacked stalks of celery.

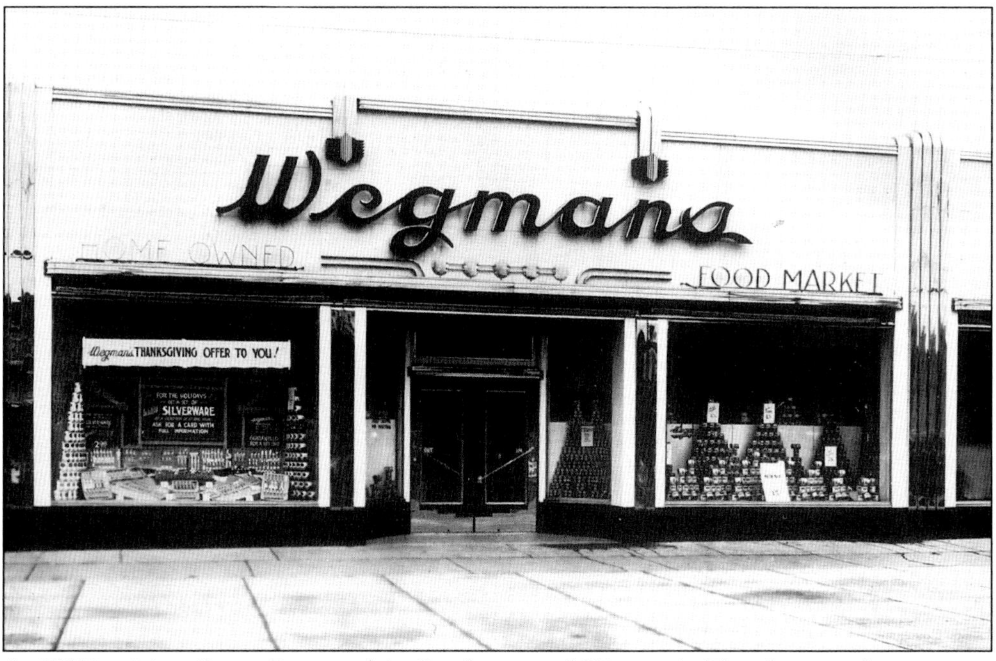

At 375 East Main Street, Raymond A. Gysel managed Wegman's. The photograph appears to have been taken at Thanksgiving time c. the 1960s. Pyramids of cans fill the show windows; some are priced at 15¢ and some at 25¢. Neon lit from behind, quarter-inch stainless steel letters proudly proclaim, "home owned food market." Ready-to-serve food was already an emerging element of Wegman's grocery store business.

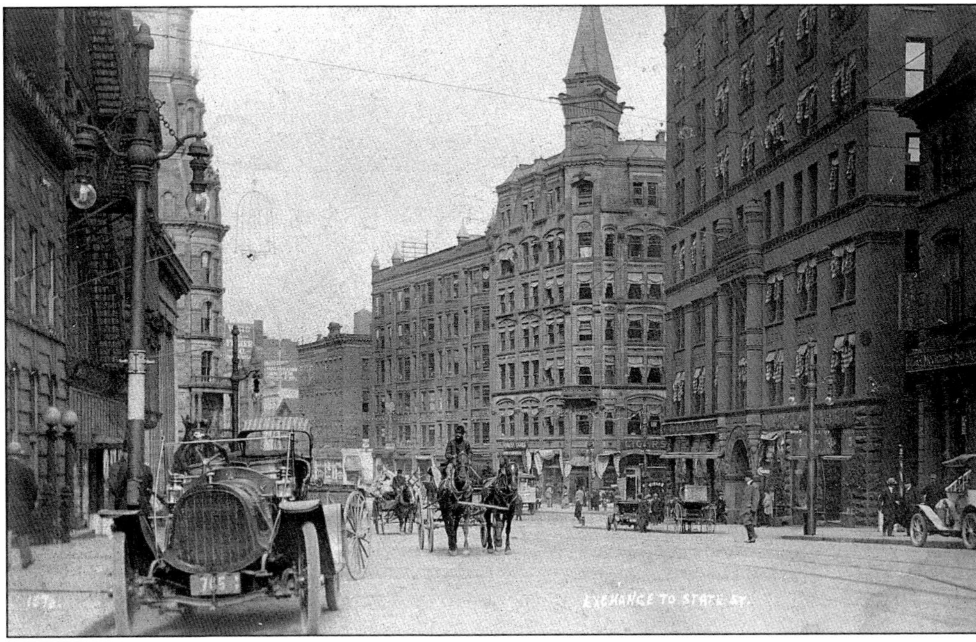

This 1910 view, looking north on Exchange Street, shows the 1887 Wilder Building on the right-hand corner of Main Street and, across the street, the 1870s Elwood Building, with the set of fearsome gargoyles peering out from its tower. The image was taken by George H. Monroe, the man who interested inventor and industrialist George Eastman in photography.

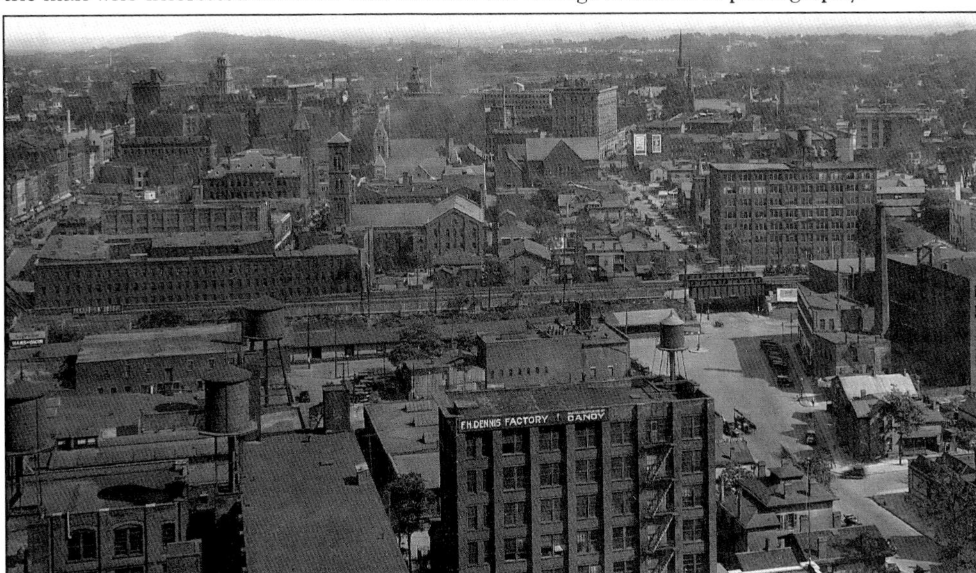

Looking south down Plymouth Avenue toward West Main Street, this vintage photograph provides a remarkable look at Rochester *c.* 1915. On the left horizon is the Power's Building tower; more centrally, the twin pyramid shapes of the old city hall; and on the right, the Hotel Rochester and the spire of the Spiritualist Church—both on Plymouth Avenue. The raised tracks of the New York Central & Hudson River Railroad run through the center of the photograph. Frontier Field now occupies the area at the lower right, opposite the Frank H. Dennis Wholesale Candy Factory, located at 7 Griffith Street.

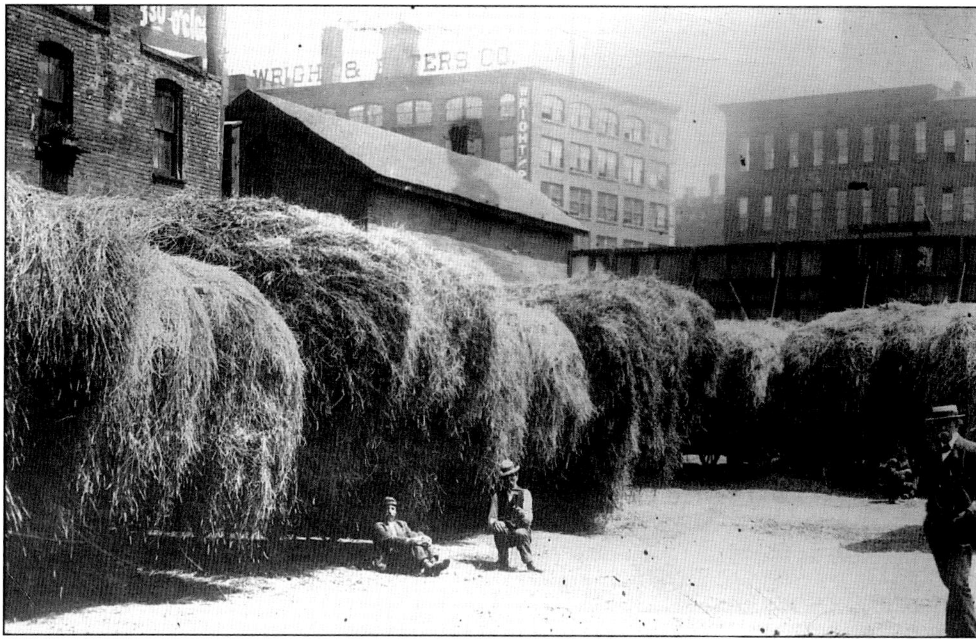

The old Hay Market, at 118 Front Street, was run by Charles H. Bidwell. For years, it provided the fuel necessary for legions of horses that played a dominant role in moving Rochester's commercial traffic and private transportation. This photograph was taken in 1914.

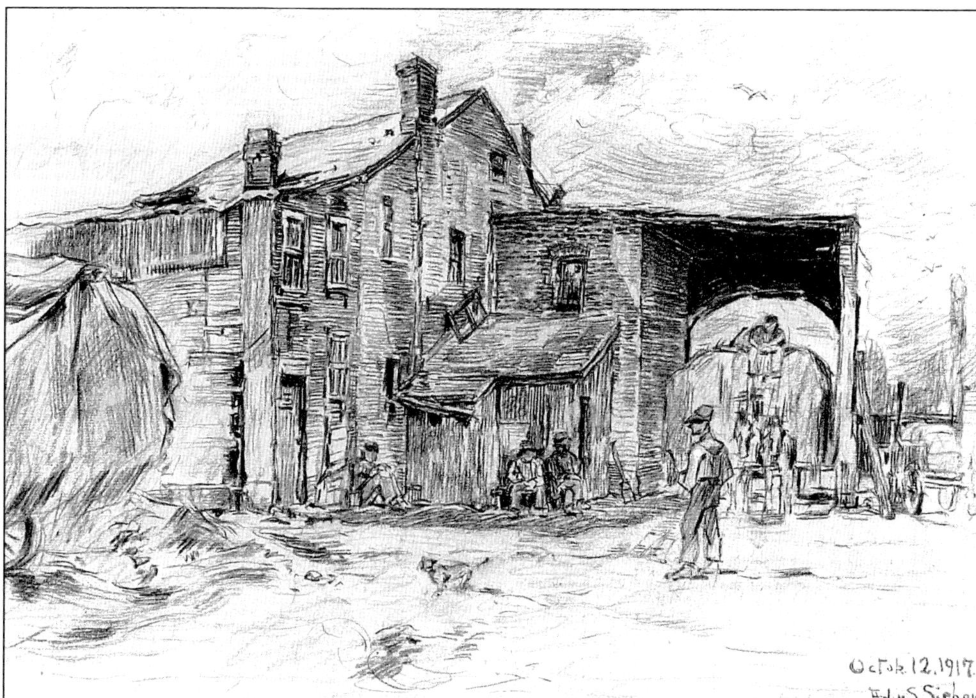

This pencil sketch of the quaint Hay Market was drawn by Edward S. Sirbert on Columbus Day 1917. It represents the period when hay was needed to feed old dobbin and a new mode of transportation, the automobile, was already gaining in popularity. (Courtesy John Topham.)

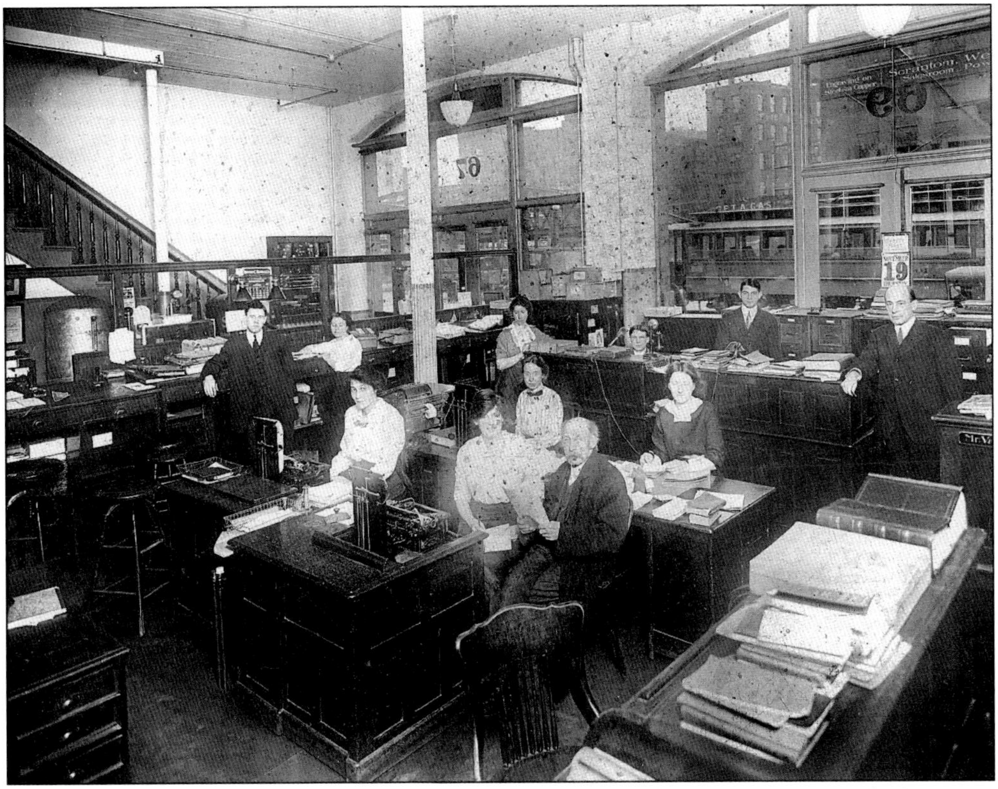

The interior of the Samuel Sloan & Company, Plumber's and Steam Fitters Supply Company reveals an office staff of 10 clerks and secretaries. The man in the center of the November 19, 1921 photograph may be Samuel Sloan. Located at 67–71 Exchange Street, the company was located across from the Scrantom, Wetmore Company, at West Main and State Streets. Street car No. 561 passes the window.

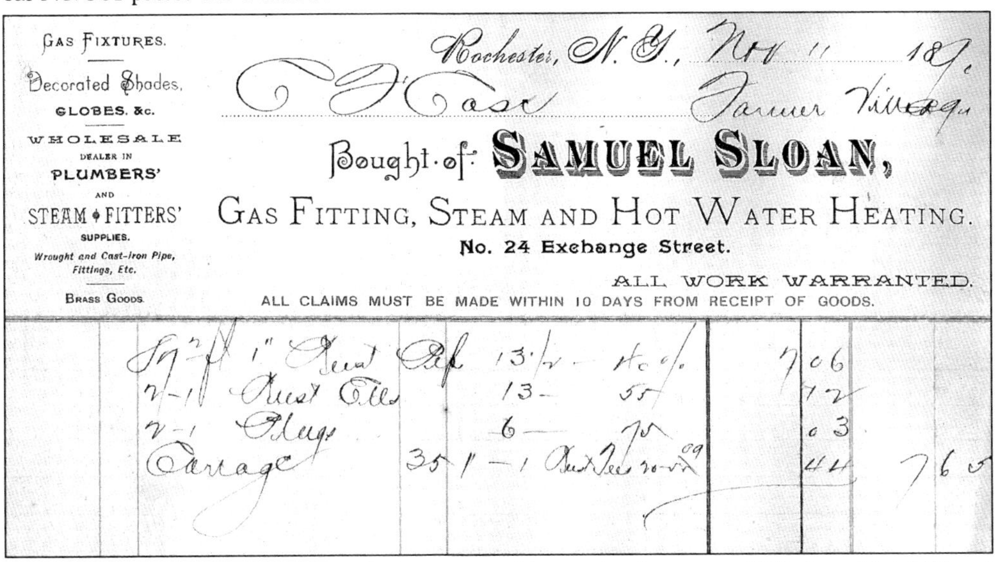

Gas Fixtures.
Decorated Shades,
GLOBES, &c.
WHOLESALE
DEALER IN
PLUMBERS'
AND
STEAM FITTERS'
SUPPLIES.
Wrought and Cast-Iron Pipe, Fittings, Etc.
Brass Goods.

Rochester, N.Y., Nov 11 1890
C. T. Case
Bought of SAMUEL SLOAN,
GAS FITTING, STEAM AND HOT WATER HEATING.
No. 24 Exchange Street.
ALL WORK WARRANTED.
ALL CLAIMS MUST BE MADE WITHIN 10 DAYS FROM RECEIPT OF GOODS.

In November 1890, Samuel Sloan & Company sold its utility fittings to C.T. Case. This billhead is a reminder of bygone times when life was a different than it is today.

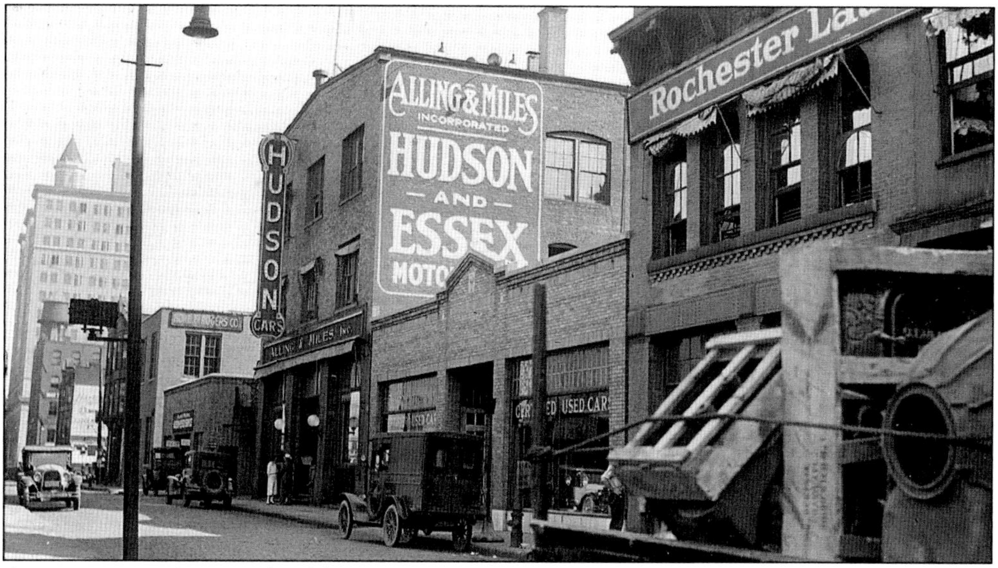

A more recent photograph of downtown reveals a section near 82 Stone Street as it appeared on July 8, 1927. Note the fancy Hudson and Essex automobiles. A truckload of cast-iron furnace parts dominates the foreground, with the Lincoln Alliance Bank Building in the distance.

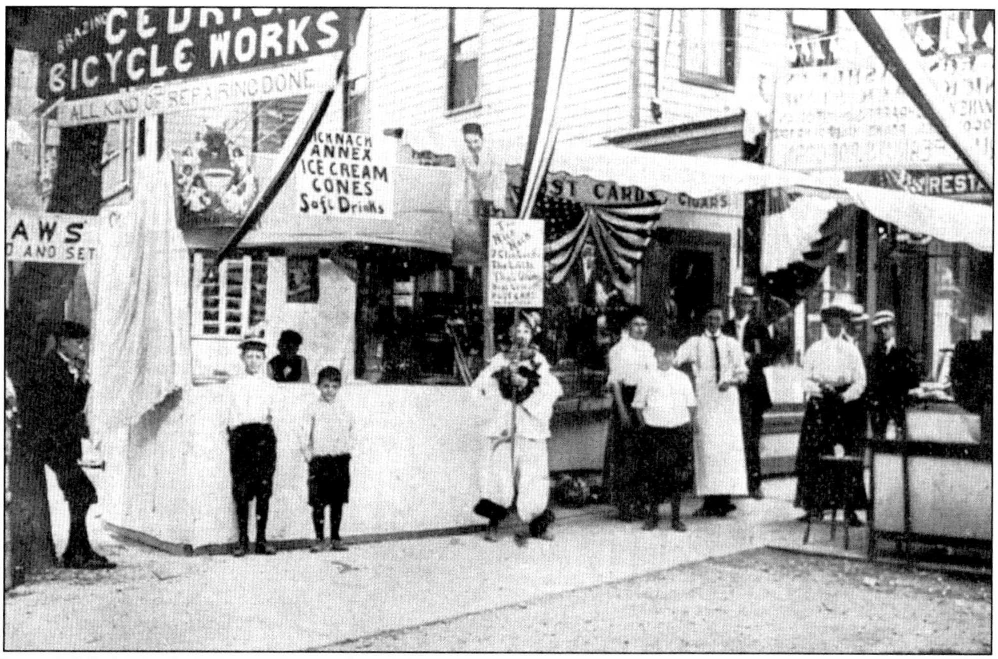

Leon's Nick Nack Store, at 7 North Clinton Avenue, was operated by one of many entrepreneurs of the day. The motto for Leon's Nick Nack was "the little store that's growing larger and better." Ice cream and postcards were among the items sold there. The 1893 city directory lists 103 confectionery stores in Rochester.

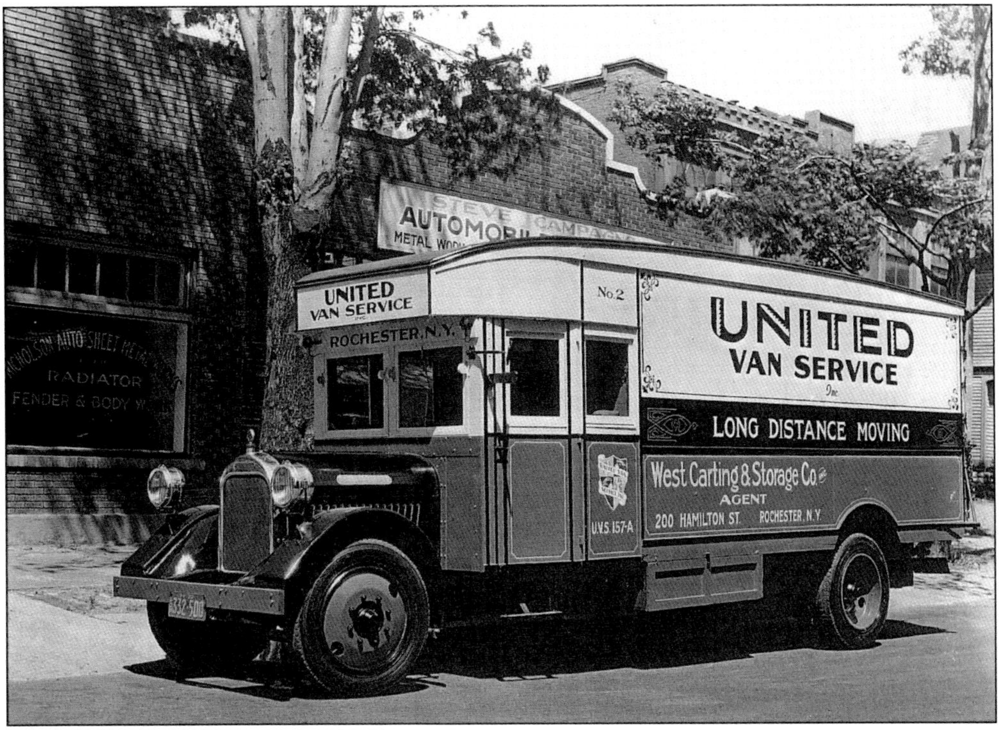

Charles A. Mongenet, president of West Carting & Storage Company, was justly proud of his shiny new moving van. The photograph was taken in the summer of 1920, just after Stephen Campagno neatly painted and lettered the van, parked in front of his shop.

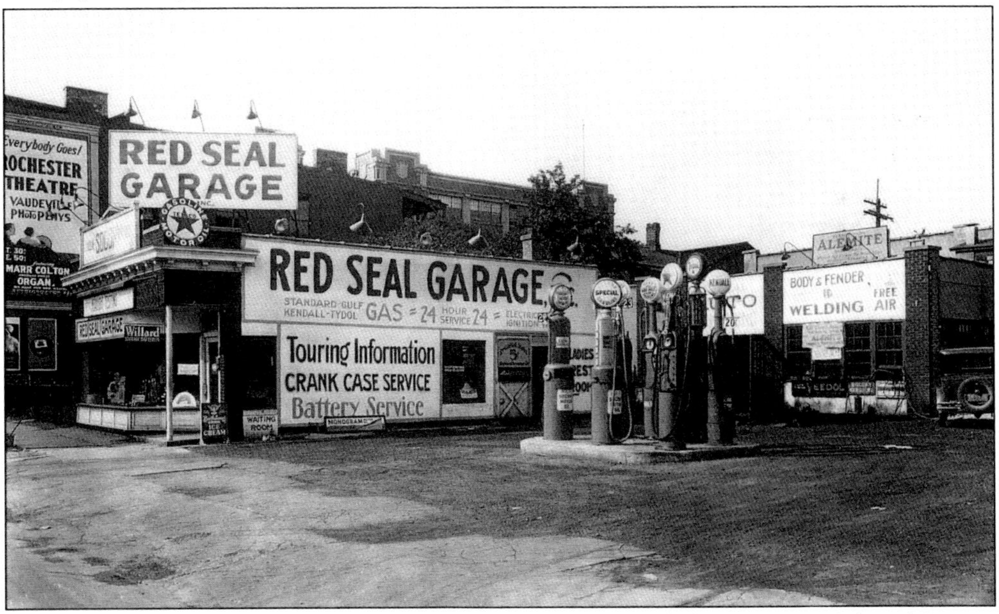

The Red Seal Garage, open for 24-hour service, sells Gulf, Kendall, Texaco, Tydol, and Socony gasoline from its seven pumps at just 20¢ to 23¢ a gallon. The poster at the left invites patrons to attend the Rochester Theatre's vaudeville and photo-plays, with the matinee price at just 30¢. The theater was cooled with "refrigerated air."

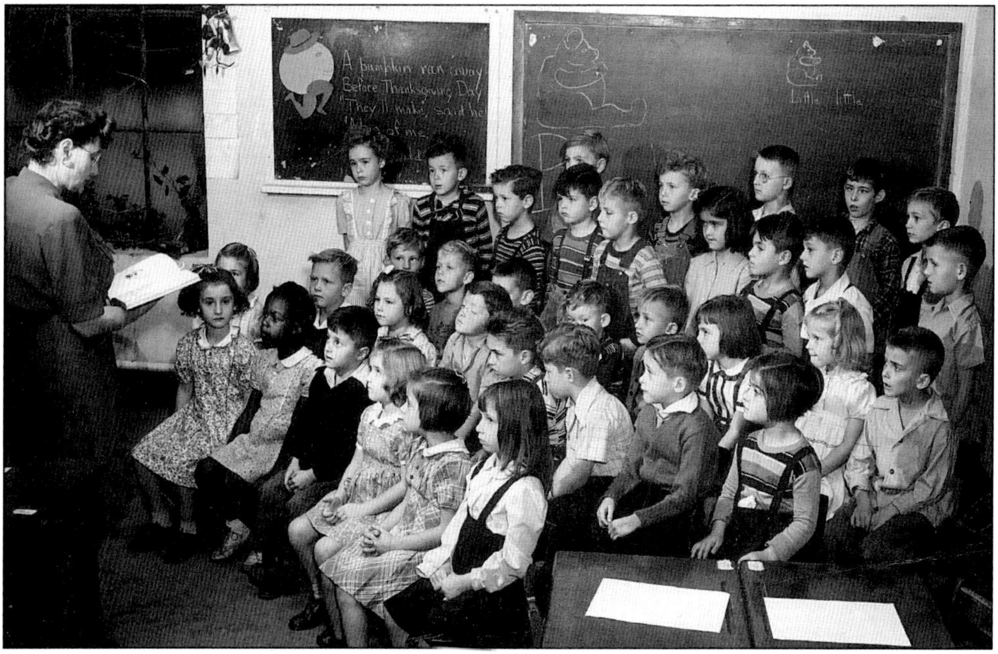

It was almost Thanksgiving *c.* the 1940s when a city school photographer captured these 37 second-graders raptly listening to a story read by their teacher. Very few children wore glasses at that time, and girls always wore dresses to school.

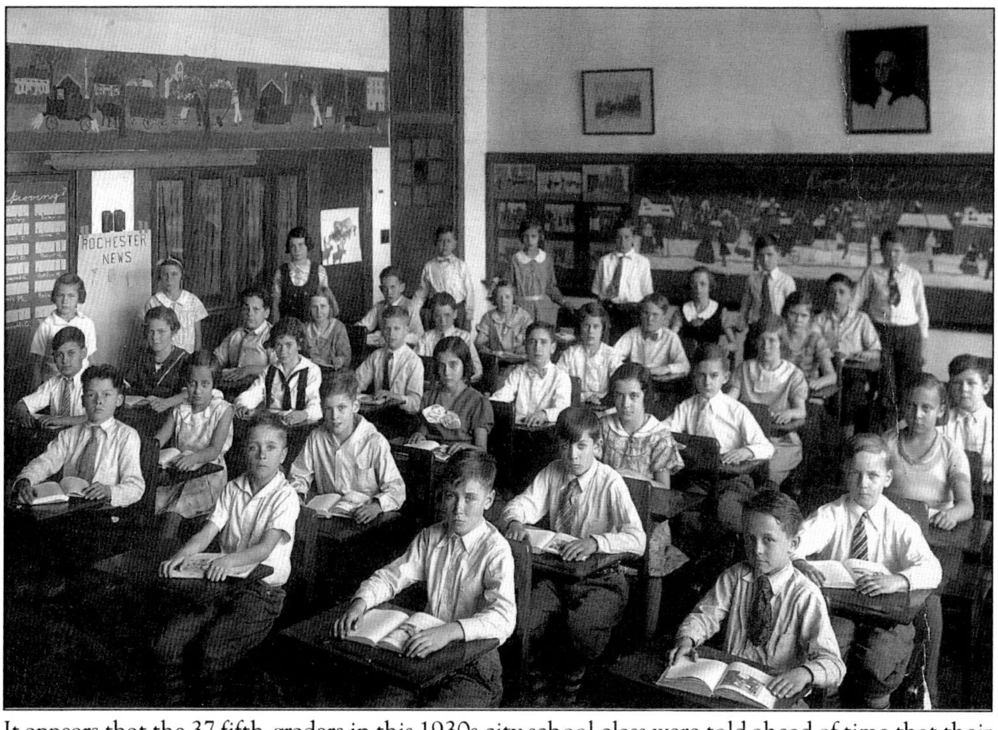

It appears that the 37 fifth-graders in this 1930s city school class were told ahead of time that their picture was going to be taken. Thus, the boys are in white shirts and ties, and the girls are in their best dresses. The back wall mural suggests that the class has been learning about Rochesterville.

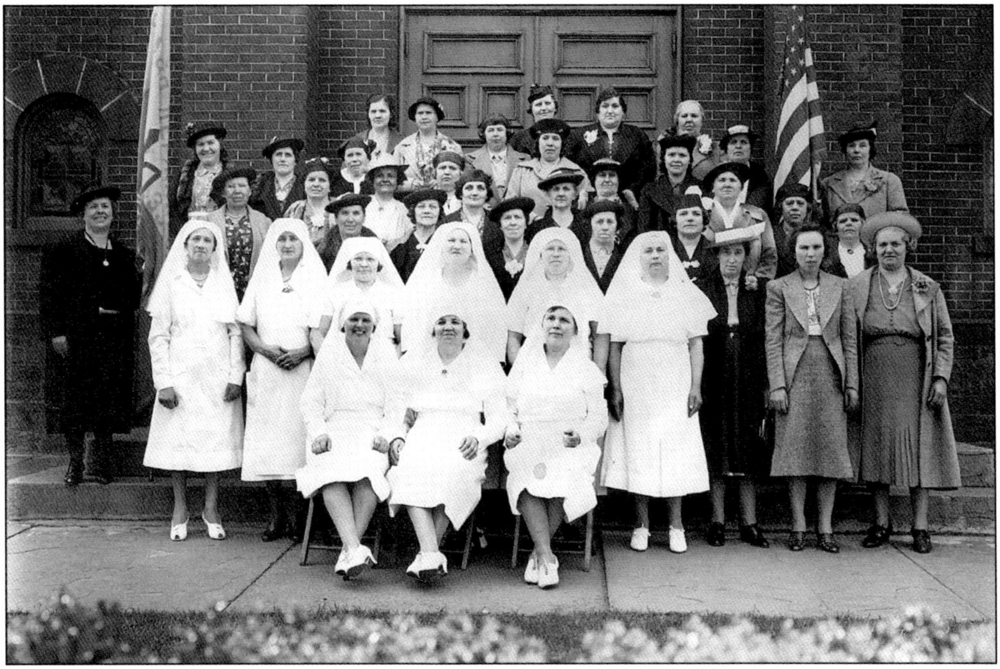

Taken in the late 1930s, this photograph shows the teaching Sisters and lady parishioners of St. Josephat Ukrainian Catholic Church. Founded in 1910, the church was located at 305 Hudson Avenue. In the 1970s, the congregation moved to a new site on Ridge Road in Irondequoit. The former church site is now the Dag Hammerschold School.

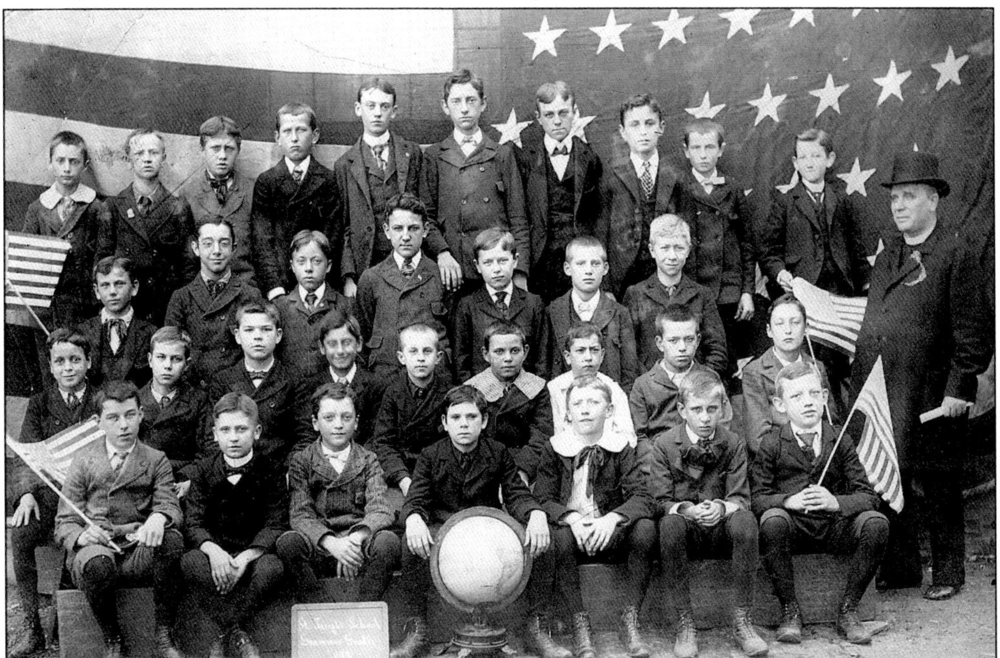

A huge American flag is the backdrop for the faces of these young boys in the 1898 "Grammar Grades" of St. Joseph's School, located at 70 Franklin Street.

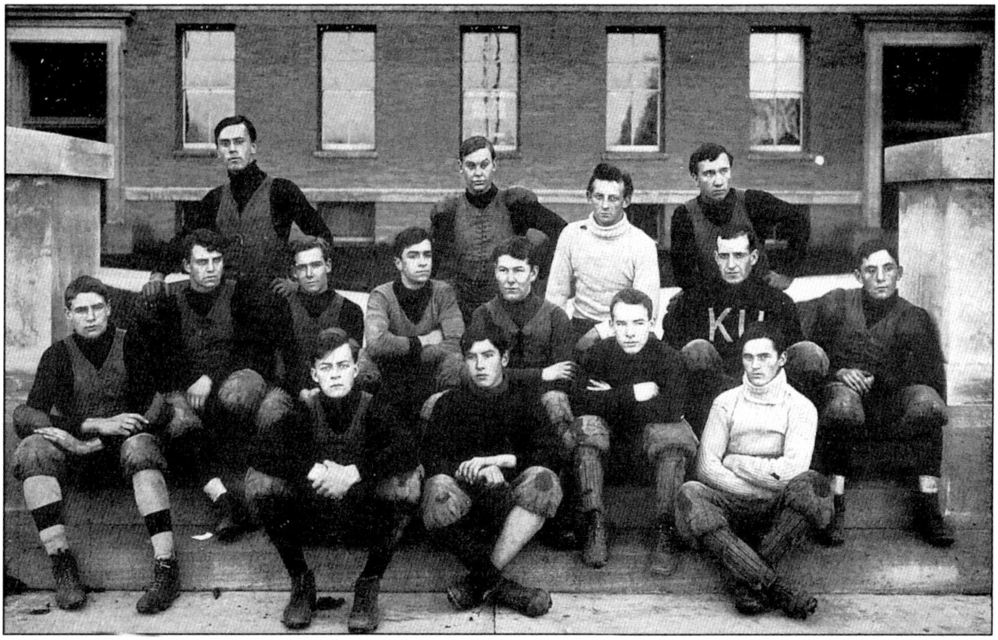

The 15 members of West High School's football team are seen in uniforms with shin guards but no shoulder pads. According to the *Occident*, the team set a 1906 record, defeating their opponents 104-0. Trouncing Geneva 47-0, they also beat Syracuse 12-0.

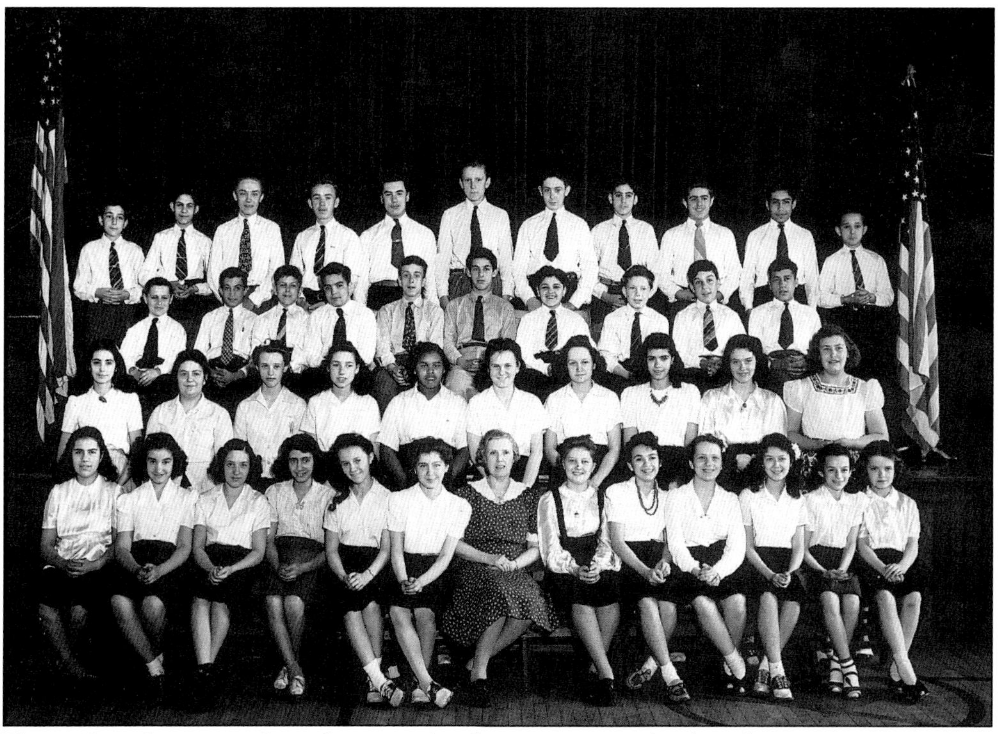

These 43 smiling seventh-graders pose for their grammar school graduation picture in June 1942. The neatly dressed students are graduating from No. 14 School, at Scio Street and University Avenue.

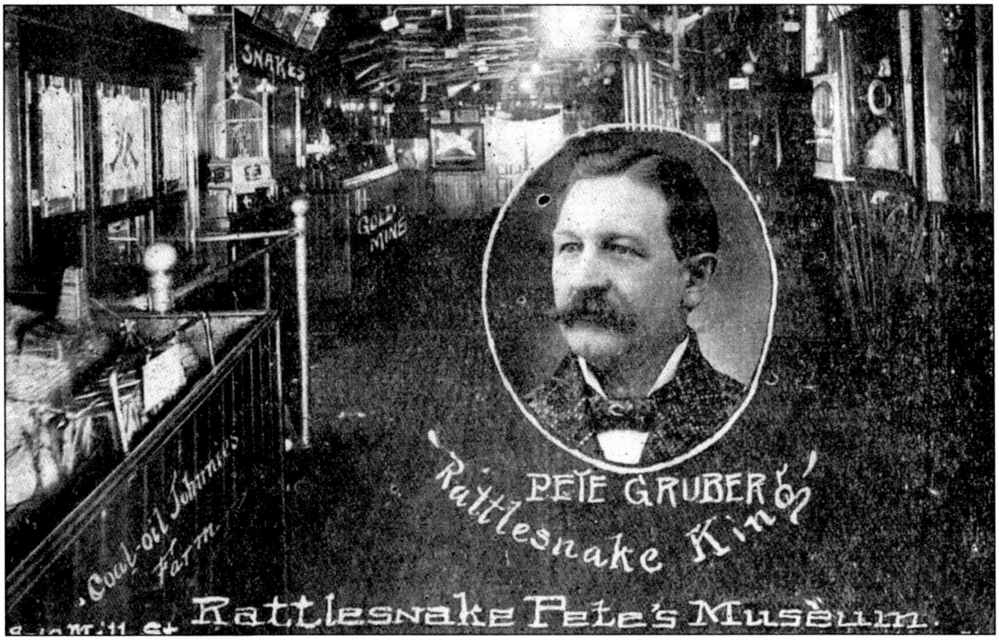

For 40 years, 1892 to 1932, Rattlesnake Pete entertained all comers at his Hall of Wonders, a combination tavern and museum. Located at 8–10 Mill Street, just around the corner from Front Street, the Hall of Wonders held not only live snakes but also an awesome collection of strange, exotic, and unique curiosities.

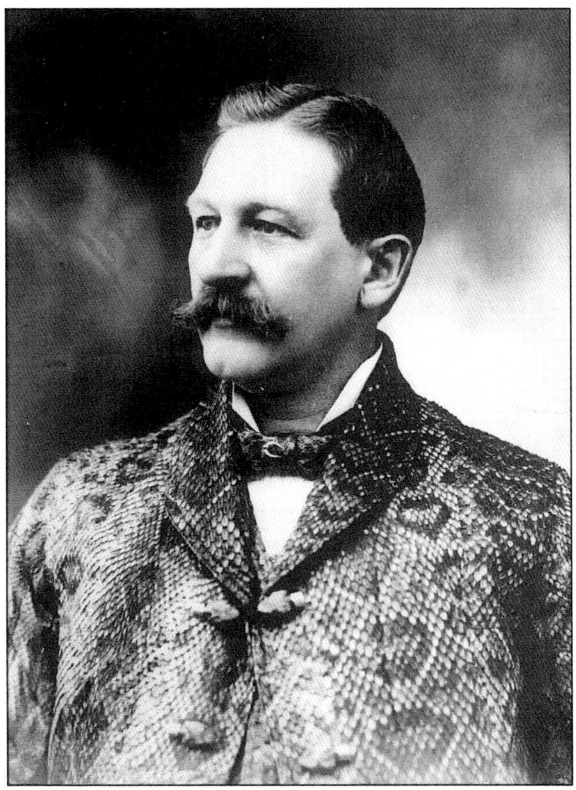

Peter Gruber, owner of the Mill Street emporium, was best known as Rattlesnake Pete. Of all the unusual characters associated with the Front Street area, he was the most colorful. Nattily attired in coat, tie, and vest, Gruber obviously made unique use of his rattlesnake skin collection.

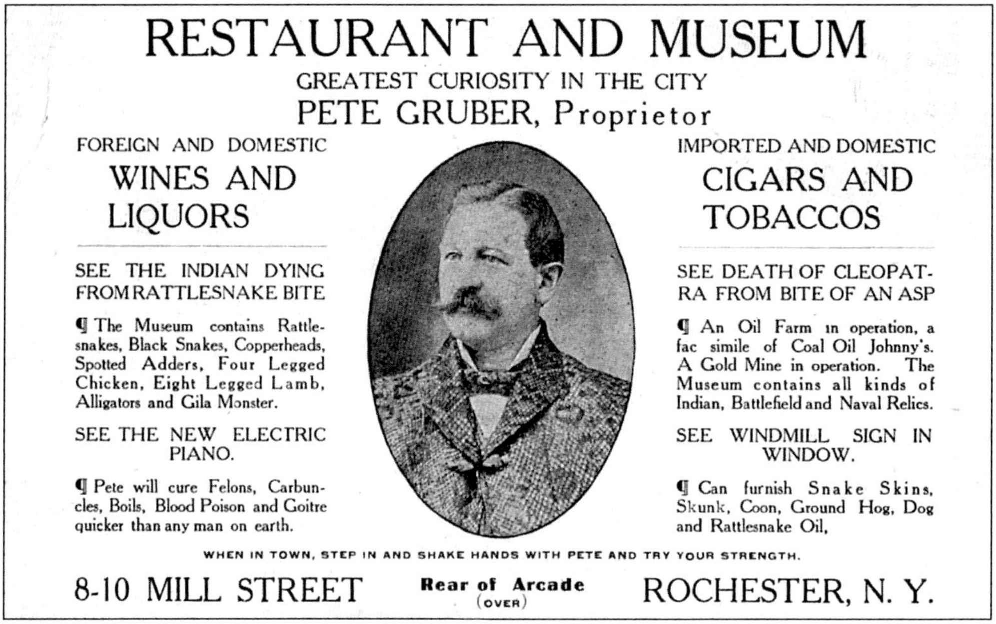

"The greatest curiosity in the city" is how Rattlesnake Pete advertised his establishment to the public. The fine print adds, "When in town, step in and shake hands with Pete and try your strength." It is said that even Buffalo Bill, accompanied by his troupe of wild Native Americans, paid Rattlesnake Pete a visit.

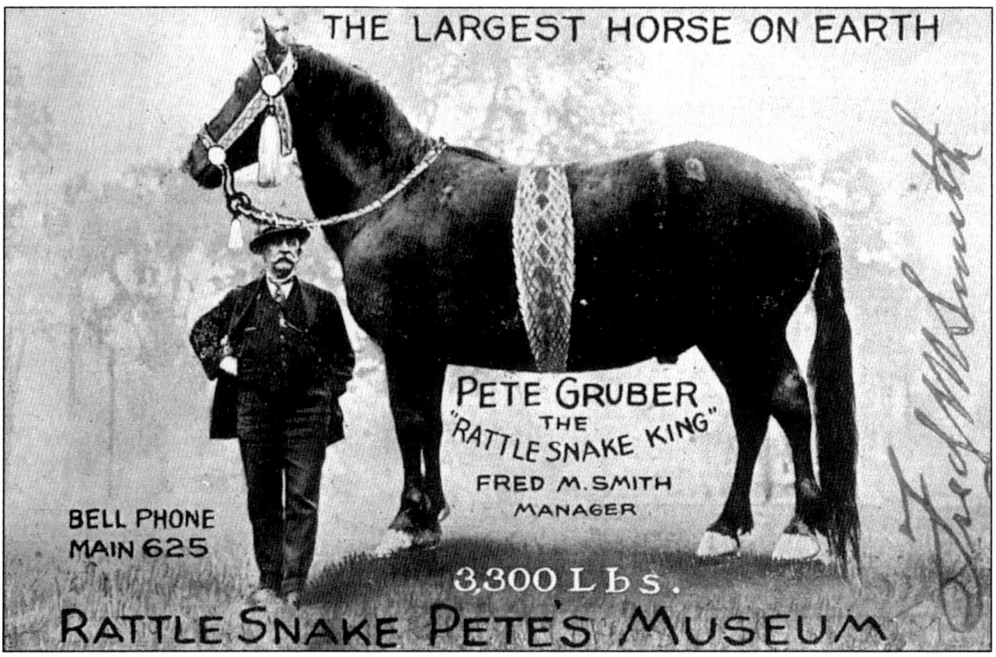

This unusual photograph illustrates one of Rattlesnake Pete's favorite museum artifacts. It is a huge Percheron horse, stuffed and placed as the centerpiece in the museum. This breed of horse was bred in France during the Crusades to support knights in full armor. The horse's weight was more than a ton and a half. The autograph at the right is that of Fred M. Smith, publicity agent for Rattlesnake Pete.

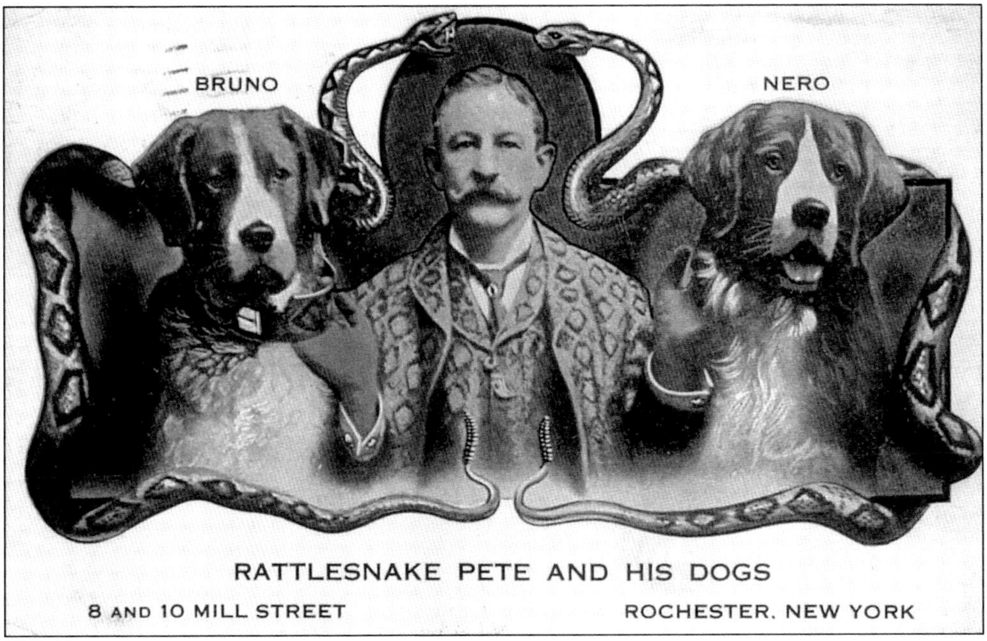

Besides rattlesnakes, Peter Gruber also had a passion for St. Bernard dogs. His "inseparable companions" included at least five of them: Bruno, Nero, Queenie, Brutus, and Markus. He taught both Bruno and Nero how to ride on the running boards of his bright red Rambler touring car. It was quite a spectacle as he drove the automobile around a corner, honking the snake-headed brass klaxon, with the two dogs leaning inward to avoid falling off.

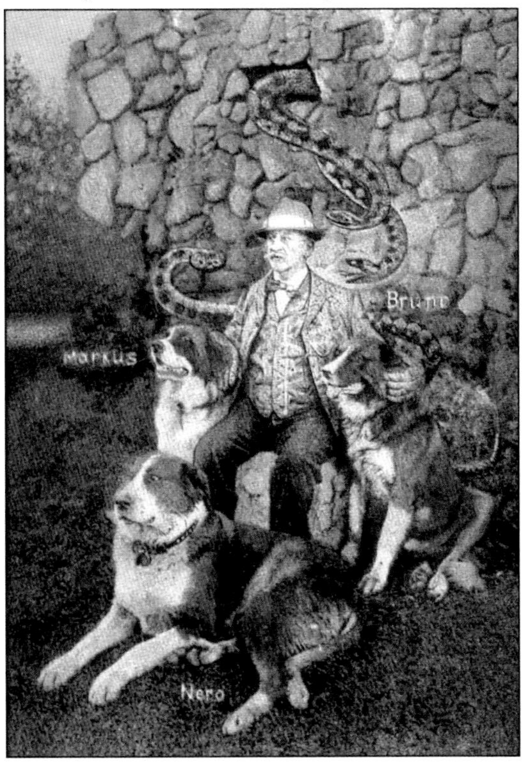

The photographer was allowed a lot of artist's license for this specially posed photograph of Rattlesnake Pete and his dogs. Peter Gruber arrived in Rochester in 1892, overseeing his unique establishment for 40 years and surviving the bites of 29 rattlers and four copperhead snakes. On October 11, 1932, Peter Gruber, 75, died of natural causes at his home on Averill Avenue.

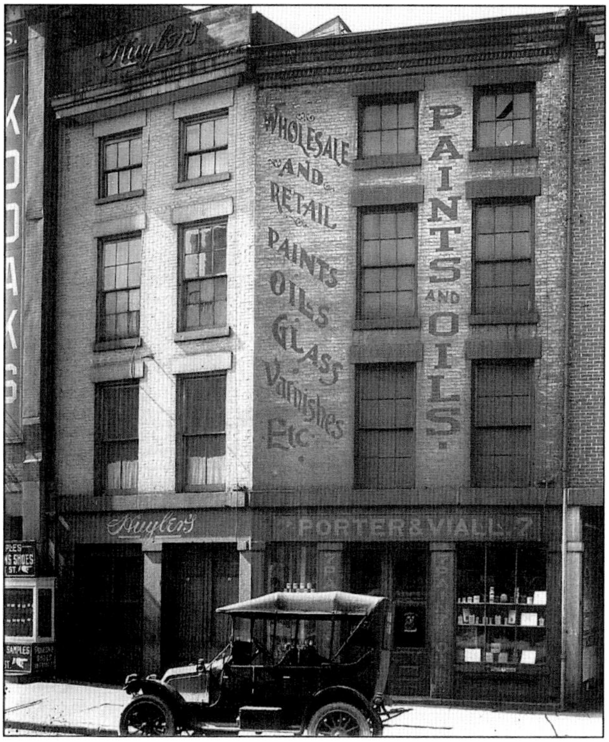

Front Street, once known as Rochester's Bowery, Barbary Coast, and Skid Row, had enormous character—and a lot of characters. A magnet for those shopping for fresh meat and poultry, and only five blocks long, the street was crammed with small markets, a pawn shop, a locksmith, a college for barbers, clothing stores, small eateries, and more than a few thirst parlors. (Courtesy Rochester Historical Society.)

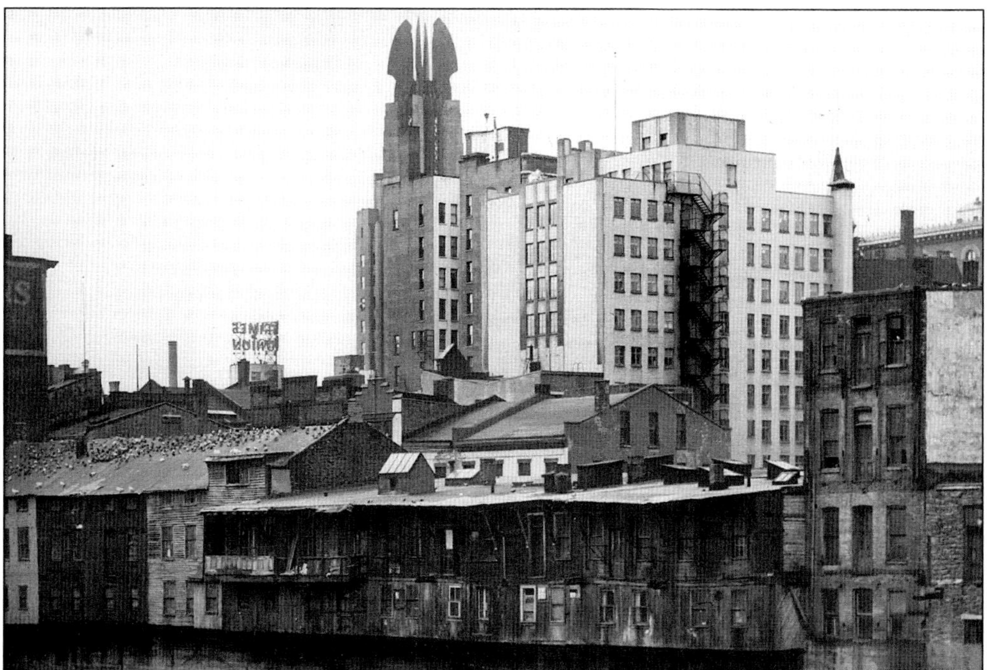

Perched above the Genesee River is this row of venerable Front Street shops. One shop owned by Archie Lipsky Poultry, at 60 Front Street, had the advantage of the river for disposing of chicken feathers. The Reynolds Arcade and the former Genesee Community Bank Building are in the background.

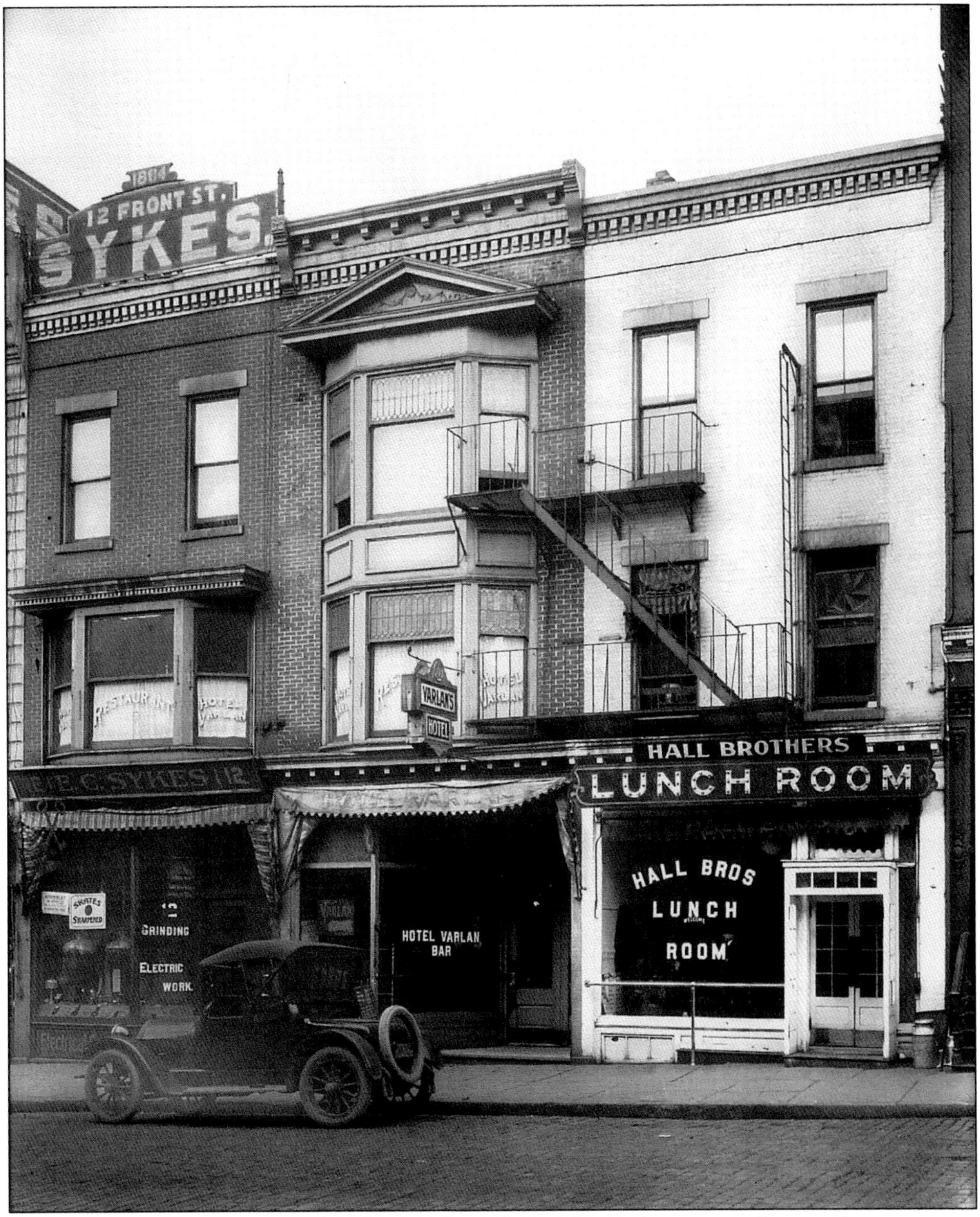

It is said that one had to try the lunch at Hall Brothers. The food was nourishing and inexpensive, and the door never closed. Henry Clune wrote, "It was a snug haven on a blustery winter night; it was cooled by whirling fans on nights of summer dog days." He added that the 20¢ chicken pie was "a concoction topped by a crust somewhat the texture of battleship plating, but tasty if one had solid teeth." Two doors down, Edwin C. Sykes would sharpen your ice skates and lawn mower blades and cutlery, do electrical repairs, and fix your locks. (Courtesy Rochester Historical Society.)

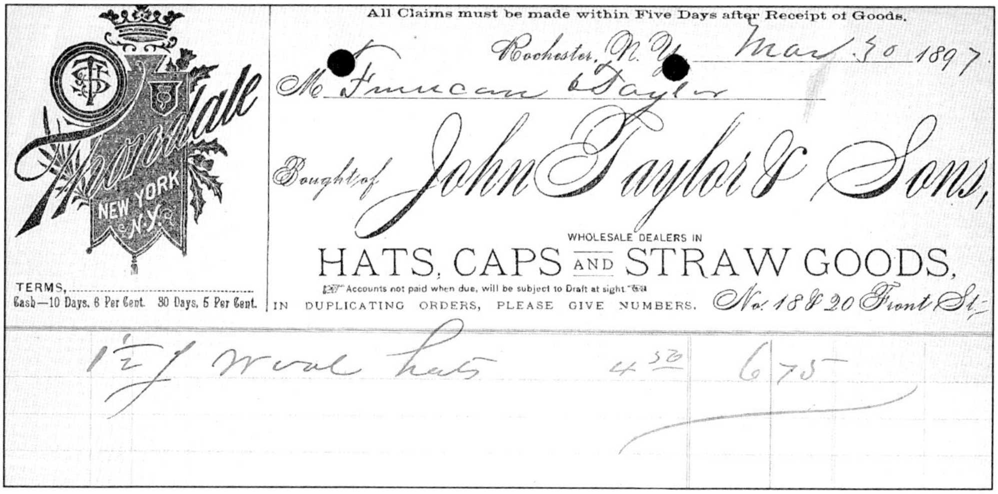

All Claims must be made within Five Days after Receipt of Goods.

Rochester, N.Y. Mar 30 1897

M Finucan & Taylor

Bought of John Taylor & Sons,

WHOLESALE DEALERS IN

HATS, CAPS AND STRAW GOODS,

Accounts not paid when due, will be subject to Draft at sight

IN DUPLICATING ORDERS, PLEASE GIVE NUMBERS. No. 18 & 20 Front St.

TERMS,

Cash—10 Days, 6 Per Cent. 30 Days, 5 Per Cent.

1½ / wool hats 4.50 6.75

From 1860 until the wrecking ball demolished Front Street in 1965, the John Taylor & Sons emporium sold the finest of hats, caps, and gloves. Located in a three-story brick building at 18–20 Front Street, Taylor & Sons was *the* place to purchase the famous Italian fedora Borselino hats.

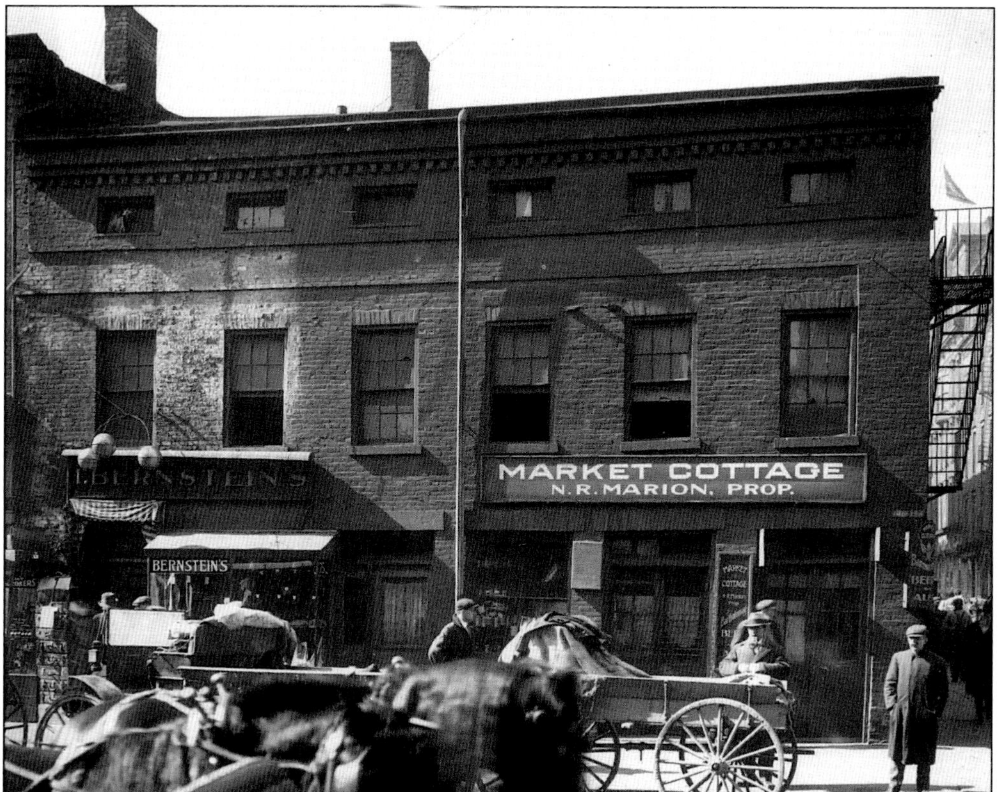

Typical of the buildings along Front Street was the one that housed Bernstein's Pawn Shop and Nicholas R. Marion's Market Cottage. This 1915 scene clearly shows the pawnbroker's symbol over the doorway, while the Bartholomay sign signifies that beer was available at the Market Cottage.

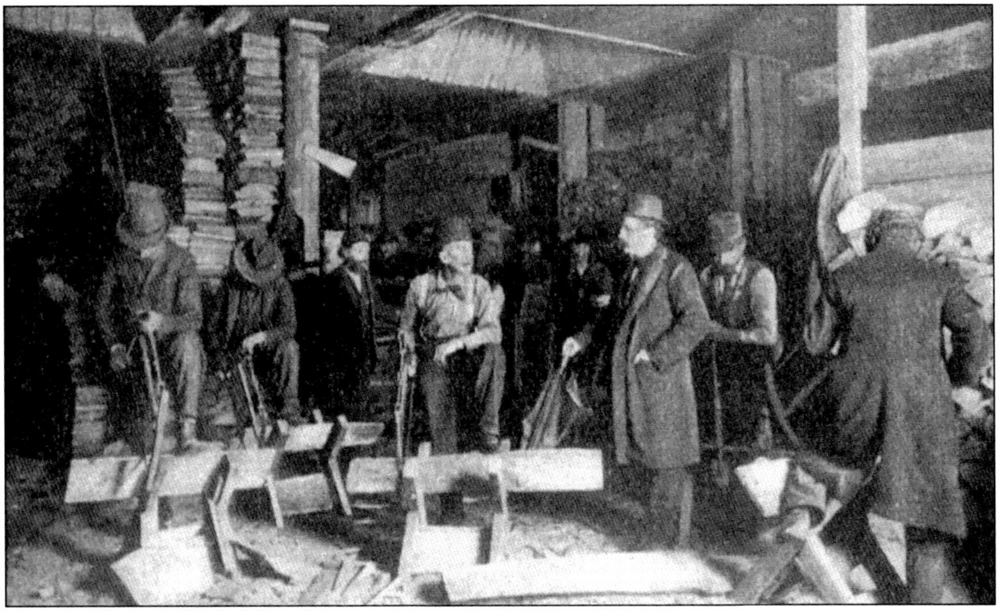

Using bucksaws and sawhorses, indigent men created firewood to be sold by the People's Rescue Mission. The labor gave the men a feeling of dignity, helping them to earn their keep at the mission, at 173 Front Street. Wooden packing crates were donated to the woodlot by Sibley's and other dry goods firms. (Courtesy George Brown.)

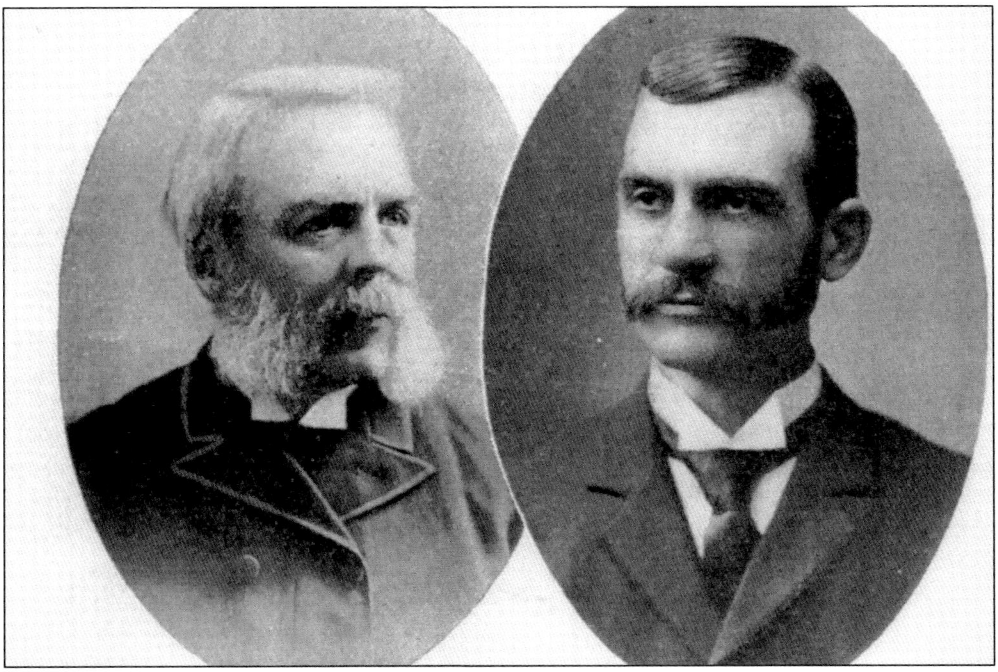

The People's Rescue Mission was established on Front Street in October 1889. It "redeemed the fallen" and helped those who "became slaves to strong drink." An unending supply of such individuals frequented the area. In 1897, Dr. Joseph H. Gilmore, a distinguished professor at the University of Rochester, was mission president. Albert F. Hines served as the superintendent. (Courtesy George Brown, a relative of Albert F. Hines.)

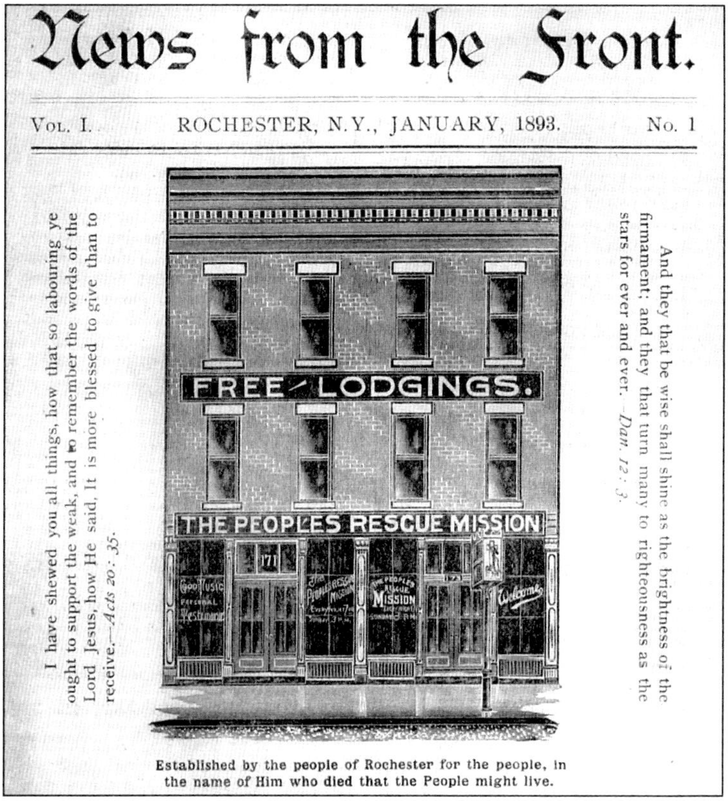

News from the Front.

VOL. I. ROCHESTER, N.Y., JANUARY, 1893. No. 1

I have shewed you all things, how that so labouring ye ought to support the weak, and to remember the words of the Lord Jesus, how He said, It is more blessed to give than to receive.—*Acts 20: 35.*

And they that be wise shall shine as the brightness of the firmament; and they that turn many to righteousness as the stars for ever and ever.—*Dan. 12: 3.*

Established by the people of Rochester for the people, in the name of Him who died that the People might live.

News from the Front was the initial publication of the People's Rescue Mission. This rare sketch shows the first mission, surrounded by appropriate Bible verses. (Courtesy George Brown.)

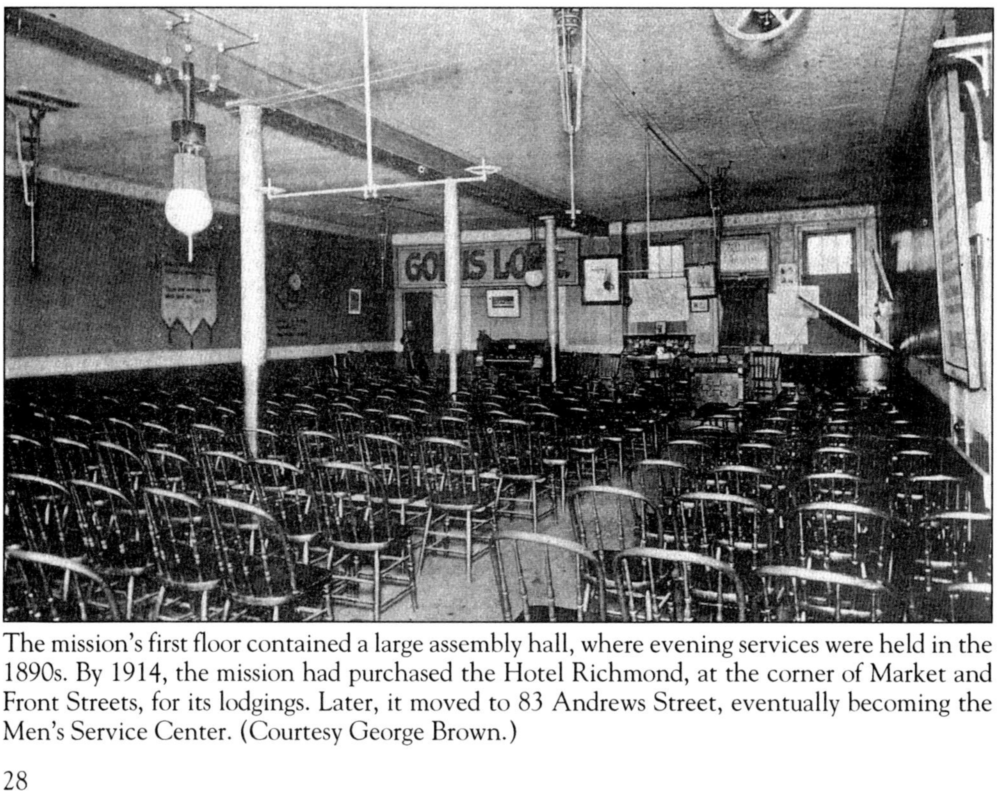

The mission's first floor contained a large assembly hall, where evening services were held in the 1890s. By 1914, the mission had purchased the Hotel Richmond, at the corner of Market and Front Streets, for its lodgings. Later, it moved to 83 Andrews Street, eventually becoming the Men's Service Center. (Courtesy George Brown.)

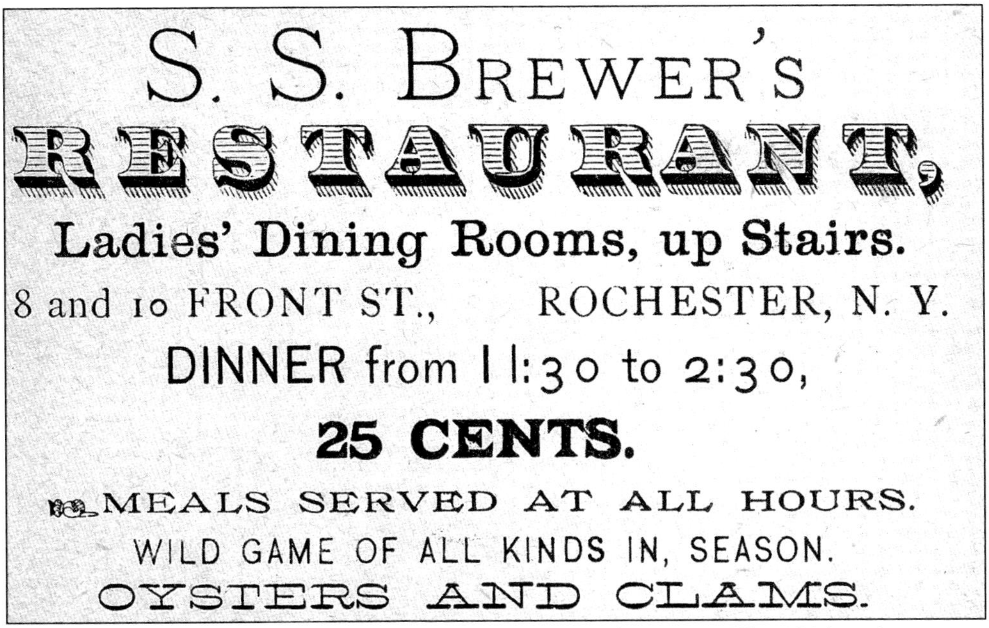

This advertisement is representative of many Front Street businesses. The 1886 card promotes the Samuel S. Brower Restaurant, at a time when food and drink were purveyed in equal quantities. Front Street also contained over a dozen meat and poultry shops in those years.

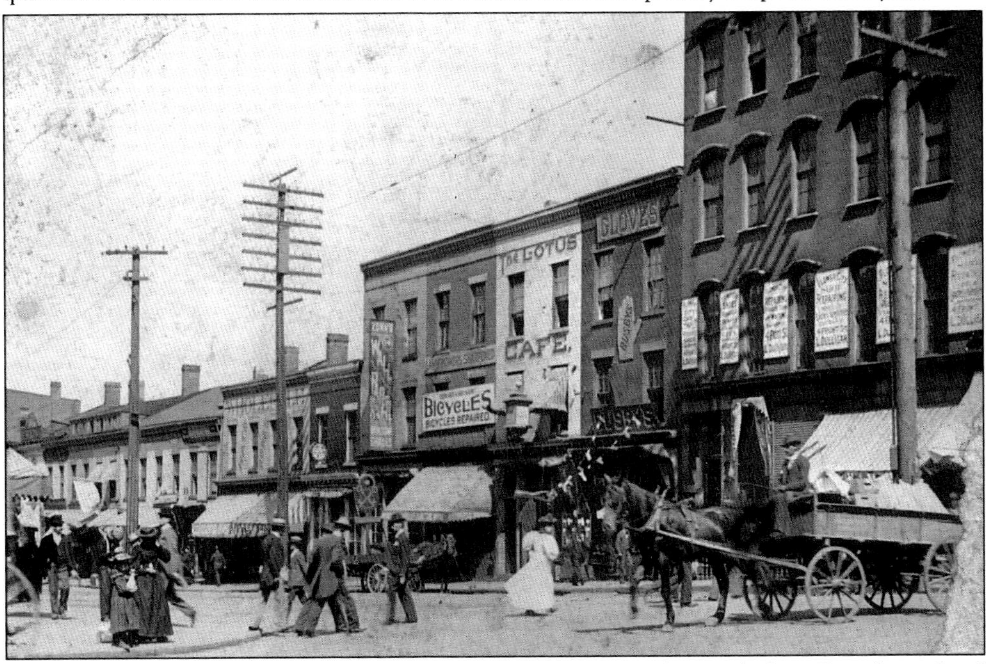

This vintage photograph captures a portion of Front Street rarely seen before. Found in a local antique shop by Len Rosenberg, the 1886 photograph was taken with a Rochester-made Premo B camera. The large mitten sign on the building to the right of the Lotus Cafe indicates where Thomas M. Busby manufactured gloves, at 14 Front Street. Sarah A. Zorn's Wall Paper Store is at the left of the Lotus Café, at 22 Front Street. Lawrence Dulligan did shoe repairing in the four-story building at the right.

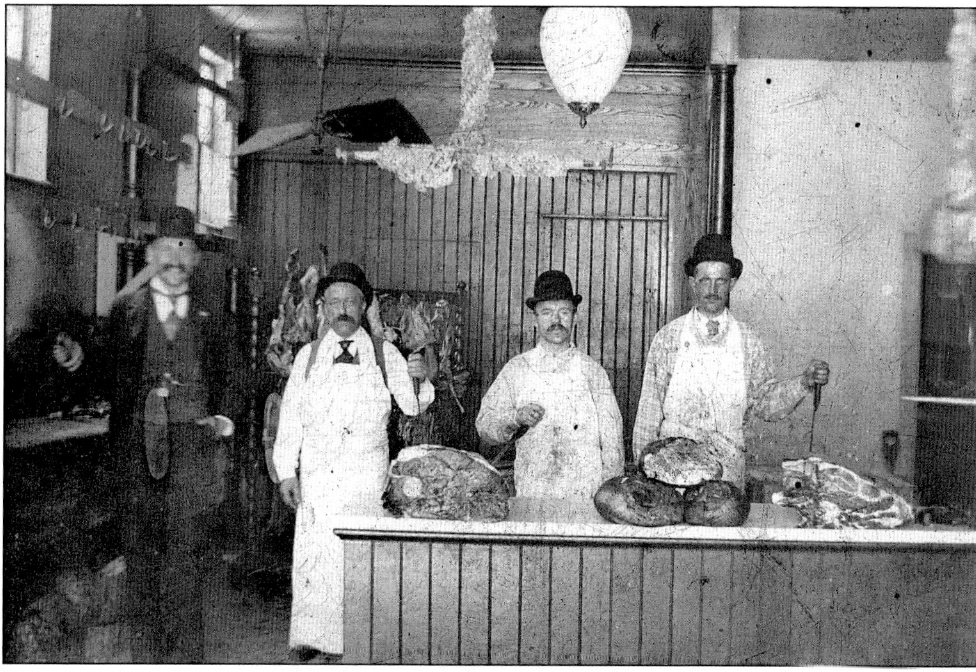

For years, Front Street was the place to purchase quality meat products. Even as early as 1893, when this photograph was taken, the James & George Brown store sold meat at 61 Front Street.

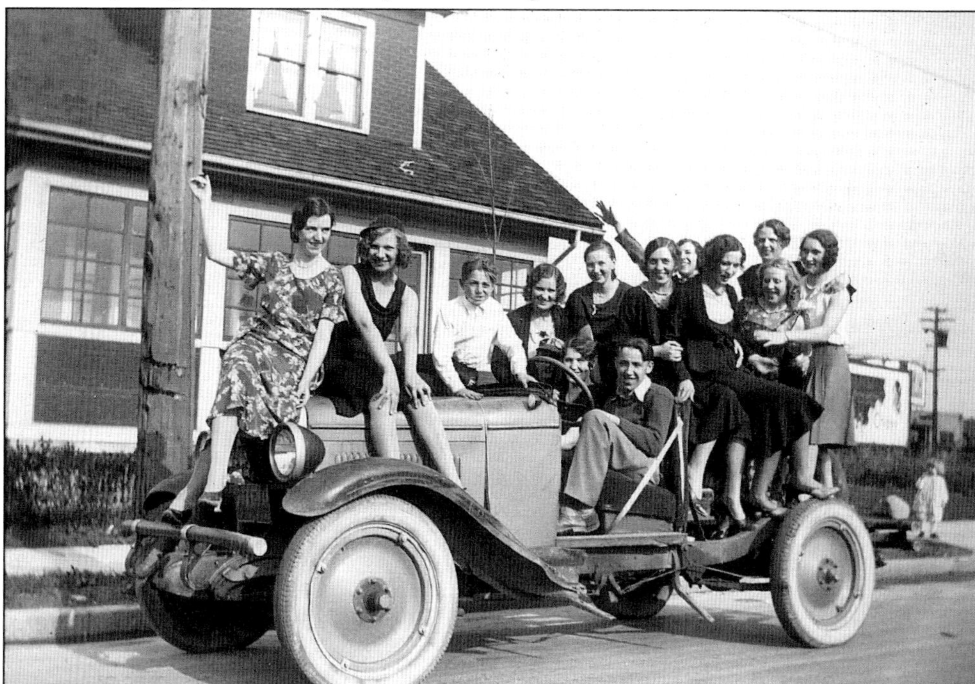

Jalopies were the rage in the Roaring Twenties. This one is a cutdown truck chassis, without seatbelts. It seems to have attracted the coeds, seen here with a young man identified as Frank S. The photograph was taken near the University of Rochester's women's campus, when it was located on University Avenue.

Two

"Rochester-Made Means Quality"

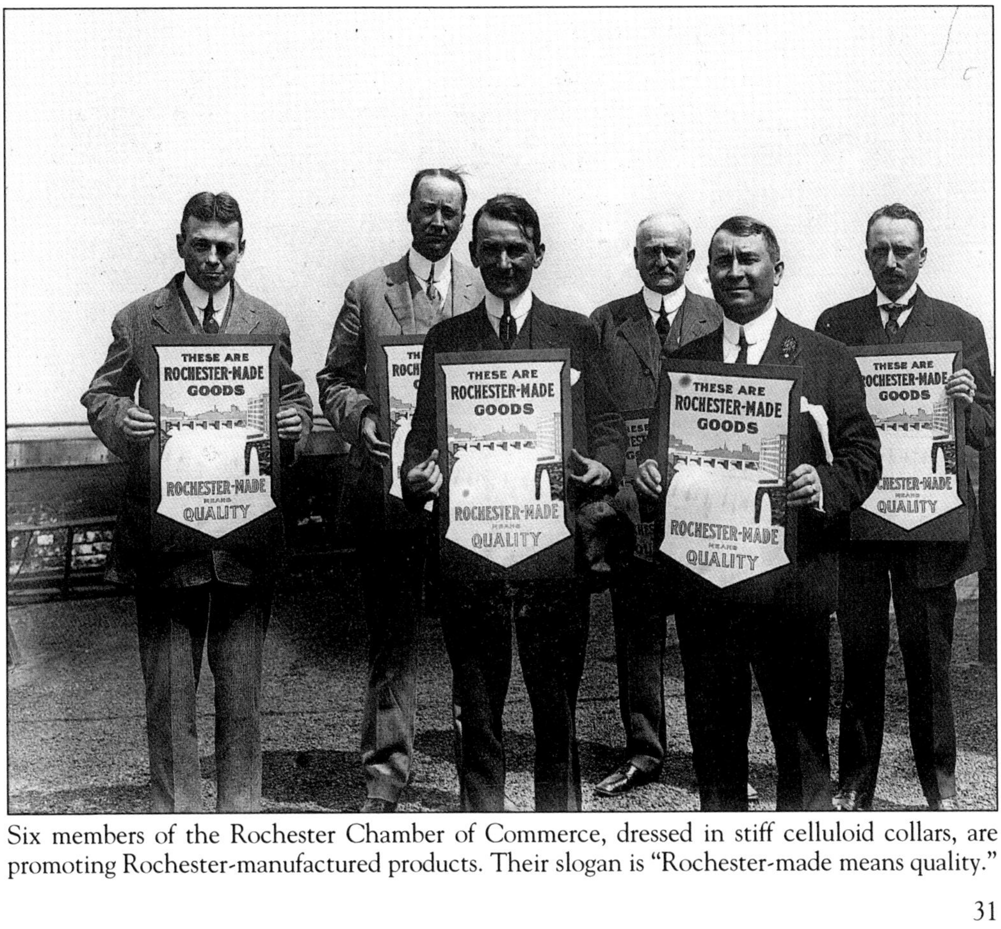

Six members of the Rochester Chamber of Commerce, dressed in stiff celluloid collars, are promoting Rochester-manufactured products. Their slogan is "Rochester-made means quality."

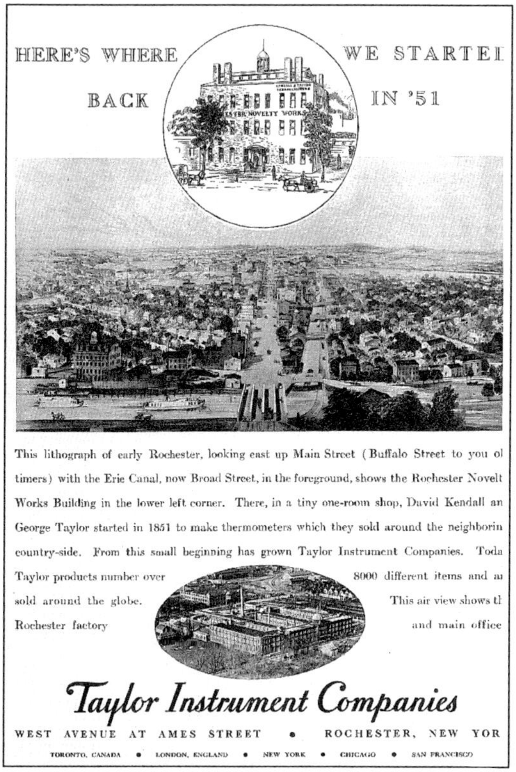

The Taylor Instrument Company was one of Rochester's early firms that grew to national prominence. The advertisement illustrates its origins and growth.

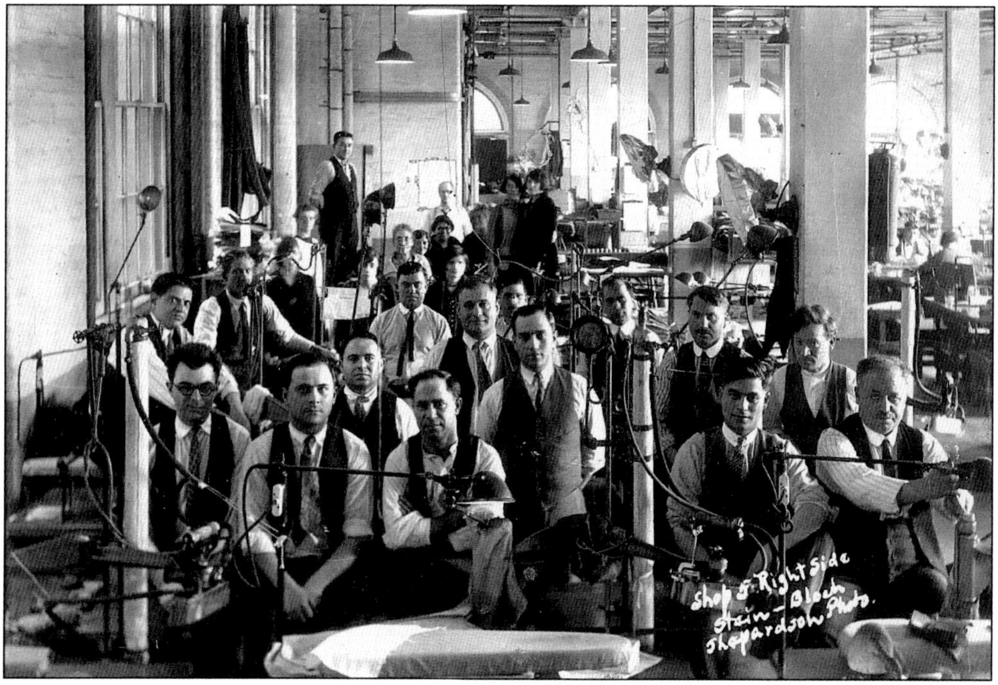

The tailors, cutters, and pressers at the Stein-Block Clothing Company, at 134 St. Paul Street, look rather natty in this the 1930s photograph. Notice that they all wore white shirts, ties, and vests when working.

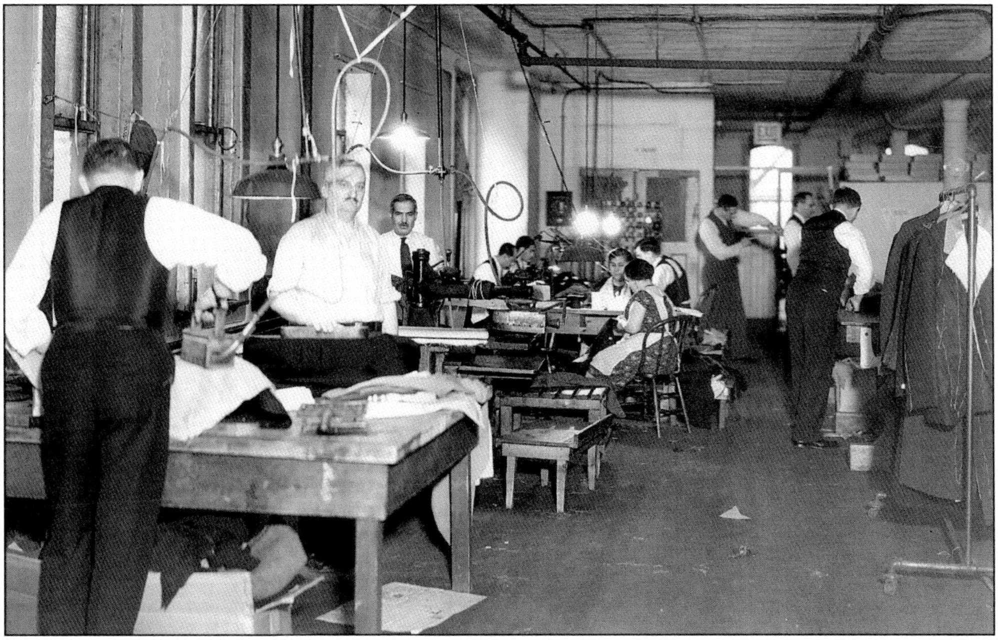

Rochester boasted numerous small clothing shops, many doing special job lots for the local industry. Shown in December 1931 is a group of skilled workers for the Rochester Raiment Company, at 208 Andrew Street. The man in the foreground using the heavy gas-fired flatiron had an especially tough job.

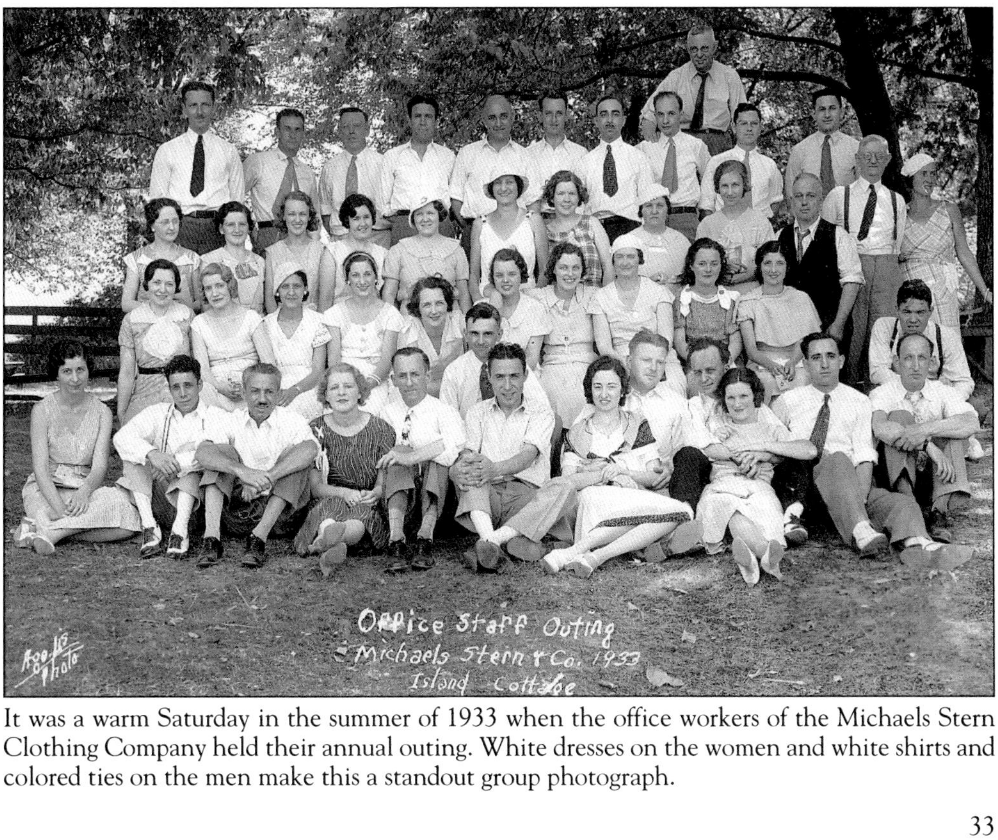

It was a warm Saturday in the summer of 1933 when the office workers of the Michaels Stern Clothing Company held their annual outing. White dresses on the women and white shirts and colored ties on the men make this a standout group photograph.

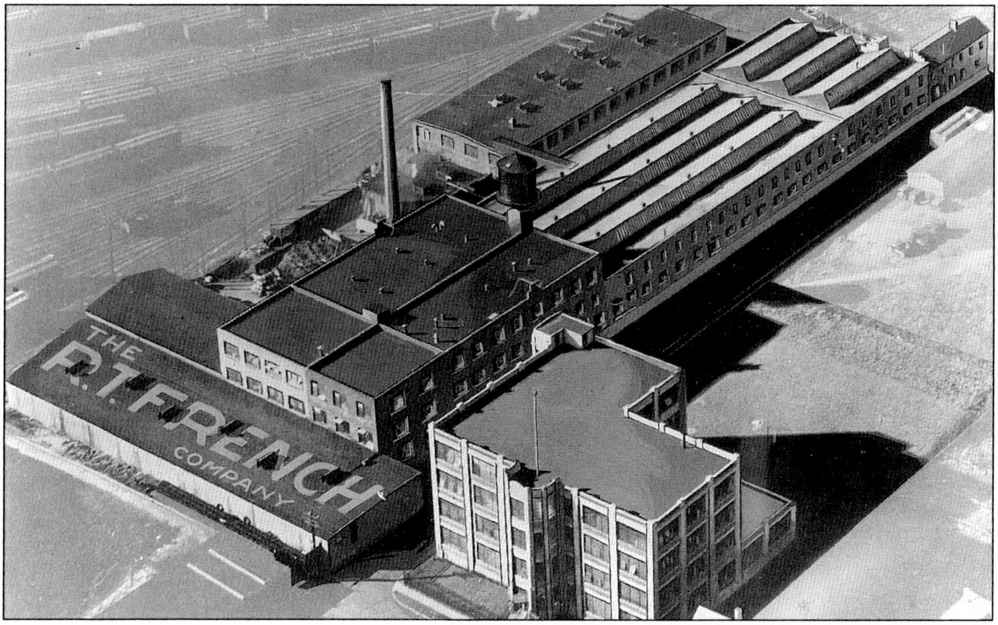

The Robert T. French Company, spice manufacturer, arrived in Fairport in 1883, moved to Brown's Race c. 1886, and to 1 Mustard Street in 1912. By 1940, the firm had grown to become one of the nation's leading spice merchants and the pacesetter in sales of creamy mustard.

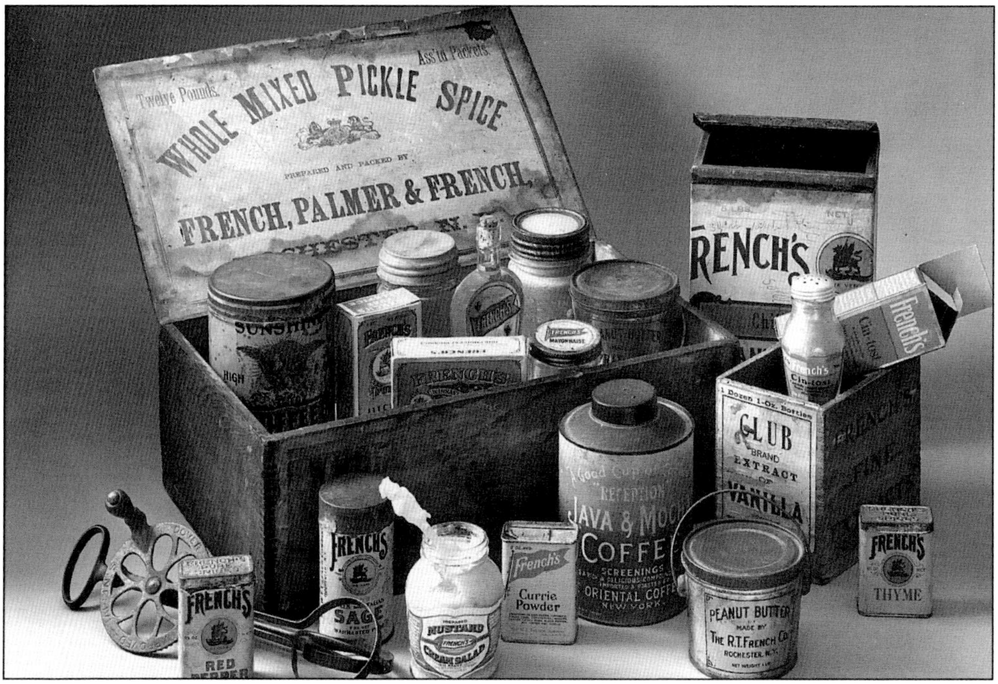

Some of French's early products, dating to the 1880s, are displayed here. The creation of creamy mustard won nationwide fame for French's. Birdseed sales helped the company weather the Great Depression. Scores of new products were added to French's line. The removal of the company to New Jersey was a dismal failure. Today, only mustard and handful of products still carry the French's name. (Photograph Len Rosenberg.)

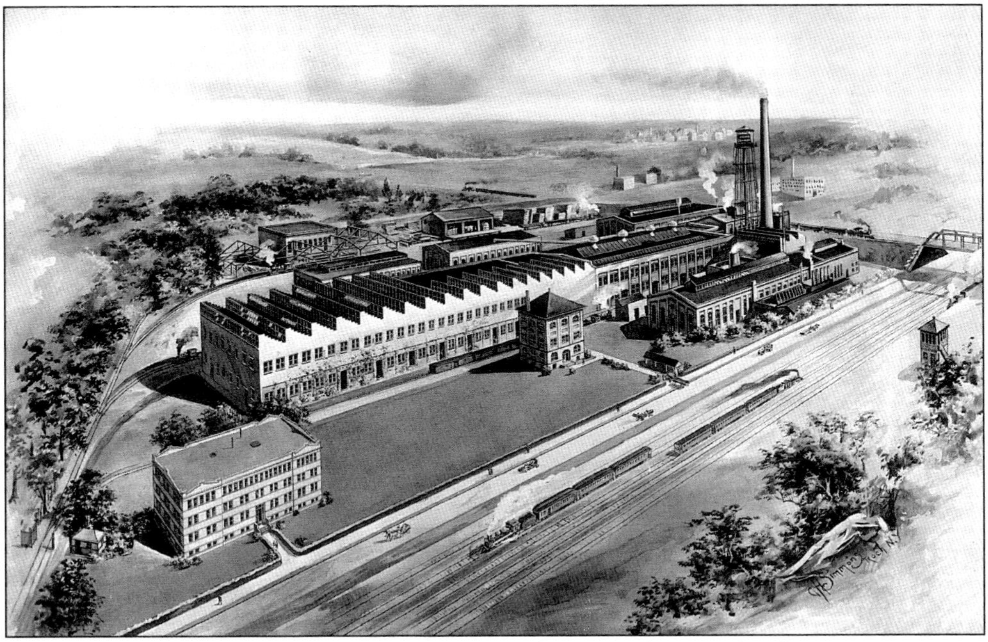

The General Railway Signal Company, seen in this 1907 drawing, has been a presence in Rochester for nearly a century. Founded in 1904, it was a merger of Buffalo's Taylor Signal Company and Rochester's Pneumatic Signal Company. Originally located at 801 West Avenue, the foundry produced castings for a wide variety of railroad safety devices.

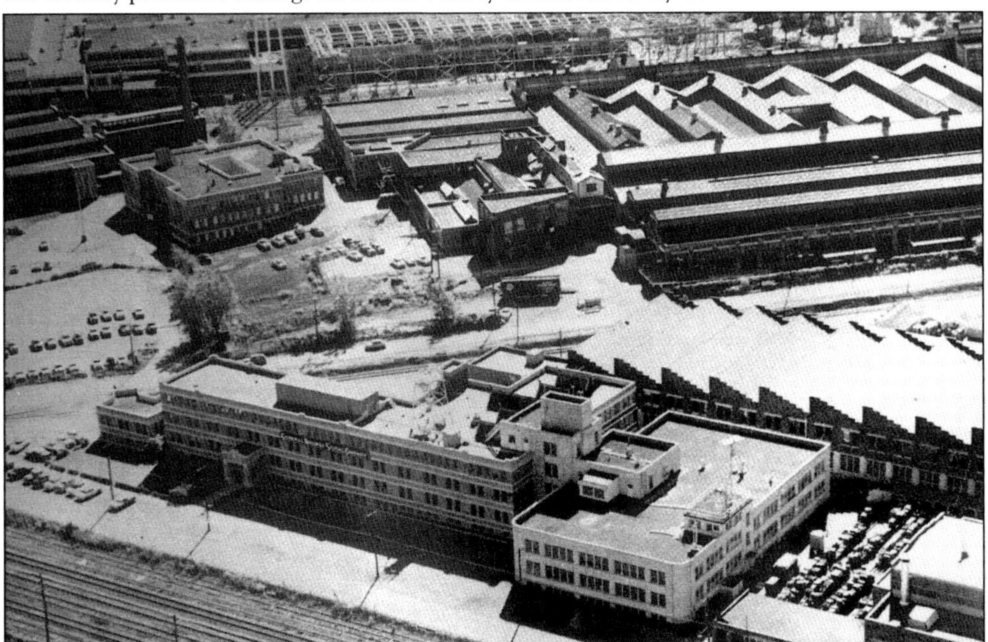

Many alterations and additions to the General Railway Signal Company can be seen when comparing this 1960s photograph with the drawing done in 1904. The Thomas H. Symington Company, manufacturer of railroad wheel journal boxes and other specialties, dominates the area just above Cairn Street.

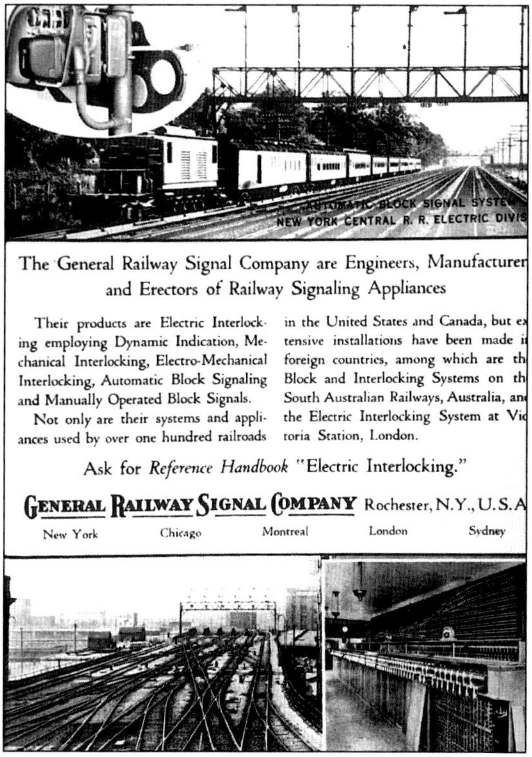

This vintage advertisement promotes automatic and manual block signaling devices that kept many railroads in the United States, Canada, and South Australia on the right track.

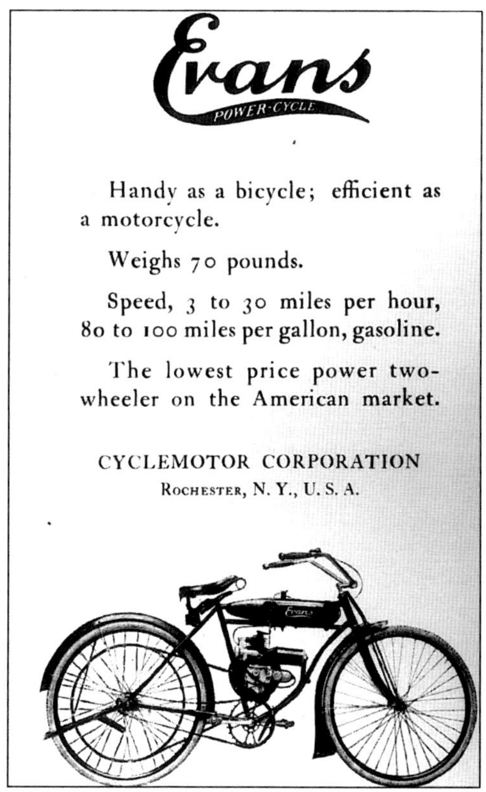

During 1915 and 1916, the General Railway Signal Company manufactured small gasoline engines for the Cyclemotor Corporation, located in the Arlington Building, at 25 East Main Street. When adapted to an ordinary diamond-frame bicycle with a rear-wheel belt transmission, the compact, air-cooled, 21-pound engine would zip along at a brisk 25 miles an hour on a level road.

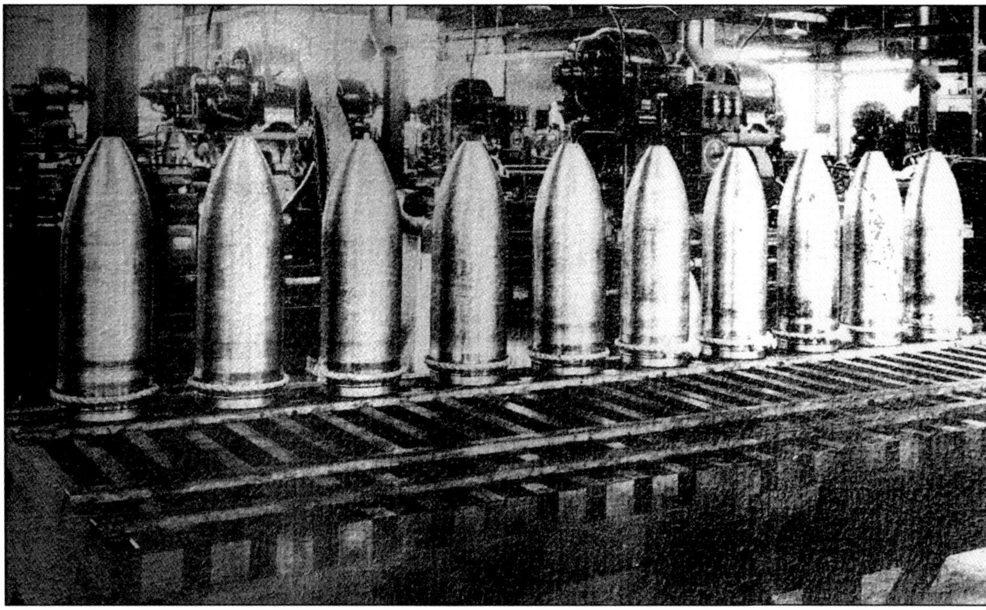

Prior to the entry of United States into World War I, the General Railway Signal Company received a rush order from the British government for artillery shells. The company erected a new building in a record 43 days and delivered 80,000 9.2-inch artillery shells to England on schedule by March 31, 1917.

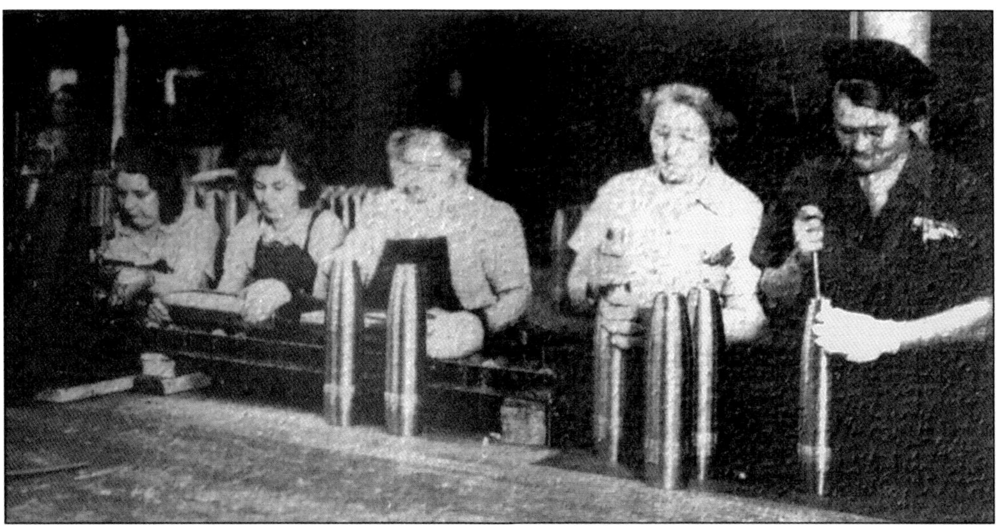

The first time in the nation that a "completely power-conveyorized system" was employed in a production line is documented in this photograph. From 1941 to 1945, the system enabled women workers to speed the assembly of 105-millimeter M-1 shells for World War II.

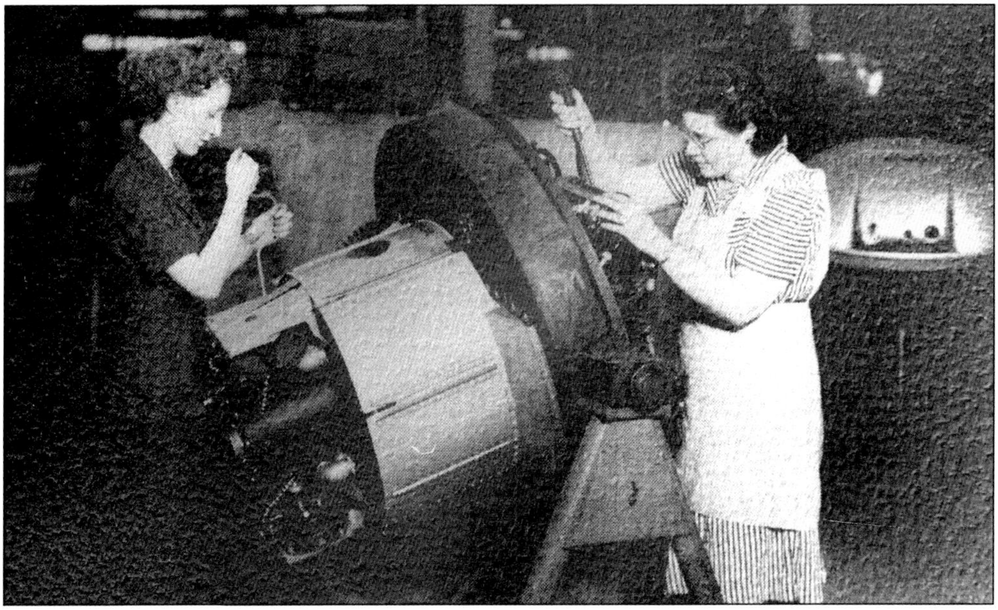

Another contract fulfilled by the General Railway Signal Company from 1942 to 1945 was the assembly of a very complex "remotely controlled turret system for B-29 long-range bombers." Women played a vital part in meeting the country's war needs. In all, they assembled 2,100 sets of the complicated turrets.

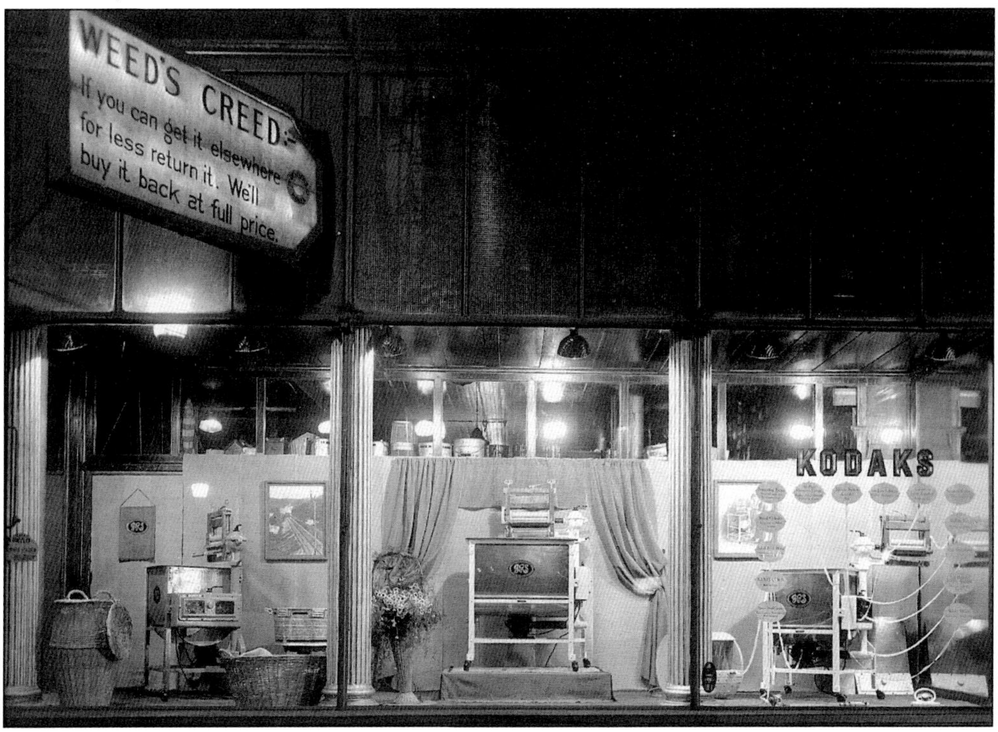

In 1920, G-R-S Products was formed as a subsidiary. Its slogan, "Good-Reliable-Servant," was chosen, using the company's initials. Weed's Hardware Store, at 15 Exchange Street, highlighted its new product, a washing machine.

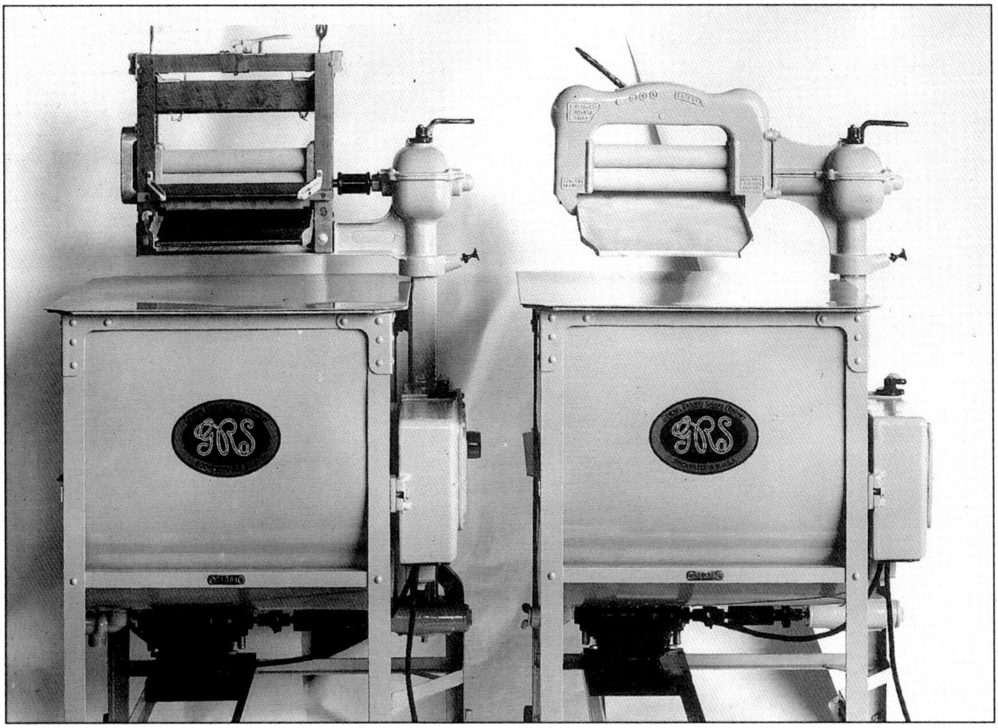

Refinements were made to the early washing machines, notably to the wringer device from a wooden to a metal frame. The machines look crude by today's standards, but they sure beat the old washtub. In 1922, G-R-S produced a dishwasher that looked much like the washing machines but came with hoses for attachment to kitchen sinks for water supply and drainage.

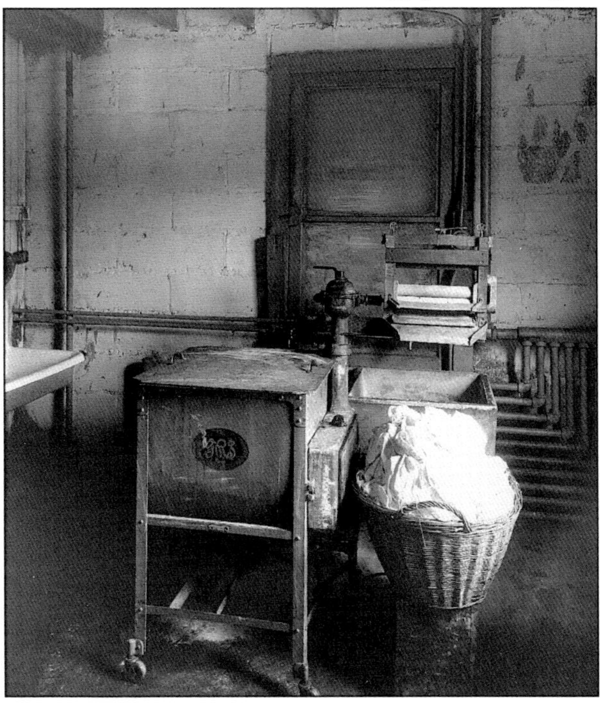

This much used machine was photographed in the cellar of a Rochester home. Although it had lost its luster, the washing machine still ran smoothly. The sturdy washing machines were produced from 1920 through 1926. They were G-R-S: Good-Reliable-Servants.

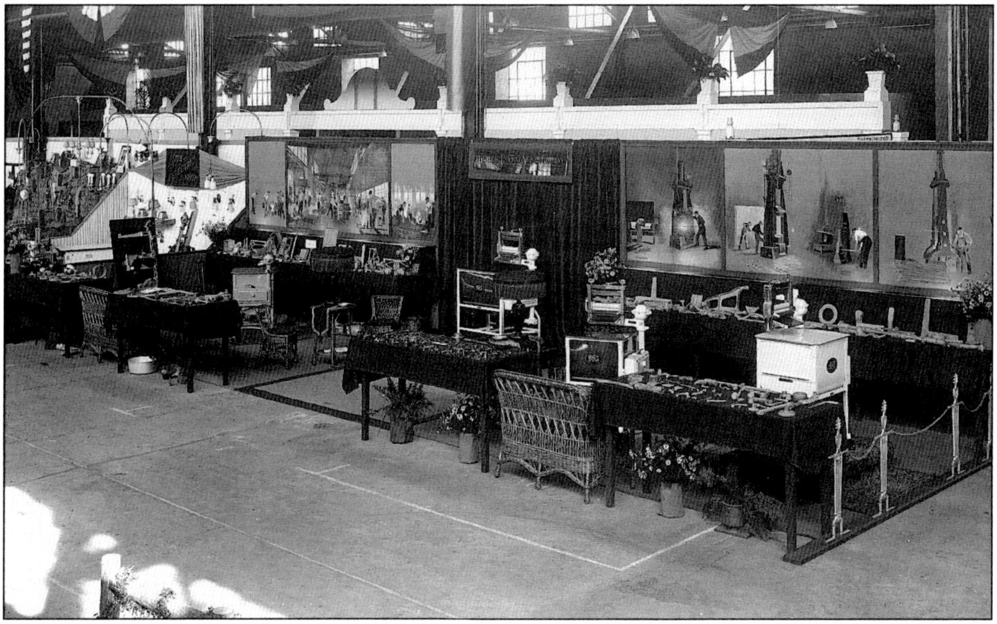

During Rochester's annual Industrial Show at Exposition Park c. 1925, the General Railway Signal Company set up a three-booth display of products manufactured at its foundry and machine shop. At the left, the Ruth Electric Shop displays the latest in lighting fixtures.

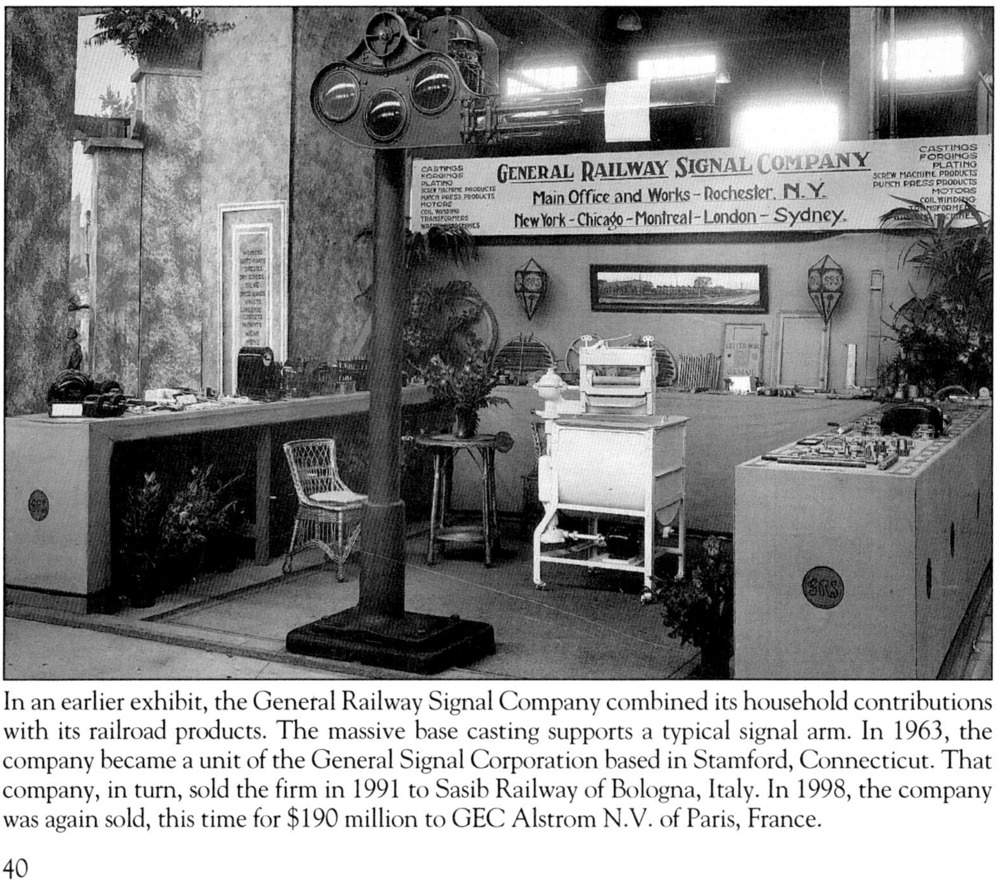

In an earlier exhibit, the General Railway Signal Company combined its household contributions with its railroad products. The massive base casting supports a typical signal arm. In 1963, the company became a unit of the General Signal Corporation based in Stamford, Connecticut. That company, in turn, sold the firm in 1991 to Sasib Railway of Bologna, Italy. In 1998, the company was again sold, this time for $190 million to GEC Alstrom N.V. of Paris, France.

Established on May 1, 1838, Kerr, Cunningham & Company opened its carriage company for the construction of cutters and buggies at 3 Canal Street. By 1865, James Cunningham owned the firm, admitting his son Joseph Cunningham as a partner. Soon, Cunningham carriages were considered "wheeled luxury." The company produced the finest in carriages, landaus, barouches, buggies, ambulances, and hearses. It was considered a great privilege to be transported in a silver-ornamented Cunningham funeral coach.

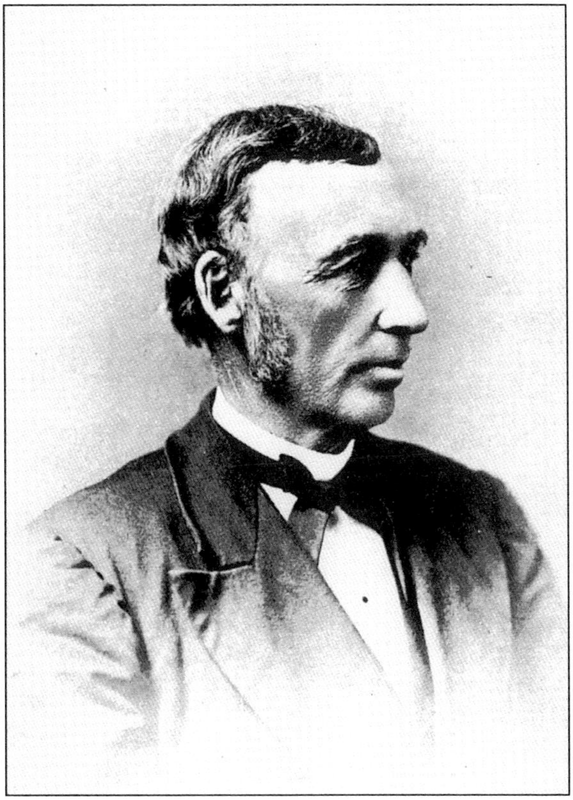

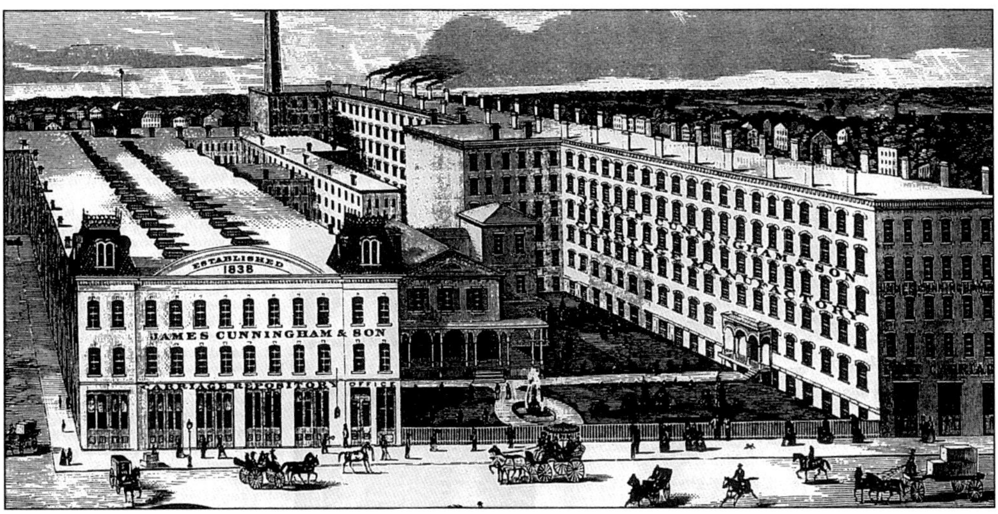

An 1882 artist's sketch of the extensive Cunningham & Son Carriage Manufactory shows the building's multistoried wings nearly engulfing the Italianate home where James Cunningham lived. It is ironic that a master craftsman of fine carriages had such a short walk to work.

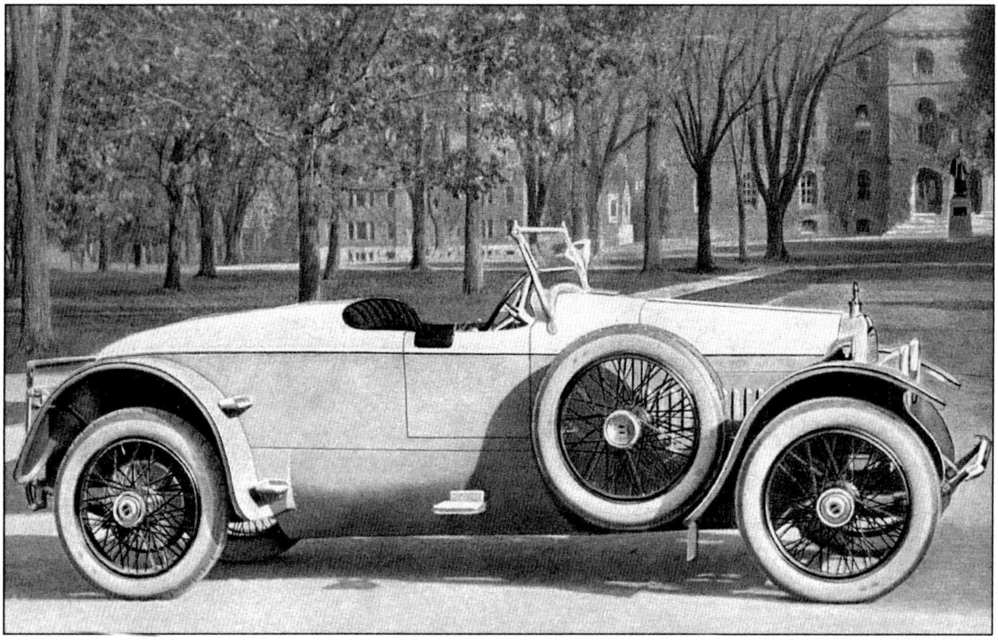

Using the former women's campus of the University of Rochester as a background, the snappy yellow 1918 Cunningham roadster looks very handsome. It must have been a genuine attraction for the college students. Note that the outside running boards were eliminated. The automobile was powered by one of world's first eight-cylinder engines.

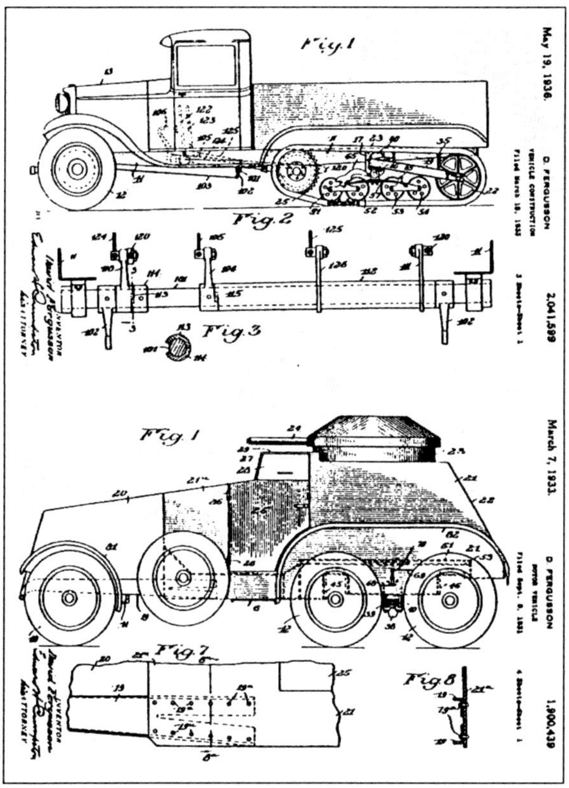

From 1928 to 1935, Cunningham produced two military vehicles. This was accomplished with the expertise of David Fergusson, an automotive genius who had worked for the Pierce Arrow Company in Buffalo. One of Fergusson's patents was a tank track with "light-weight rubber-block treads." Fitting these to civilian trucks made them useful for military purposes. The other was a high-speed armored vehicle. The 9,800-pound machine cruised at 55 miles per hour, powered by a 133-horsepower Cunningham V-8 engine. Fergusson is also remembered for developing the V-8 engine and establishing the prestigious Rochester Engineering Society.

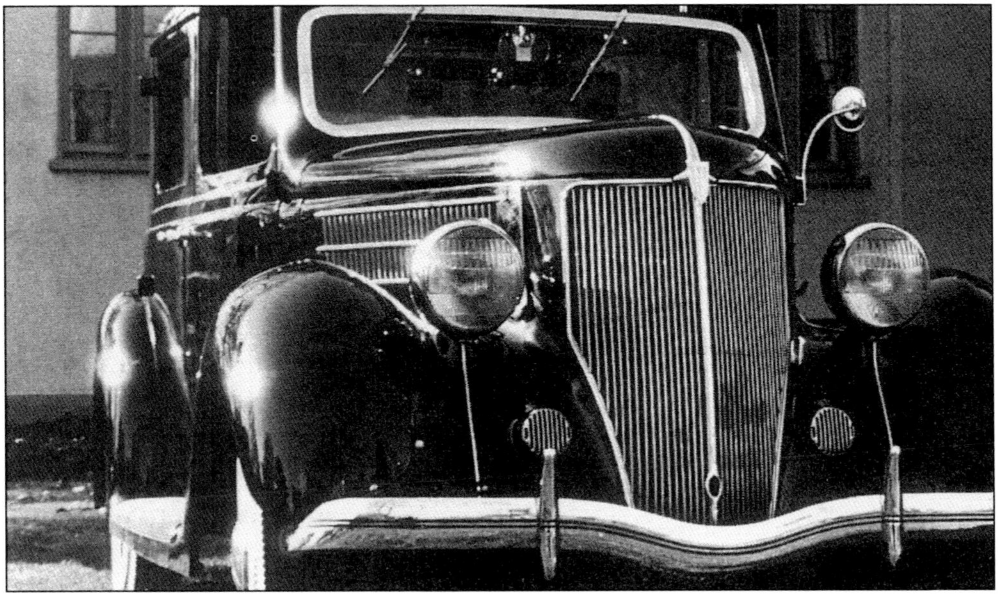

The 1936 Cunningham-Ford town car, once owned by Charlotte Whitney Allen of Oliver Street, is now in the possession of the Rochester Museum and Science Center. Just 36 of these rare cars with a Ford chassis and Cunningham custom-built body were manufactured in 1936. (Photograph William Frank.)

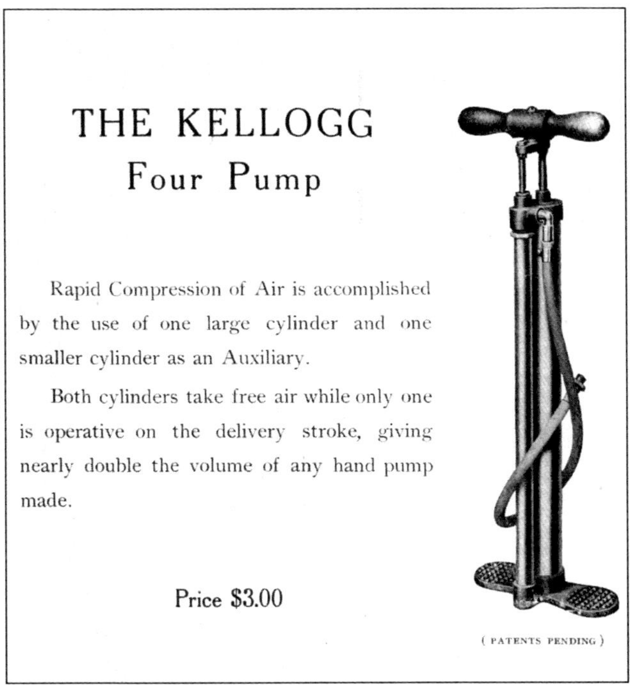

THE KELLOGG

Four Pump

Rapid Compression of Air is accomplished by the use of one large cylinder and one smaller cylinder as an Auxiliary.

Both cylinders take free air while only one is operative on the delivery stroke, giving nearly double the volume of any hand pump made.

Price $3.00

(PATENTS PENDING)

The Kellogg Manufacturing Company, at East Main and Circle Streets, was in the forefront of the automobile age. The company's 1909 catalog illustrated its line of tire-inflating pumps. Some may remember the era of those "pesky" red rubber inner tubes.

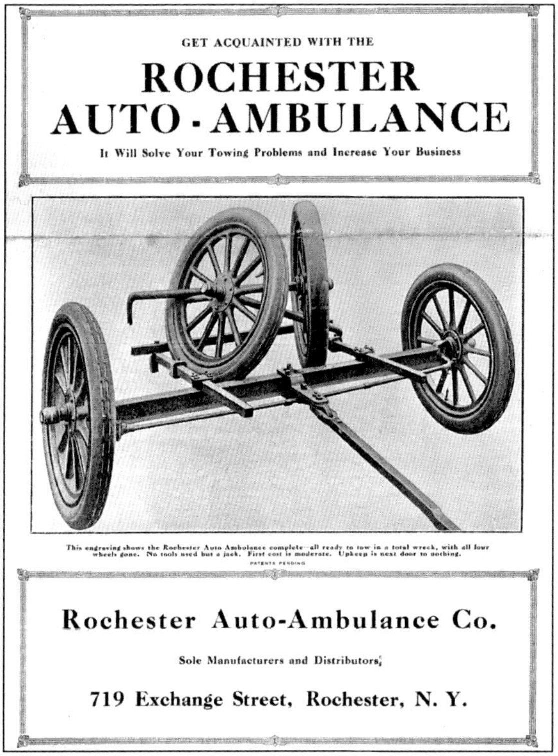

Other, lesser-known entrepreneurs made contributions to the auto industry. The Rochester Auto-Ambulance Company prompted a brief flurry of interest in its device for towing "a total wreck, with all four wheels gone." The two-wheeled trailer was a short-lived venture *c.* 1920.

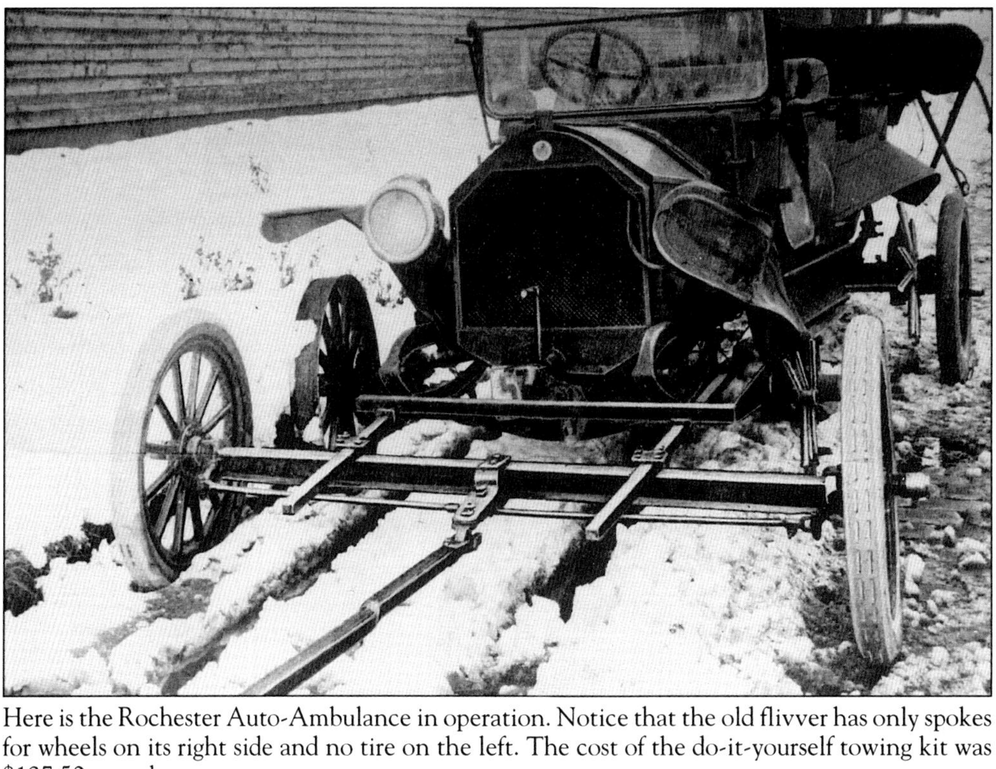

Here is the Rochester Auto-Ambulance in operation. Notice that the old flivver has only spokes for wheels on its right side and no tire on the left. The cost of the do-it-yourself towing kit was $127.50 complete.

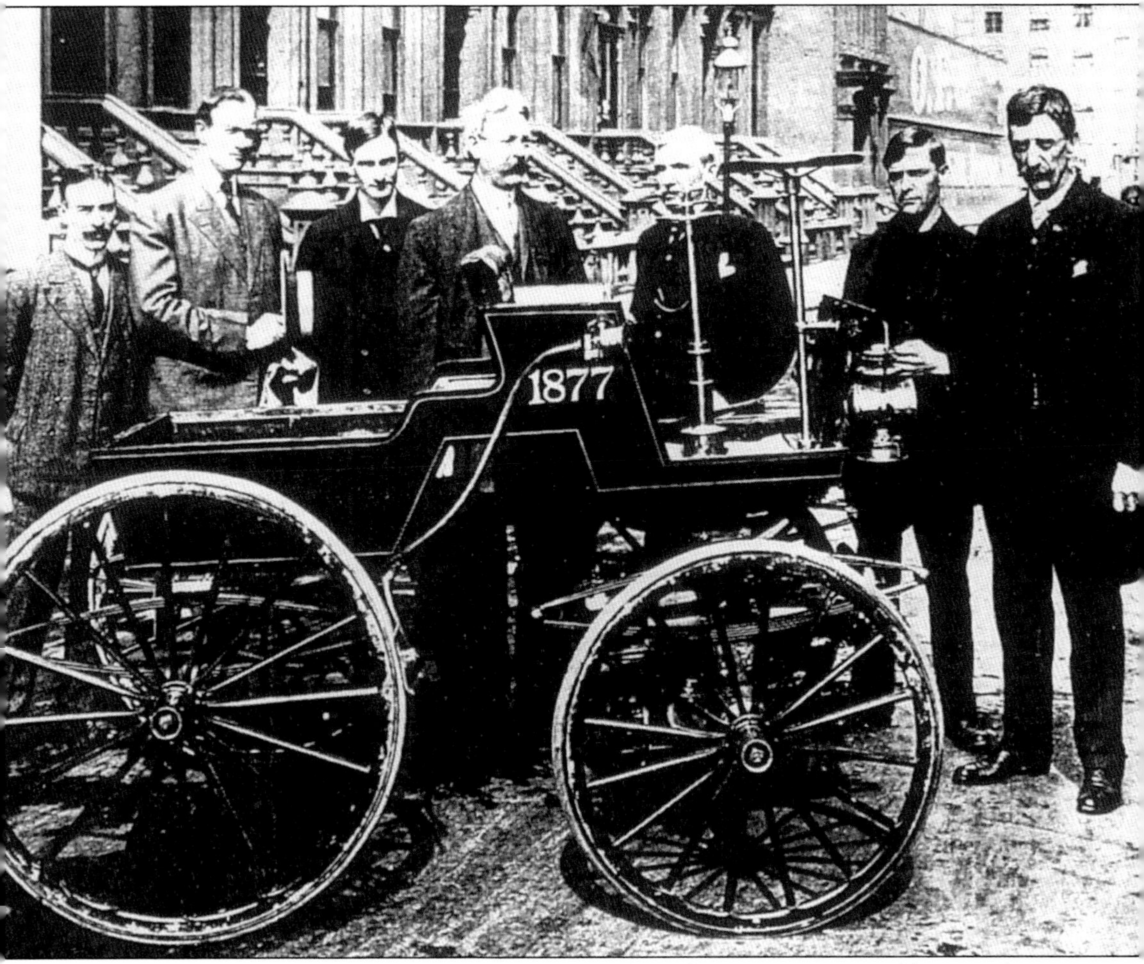

In 1905, George Selden demonstrated his invention, a horseless carriage powered by a gasoline engine. George B. Selden Sr., third from right, Henry Reichenbach, and a young Henry R. Selden are seen, accompanied by drivers and guards.

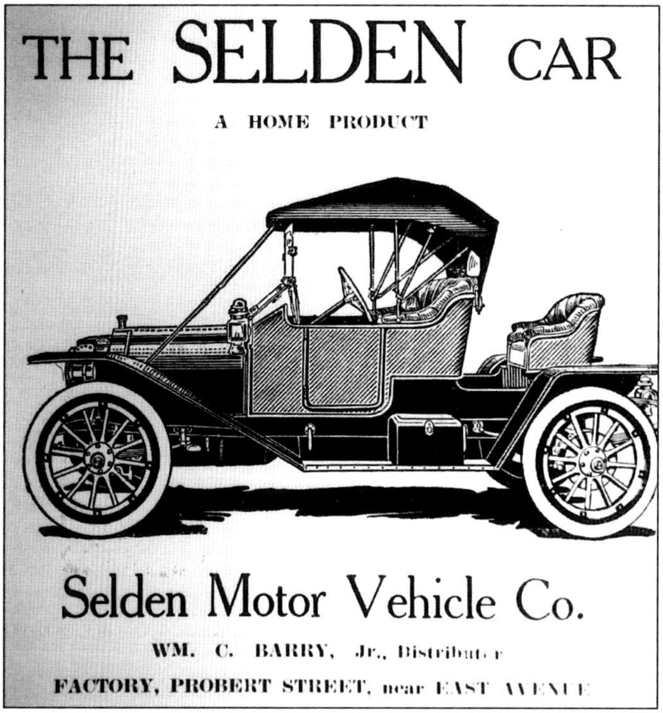

In a factory at University Avenue and Probert Street, workmen produced a more modern Selden car. George Selden, after moving to Gibbs Street in 1859, worked with Frank Clement to invent the nation's first gasoline-powered, one-cylinder internal combustion engine in 1878. Called the Father of the Automobile, Selden held a monopoly on patents covering the production of automobiles in America for nearly 12 years.

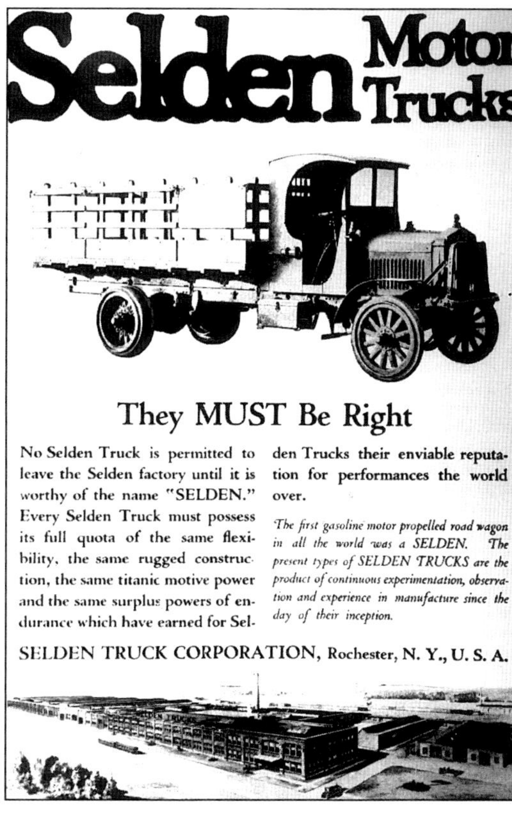

The advertisement for the Selden Motor Truck appeared *c.* 1917, about the time the company added trucks to its automobile production line. Selden's Victory trucks were used in France during World War I. A blue letter S on a white background was the company's famous symbol. It is estimated that by 1922, the year of George Selden's death, the company had produced 10,000 vehicles.

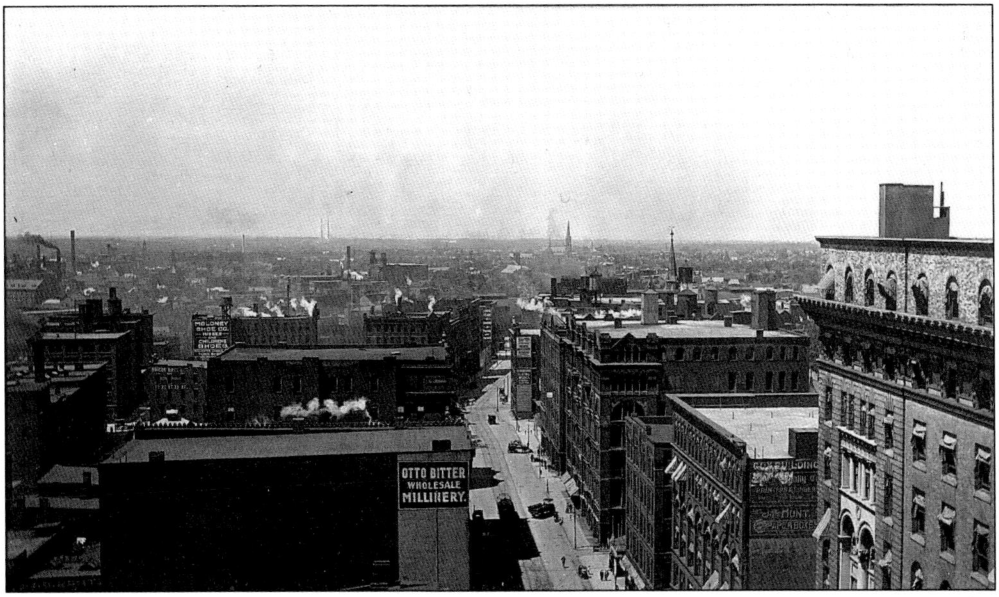

This unusual view of downtown was taken *c.* 1911 looking north from the 11th floor of the Commerce Building (Convention Center Site). Shown at the left are the bygone firms of Bittner's Millinery, at 35 St. Paul Street, and Maloney Shoe Company, at 25 Otsego Street. At the right are the Granite, Cox, and Archer Buildings. Next, at 82 St. Paul Street, is the H.H. Warner's Safe Yeast Company, or Absolute Cure Company. (Photograph S.P. Hines; courtesy George Brown.)

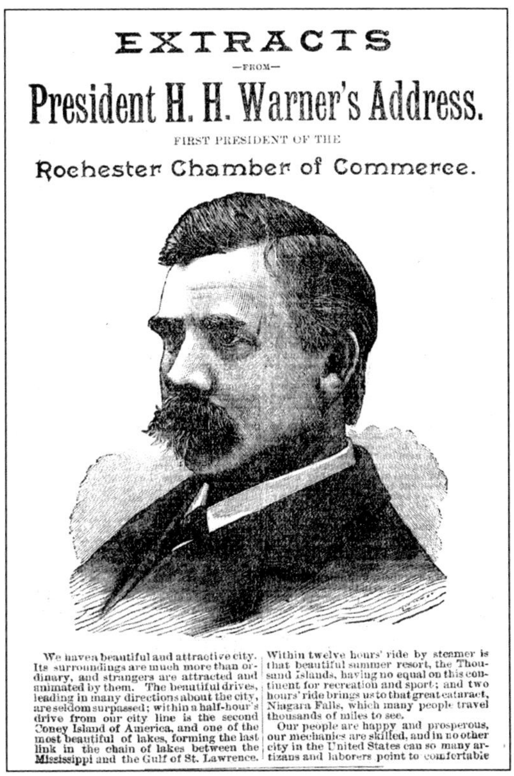

EXTRACTS

—FROM—

President H. H. Warner's Address.

FIRST PRESIDENT OF THE

Rochester Chamber of Commerce.

We have a beautiful and attractive city. Its surroundings are much more than ordinary, and strangers are attracted and animated by them. The beautiful drives, leading in many directions about the city, are seldom surpassed; within a half-hour's drive from our city line is the second Coney Island of America, and one of the most beautiful of lakes, forming the last link in the chain of lakes between the Mississippi and the Gulf of St. Lawrence. Within twelve hours' ride by steamer is that beautiful summer resort, the Thousand Islands, having no equal on this continent for recreation and sport; and two hours' ride brings us to that great cataract, Niagara Falls, which many people travel thousands of miles to see.

Our people are happy and prosperous, our mechanics are skilled, and in no other city in the United States can so many artizans and laborers point to comfortable

Two decades before George Eastman arrived on the scene, Hubert Harrington Warner was lauded in local newspapers for his Warner's Safe Cure and his Warner's Safe Pills. By the age of 45, Warner was one of the wealthiest and most respected men in the city. His patent medicines were sold throughout the world. Warner's advertising costs rose to $500,000 a year.

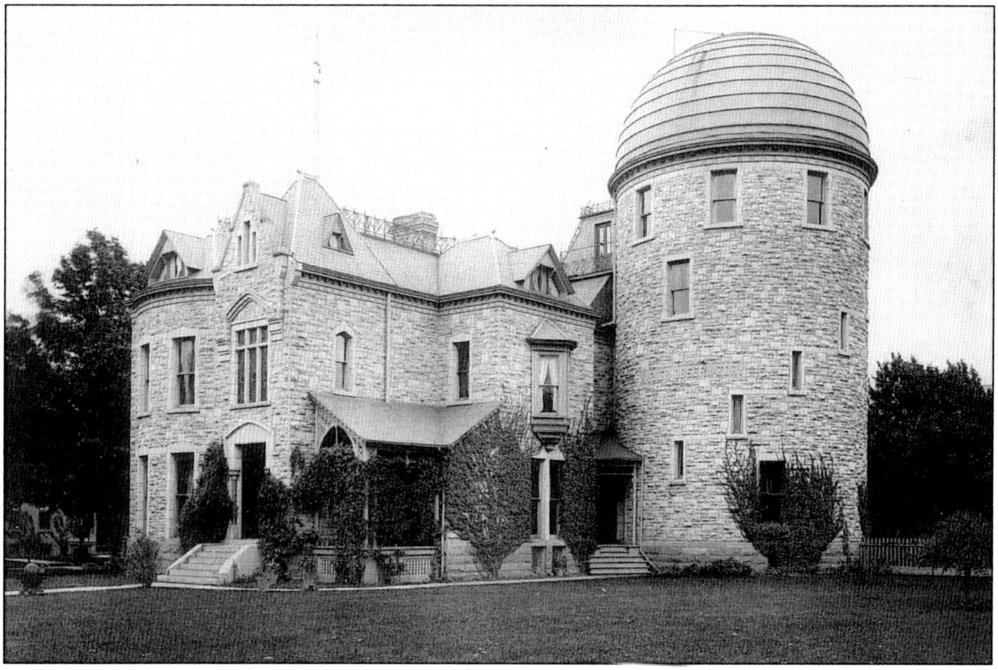

H.H. Warner built an observatory on Arnold Park and East Avenue in 1883 for Lewis Swift's 16-inch, 22-foot-long telescope. For 25¢, members of the public could observe the wonders of the universe. The popular observatory brought Warner immense publicity.

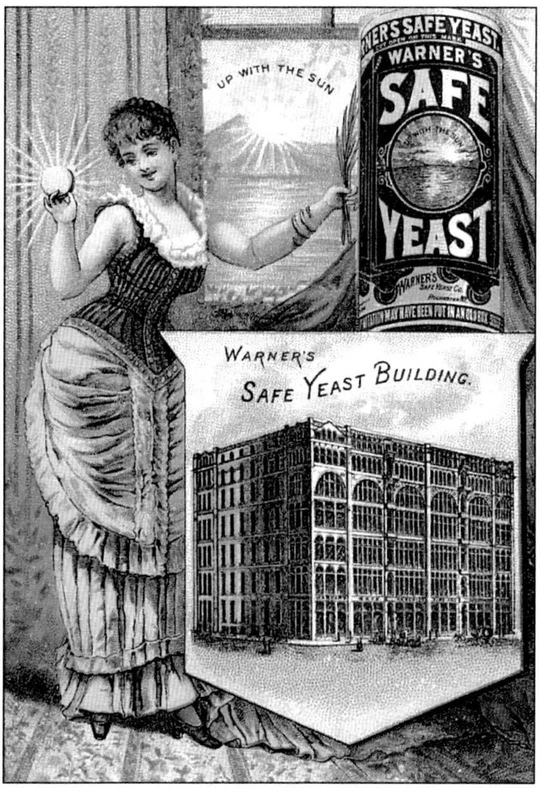

This advertisement illustrates the product and H.H. Warner's half-acre, eight-story building, erected in 1883 at a cost of $250,000. The company produced patent medicines at the rate of 7,000 gallons per day to fill 56,000 brown glass pint bottles selling for $1.25 each.

In 1887, Warner brought out a new line of medicinal miracles, omitting the word "cure." The products became Log Cabin "remedies." A compassionate frontiersman is pictured assisting an ailing Native American to his cabin for treatment with a Warner product.

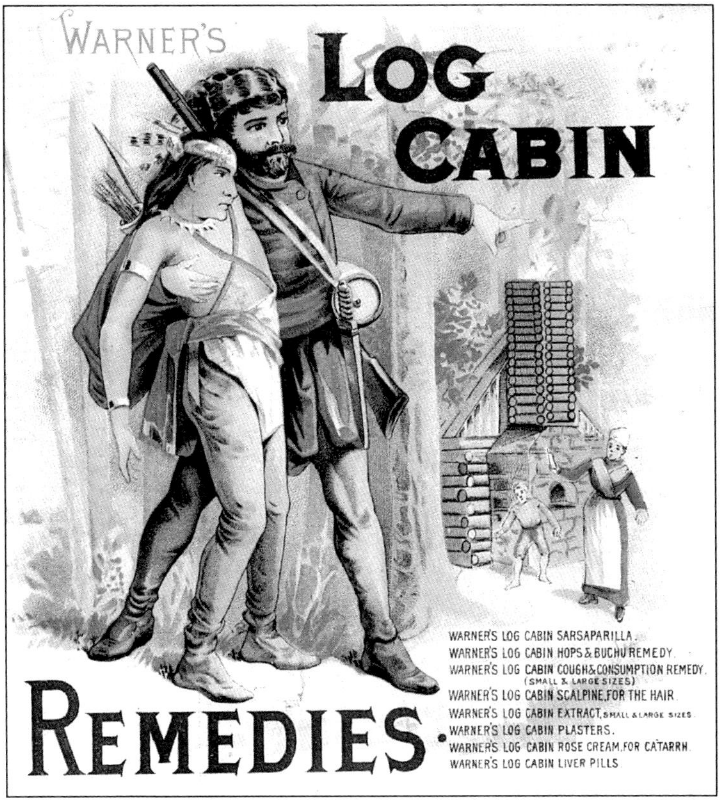

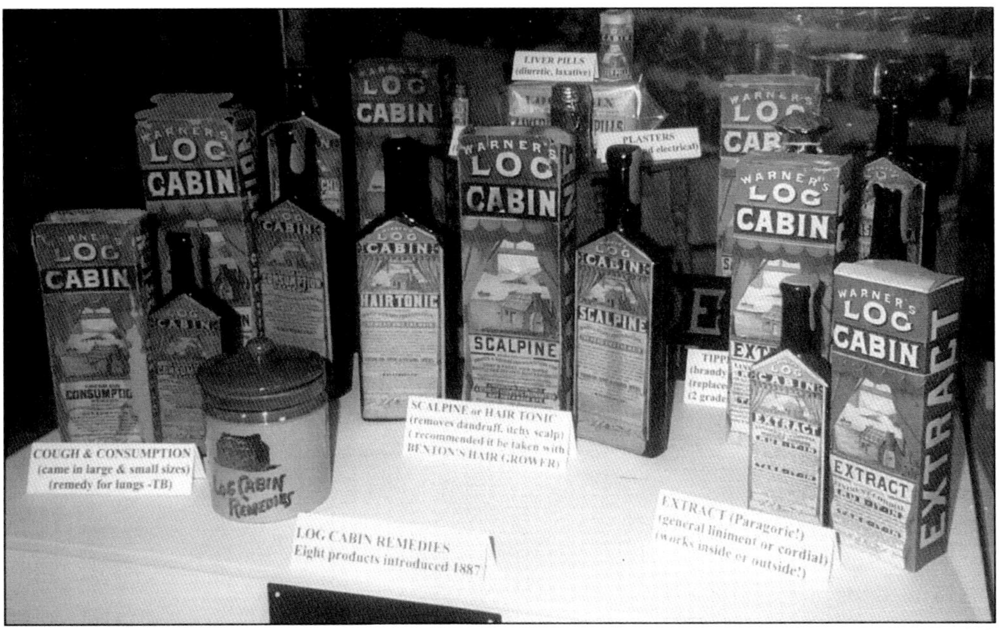

A unique collection of Warner's Log Cabin products is displayed at a Rochester Bottle Club show. Early bottles with labels intact and still within their pasteboard boxes makes the rare collection even more unusual.

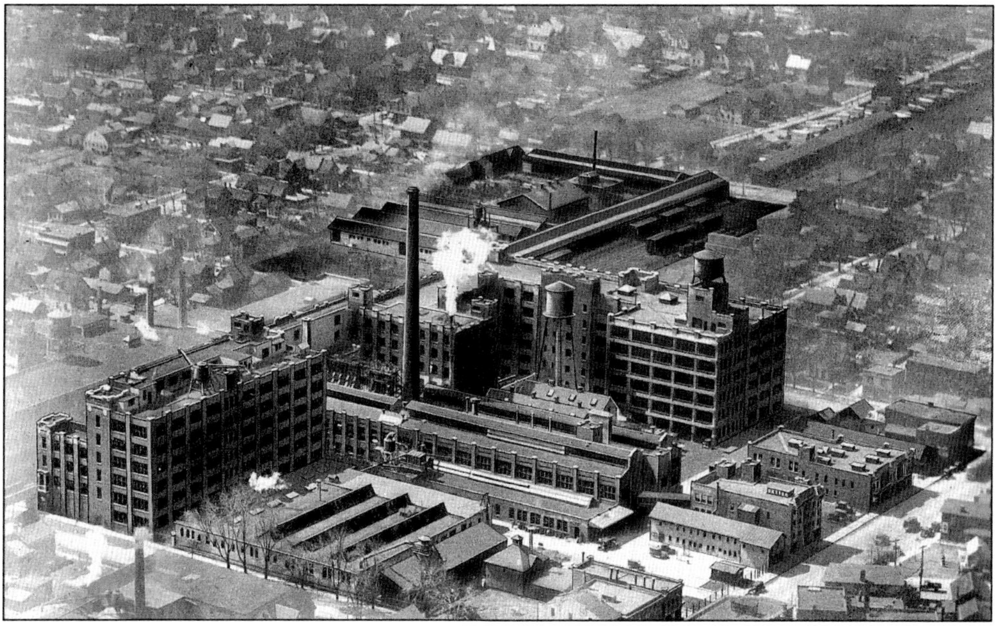

This 1920s bird's-eye view of the North East Electric Company shows the extensive plant at 379 Lyell Avenue. The avenue is at the lower right of the photograph. Edward Halbleib and Thomas Lee started the firm in 1908 to produce horns, starters, speedometers, and other automotive accessories. In 1930, the firm became the Delco Appliance Company.

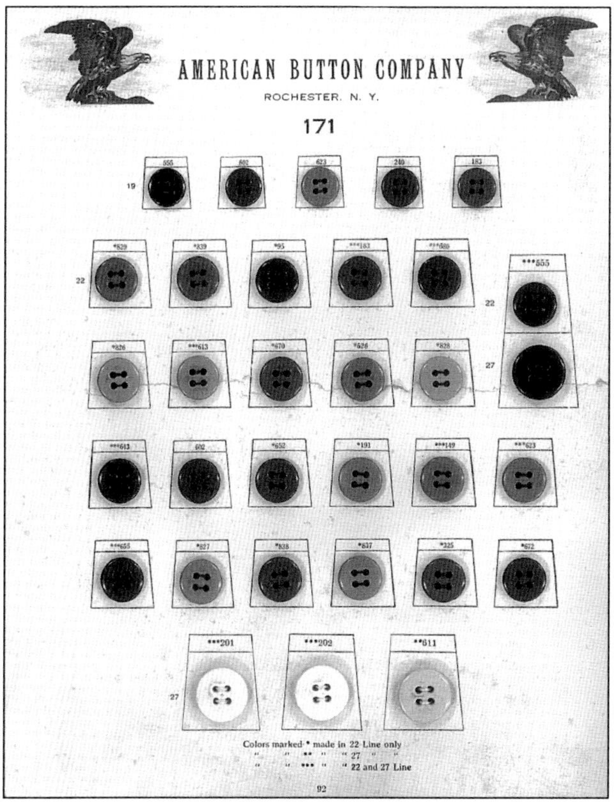

Rochester was not only a garment- and shoe-manufacturing city but also a button-making center. Shown is a salesman's sample card of trouser and shirt fasteners made *c.* 1905 by the American Button Company, located on Champeney Terrace off North Union Street.

Three

INDUSTRIES ON THE GENESEE

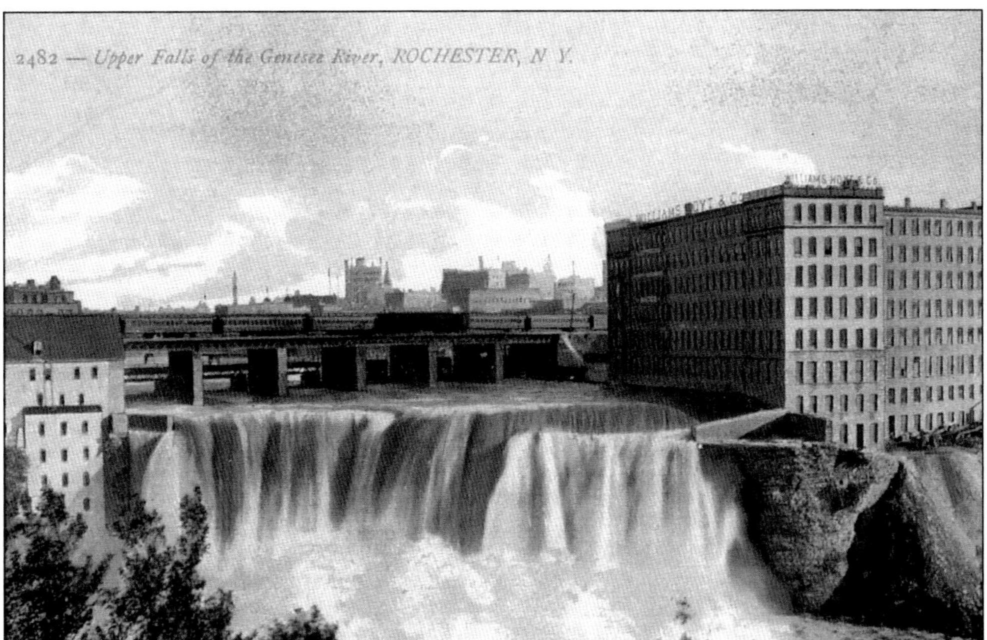

Tons of water surging and crashing over the Upper Falls of the mighty Genesee River provided the power that turned huge waterwheels and mill wheels, giving birth to Rochester's industrial beginnings. The Gorseline Building is on the right. The Brush Electric Light Company building, housing turbines for generating electricity, is on the left.

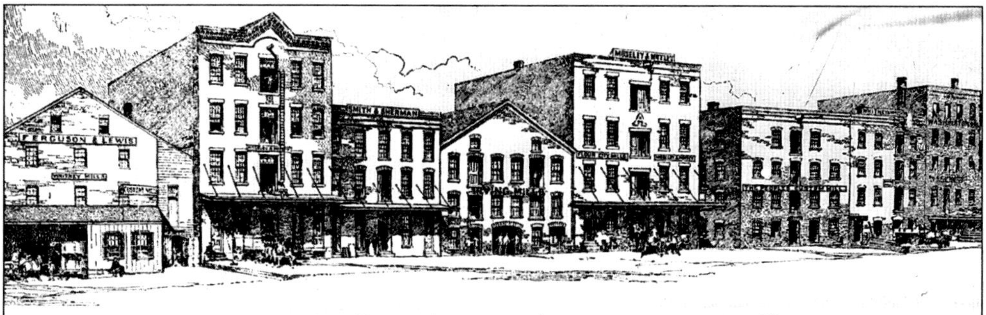

FLOUR MILLS FRONTING ON BROWN'S RACE, ROCHESTER: 1880

The mills that were constructed along Brown's Race and Mill Street used water drawn from the Genesee River. By 1870, a total of 21 mills were operating in Rochester. Seen here are two of the early mills, those belonging to Moseley and Motley; one is identified with the large letter A and the other with a B. In 1888, the B mill boasted that it ground 800 barrels of flour daily.

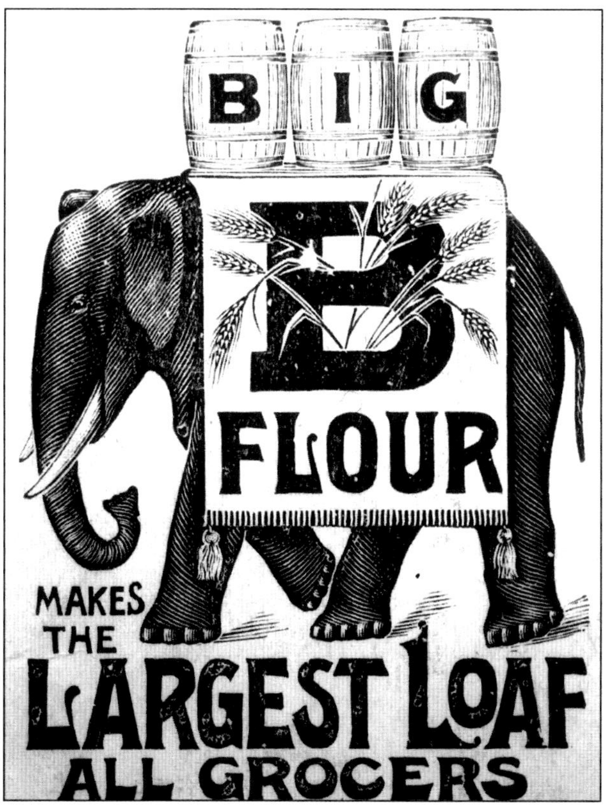

Most Rochester grocery stores carried Moseley and Motley's Big B Flour from 1910 through 1930. The flour that made elephant-sized loaves of bread was a kitchen favorite.

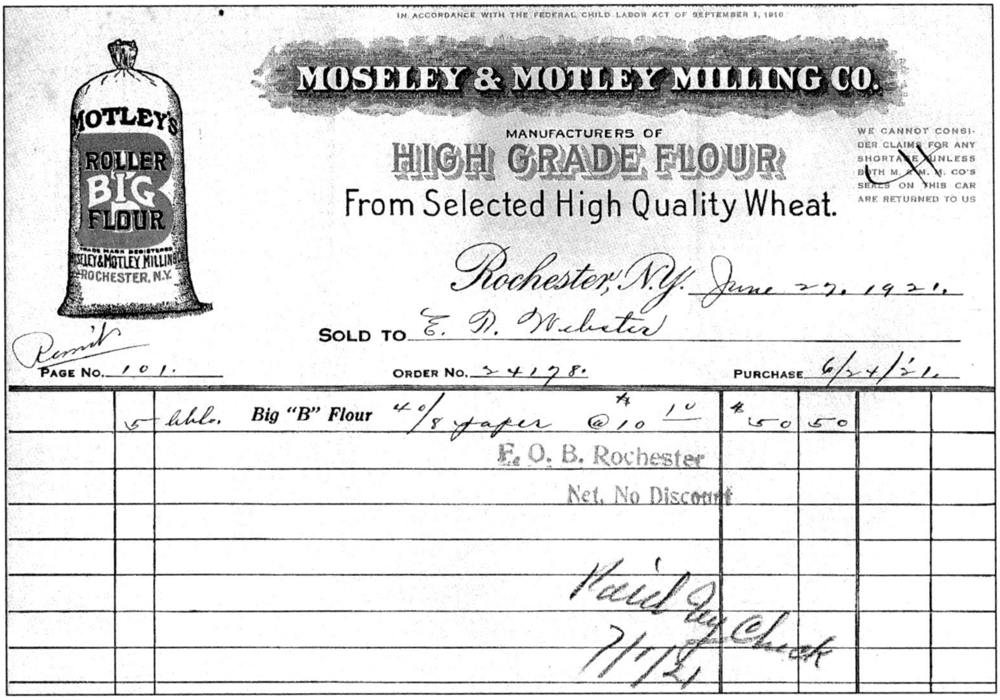

IN ACCORDANCE WITH THE FEDERAL CHILD LABOR ACT OF SEPTEMBER 1, 1916

MOSELEY & MOTLEY MILLING CO.

MANUFACTURERS OF

HIGH GRADE FLOUR

From Selected High Quality Wheat.

WE CANNOT CONSIDER CLAIMS FOR ANY SHORTAGE UNLESS BOTH M. & M. M. CO'S SEALS ON THIS CAR ARE RETURNED TO US

MOTLEY'S ROLLER BIG FLOUR — MOSELEY & MOTLEY MILLING — ROCHESTER, N.Y.

Rochester, N.Y. June 27, 1921.

SOLD TO E. D. Webster

Remit

PAGE NO. 101. ORDER NO. 24178. PURCHASE 6/24/21.

5 bbls. Big "B" Flour 4/8 paper @ 10.10 $50.50

F. O. B. Rochester

Net, No Discount

Paid by Check 7/1/21

This Moseley & Motley Milling Company billhead is dated June 1921. A barrel of Big B Flour cost $10 at that time. The Moseley & Motley mill was one of the first in America to replace its stone grist wheels with steel rollers to crush the wheat grains into flour.

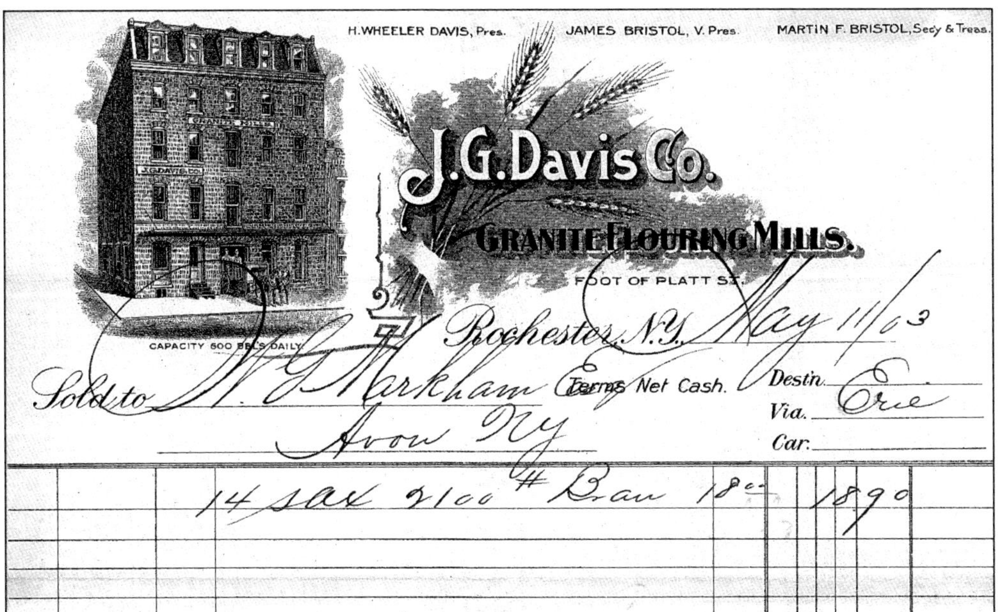

H. WHEELER DAVIS, Pres. JAMES BRISTOL, V. Pres. MARTIN F. BRISTOL, Sec'y & Treas.

J.G. Davis Co.

GRANITE FLOURING MILLS,

FOOT OF PLATT ST.

CAPACITY 600 BBLS DAILY

Rochester, N.Y. May 11/03

Sold to W. G. Markham Terms Net Cash. Destn. Erie

Avon NY Via. Car.

14 sax 2100# Bran 18.00 18.90

A five-story gristmill once stood where Platt Street joins Brown's Race. Built of solid stone in 1838, the huge mill was named the Granite Mill. The mill was operated by Joel G. Davis, and it produced more than 600 barrels of flour a day. Its office, still in use, is across Brown's Race on the corner of Platt Street.

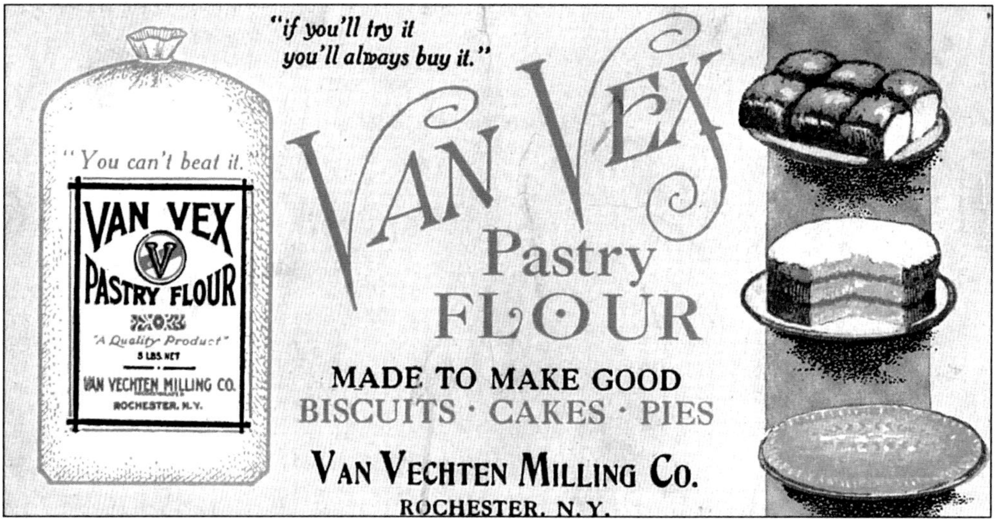

The Van Vechten Milling Company was located at 196 Smith Street. The mill produced wheat and rye flour and horse and poultry feeds. Like that of the Moseley & Motley Mills, Van Vechten flour was popular for making bread and pancakes. The last to operate within the city, Van Vechten mill closed during World War II.

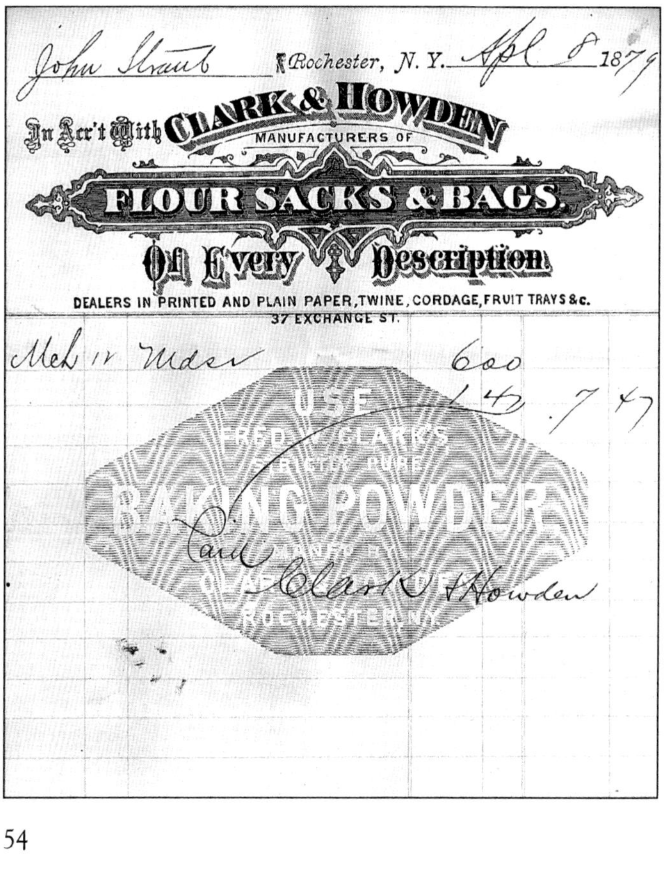
Rochester, N. Y. 187
In Acc't With CLARK & HOWDEN
MANUFACTURERS OF
FLOUR SACKS & BAGS,
Of Every Description
DEALERS IN PRINTED AND PLAIN PAPER, TWINE, CORDAGE, FRUIT TRAYS &c.
37 EXCHANGE ST.
USE
FRED W. CLARK'S
STRICTLY PURE
BAKING POWDER
MANUF'D BY
CLARK & HOWDEN
ROCHESTER, N.Y.

When mills were first built, most flour was shipped from Rochester in barrels. Later, shipments were made in burlap sacks. Clark & Howden, at 37 Exchange Street, was one of the chief sources for flour sacks and bags. Fred W. Clark also manufactured "strictly pure" baking powder.

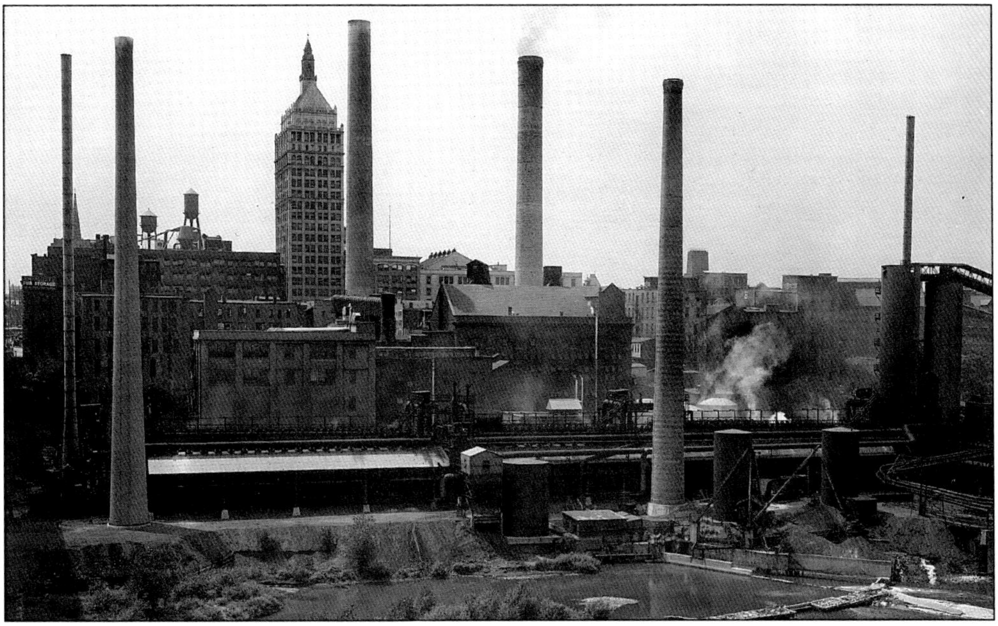

Many mills along Brown's Race disappeared and were replaced by Rochester Light and Power Company structures *c.* 1904. Later, the utility became the Rochester Railway & Light Company and, in 1919, the Rochester Gas & Electric Company. This 1939 photograph shows Station No. 3 (the Alexander M. Beebee Station). An immense complex, it utilized Genesee Falls water for hydroelectric power and coal to produce steam for electrical generation. The Kodak office building towers in the background.

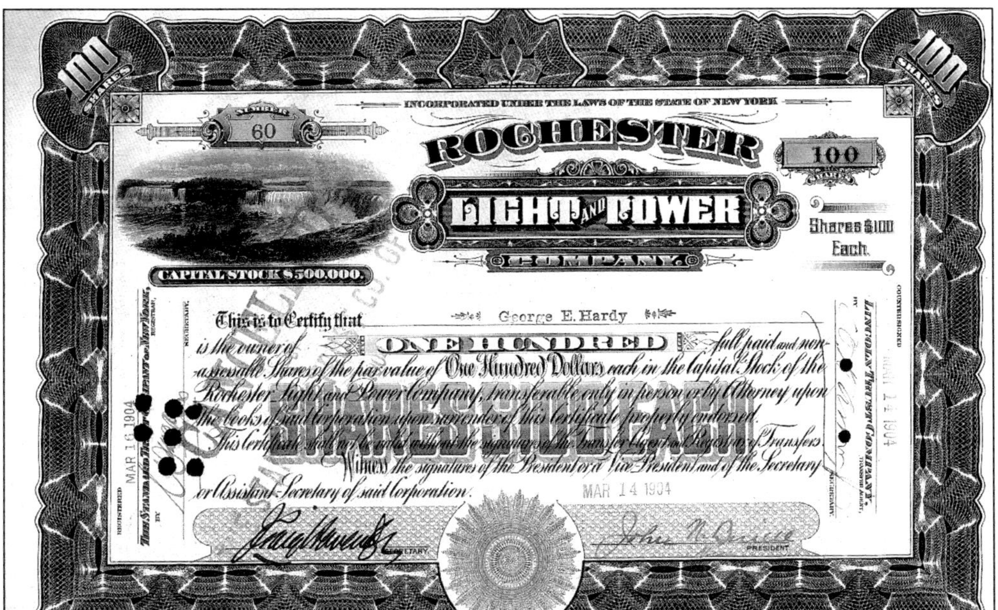

In 1904, the Rochester Light and Power Company issued stock certificates in a fledgling company, which in 1919 became the Rochester Railway & Light Company. The name of the company was later changed to Rochester Gas & Electric Company.

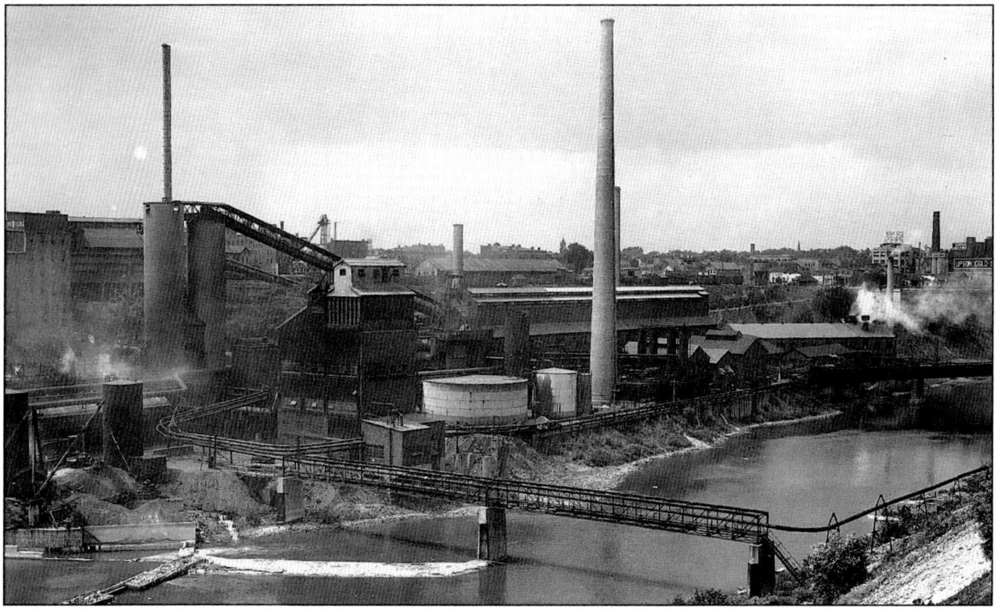

Trainload after trainload of coal was received, stored, and crushed to powder by the Rochester Gas & Electric facilities, photographed in 1939 from the east shore of the Genesee River. The buildings seen here were a part of the West Gas Station, a plant that manufactured gas for homes and industry. The pipeline over the river carried gas to be stored in enormous gas holders just north of the Smith Street Bridge.

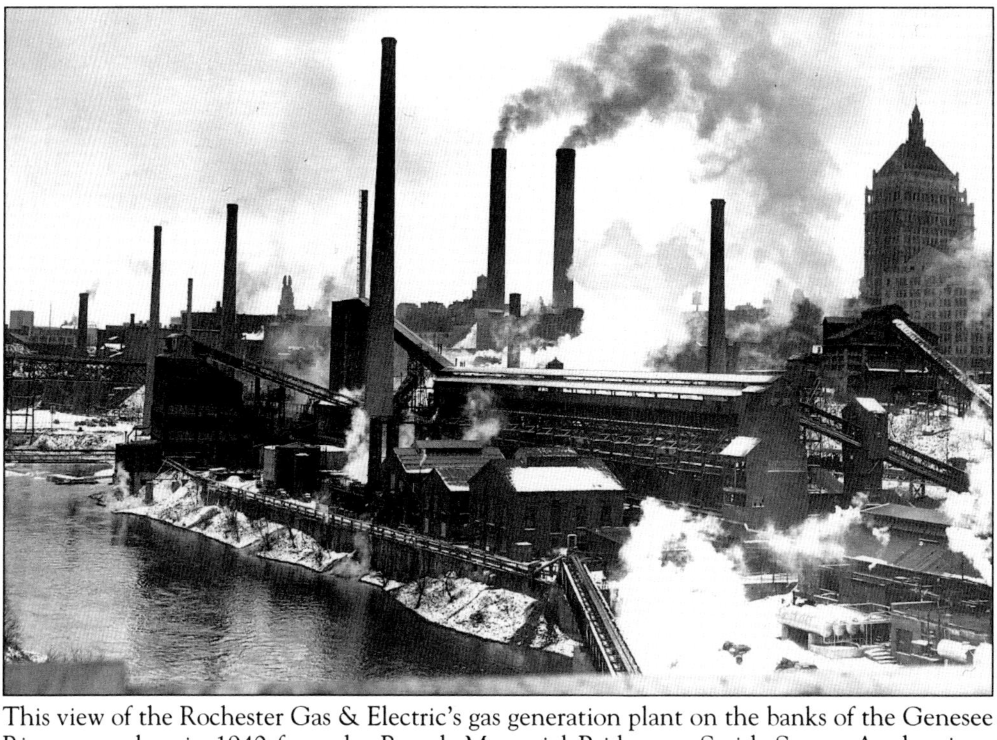

This view of the Rochester Gas & Electric's gas generation plant on the banks of the Genesee River was taken in 1940 from the Bausch Memorial Bridge, on Smith Street. At the time, smoking chimneys were considered a sign of wealth and prosperity for a community.

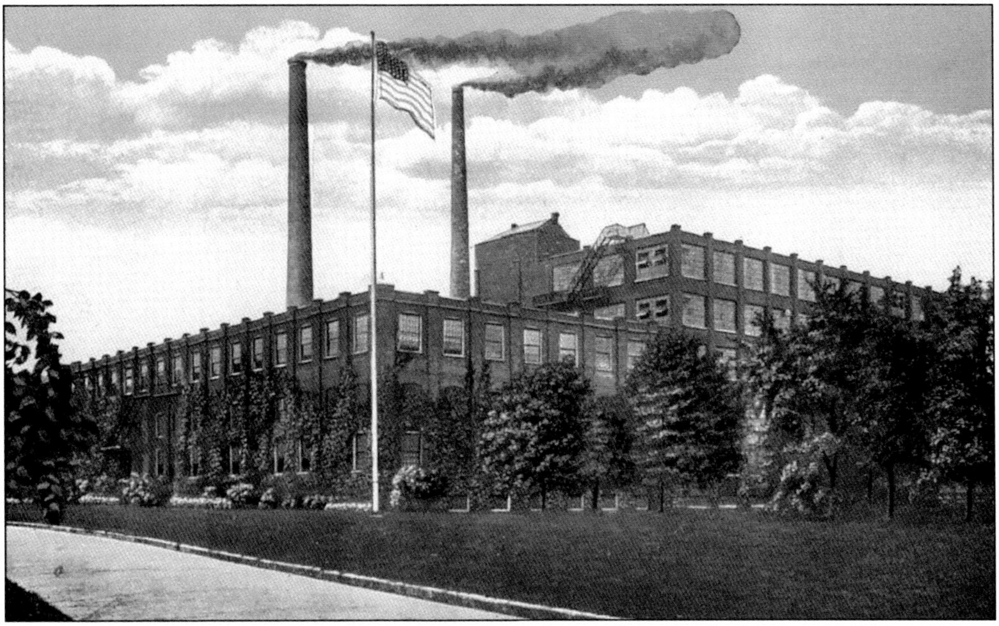

George Eastman wanted the enterprise he named Kodak to be built in a parklike setting. Rochester's major industry continues its operations in Kodak Park. Eastman Kodak's smokestacks were the "tallest in the United States" when this photograph was taken *c.* 1925.

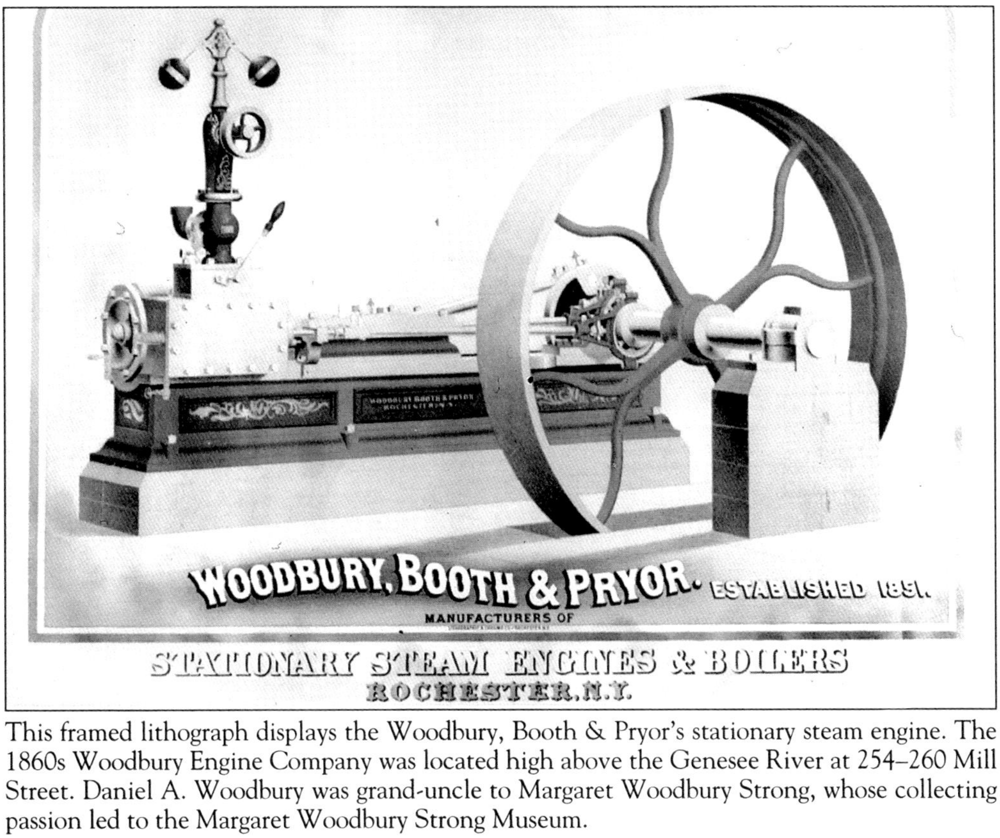

This framed lithograph displays the Woodbury, Booth & Pryor's stationary steam engine. The 1860s Woodbury Engine Company was located high above the Genesee River at 254–260 Mill Street. Daniel A. Woodbury was grand-uncle to Margaret Woodbury Strong, whose collecting passion led to the Margaret Woodbury Strong Museum.

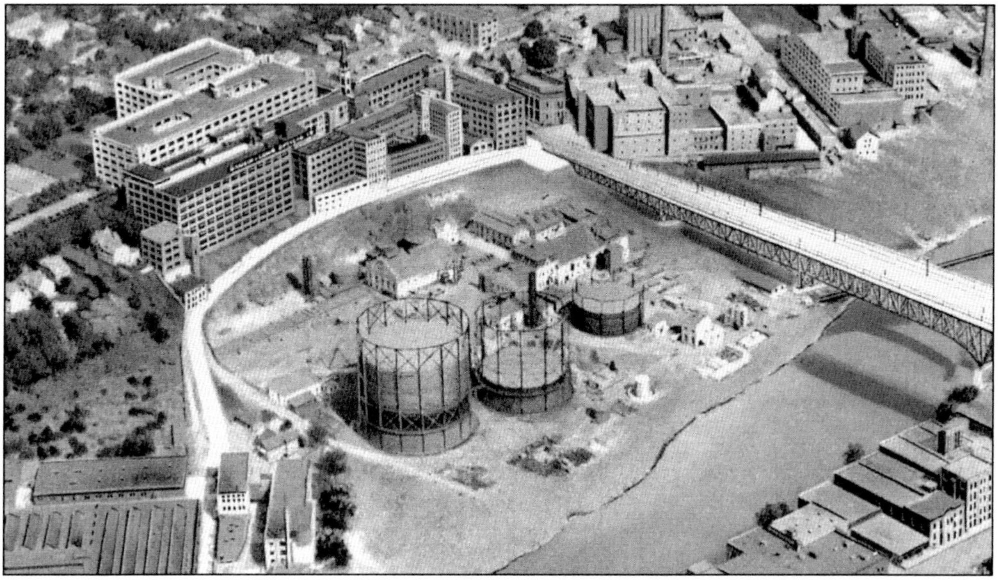

When this 1930s photograph was taken, the Bausch & Lomb Optical Company had become America's largest manufacturer of optical products. The gas holders in the foreground belonged to the Rochester Gas & Electric Company, but the city's largest consumer of that convenient gas supply was Bausch & Lomb. Their manufacturing buildings are seen at the upper left. During evening hours, the glass plant, seen on the lower left, used large volumes of gas to fire the ovens that produced tons of optical-quality glass.

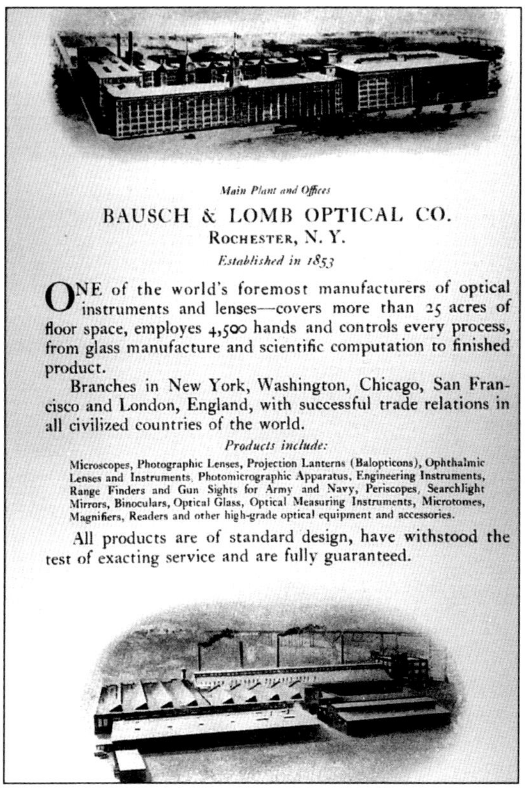

By 1918, Bausch & Lomb had expanded to 25 acres in Rochester, with branches in major cities in America and England.

Seated at rows of lens-grinding machines, these high school–aged trainees were given practical experience in the delicate art of making eyeglass lenses for the Bausch & Lomb Optical Company in the early 1900s.

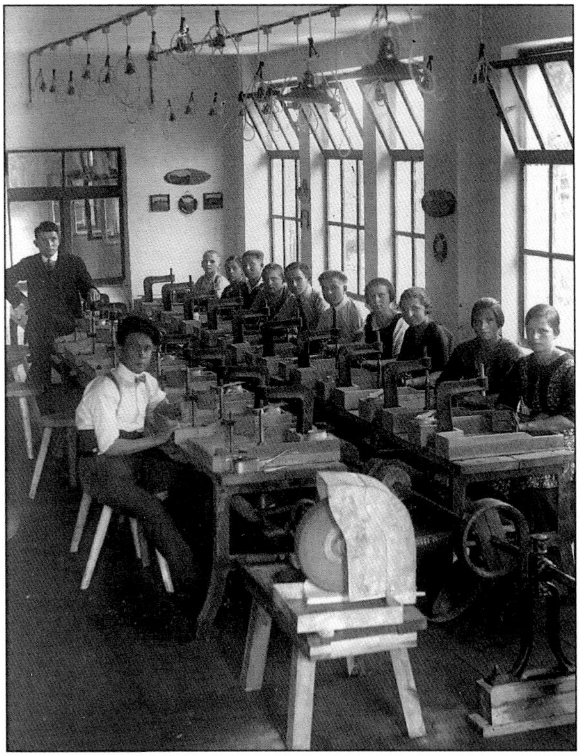

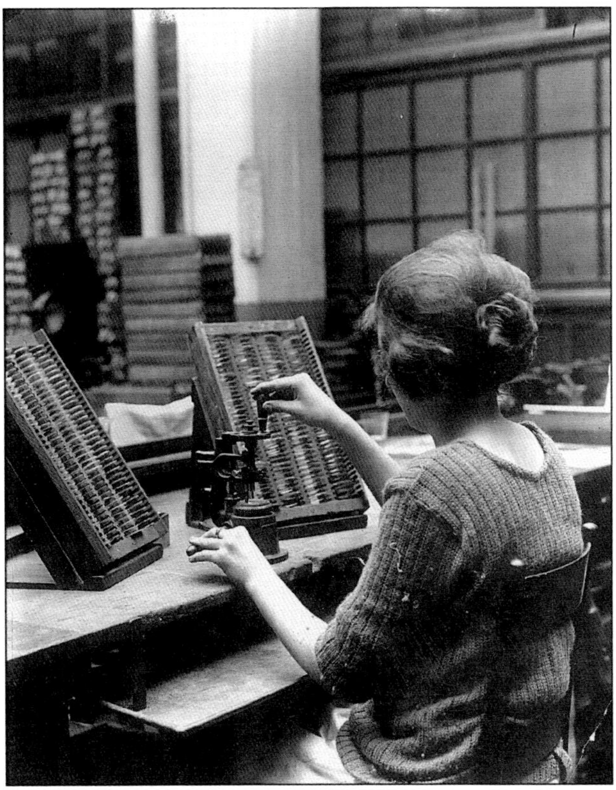

This young woman is delicately drilling holes in eyeglass lenses to enable them to be attached to nosepieces. Bausch & Lomb employed many skilled workers.

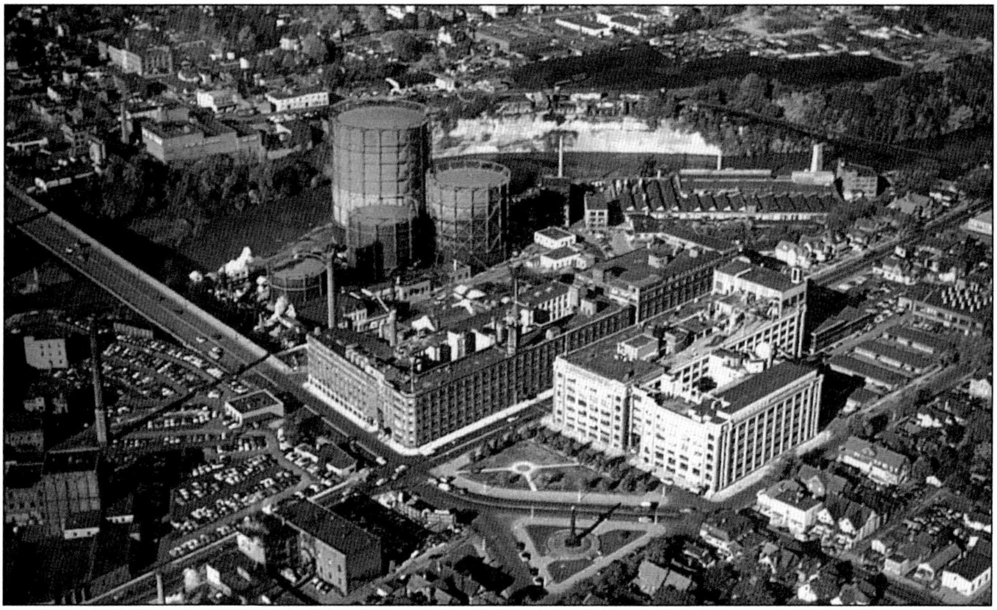

This aerial view of the Bausch & Long Optical Company originated from an ektachrome transparency made in the 1950s. In the background, the Genesee River flows around four gas holders. The company's building complex is at the center. In the lower foreground, two triangles created by surrounding streets form Lomb Memorial Park. The smaller triangle is the location of a towering column, a tribute to Henry Lomb.

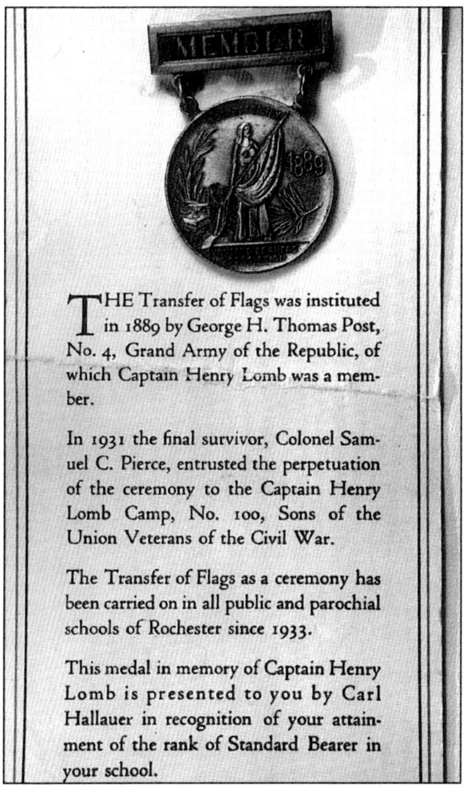

THE Transfer of Flags was instituted in 1889 by George H. Thomas Post, No. 4, Grand Army of the Republic, of which Captain Henry Lomb was a member.

In 1931 the final survivor, Colonel Samuel C. Pierce, entrusted the perpetuation of the ceremony to the Captain Henry Lomb Camp, No. 100, Sons of the Union Veterans of the Civil War.

The Transfer of Flags as a ceremony has been carried on in all public and parochial schools of Rochester since 1933.

This medal in memory of Captain Henry Lomb is presented to you by Carl Hallauer in recognition of your attainment of the rank of Standard Bearer in your school.

Capt. Henry Lomb, a veteran of the Civil War, was greatly admired. As a member of the Grand Army of the Republic, he was honored by Camp No. 100, Sons of the Union Veterans of the Civil War. This group promoted the annual Transfer of Flags ceremony in Rochester's public and parochial schools. The medal went to the student in each school who was chosen as standard bearer.

On May 30, 1932, city officials and Bausch and Lomb dignitaries gathered on a small triangle of ground once formed by Bausch, Martin, and Lowell Streets. There, they dedicated the Lomb Memorial Monument in memory of Capt. Henry Lomb, partner of John J. Bausch. Lomb and Bausch were cofounders of the optical empire. Black Minnesota granite covers the 48-foot-high shaft. Four recessed hexagons once held plaques bearing informative inscriptions. At night, the shaft and its top portion were illuminated to produce "a soft glow." Buildings of the optical firm form the background.

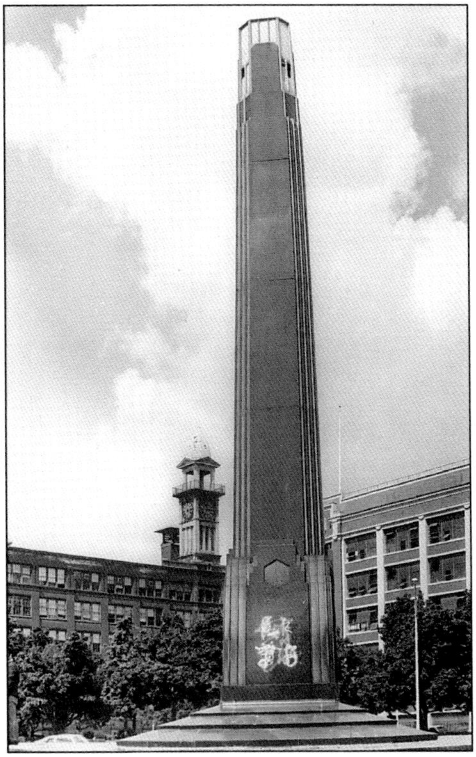

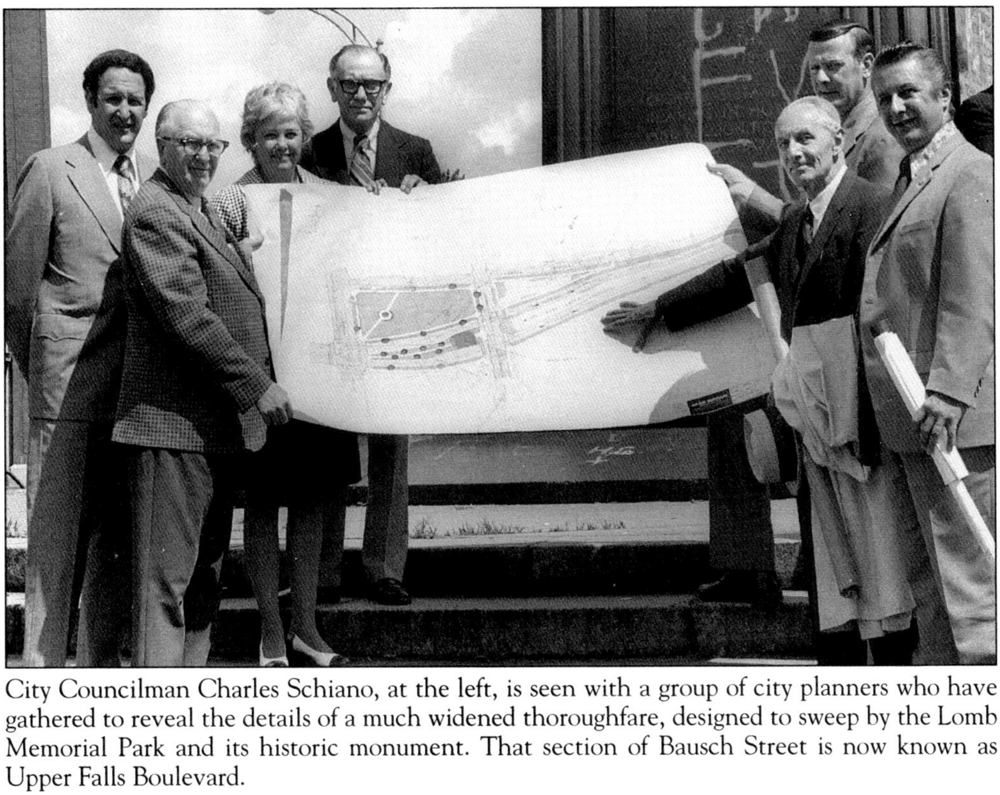

City Councilman Charles Schiano, at the left, is seen with a group of city planners who have gathered to reveal the details of a much widened thoroughfare, designed to sweep by the Lomb Memorial Park and its historic monument. That section of Bausch Street is now known as Upper Falls Boulevard.

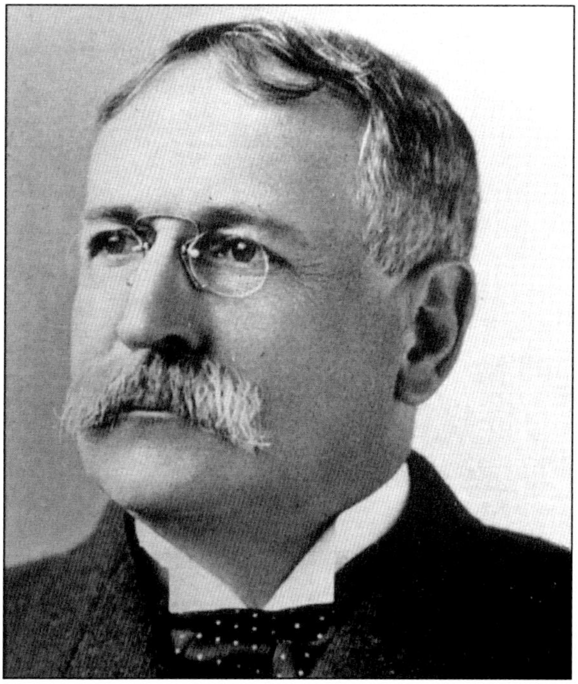

This distinguished-looking gentleman, William Smith Kimball, headed the nation's most prestigious tobacco company. Organized in 1867, it was called the William S. Kimball & Company, Peerless Tobacco Company. The company ranked as the world's largest tobacco manufacturer by 1880. Annual production was over 750 million cigarettes in various brands. Packs of Kimball's cigarettes were sold in markets throughout the world.

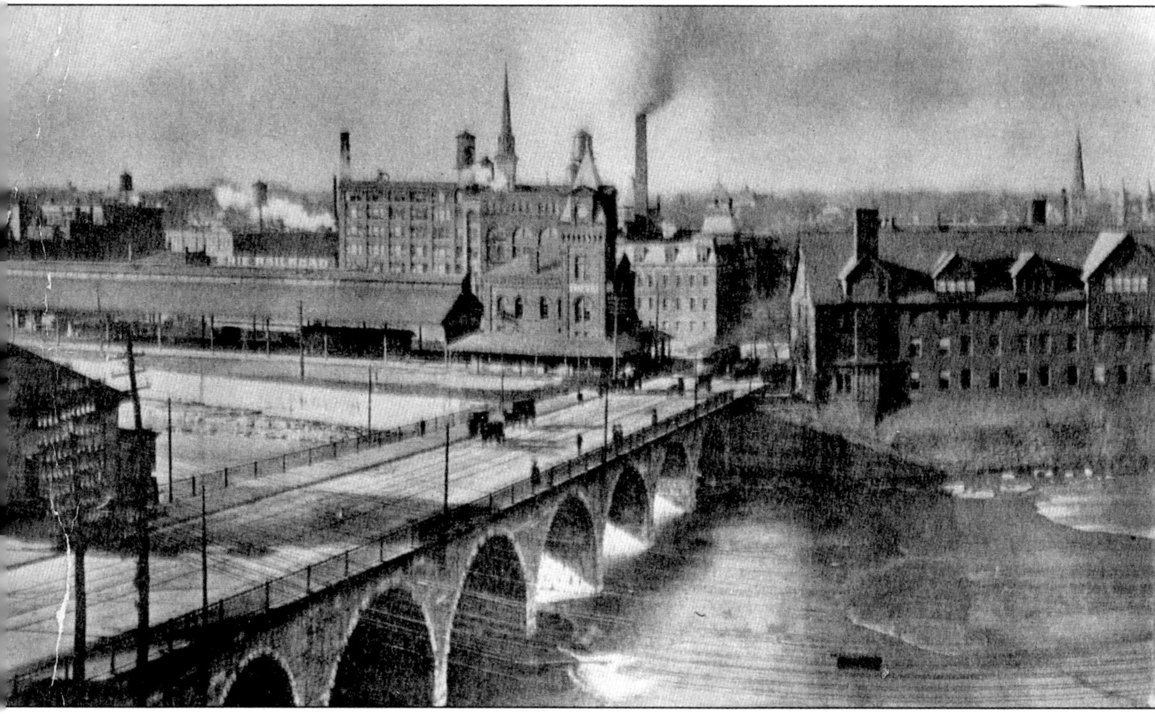

This panoramic view of the Genesee River brackets William S. Kimball's Peerless Tobacco Company on the west bank of the river squarely between the Court Street Bridge on the left and the Erie Canal aqueduct on the right. Taken in 1911, the view is from South St. Paul Street, now South Avenue, looking west. The towering tobacco company smokestack dominates the city horizon, bearing a statue of Mercury. The huge, triangular shape of the

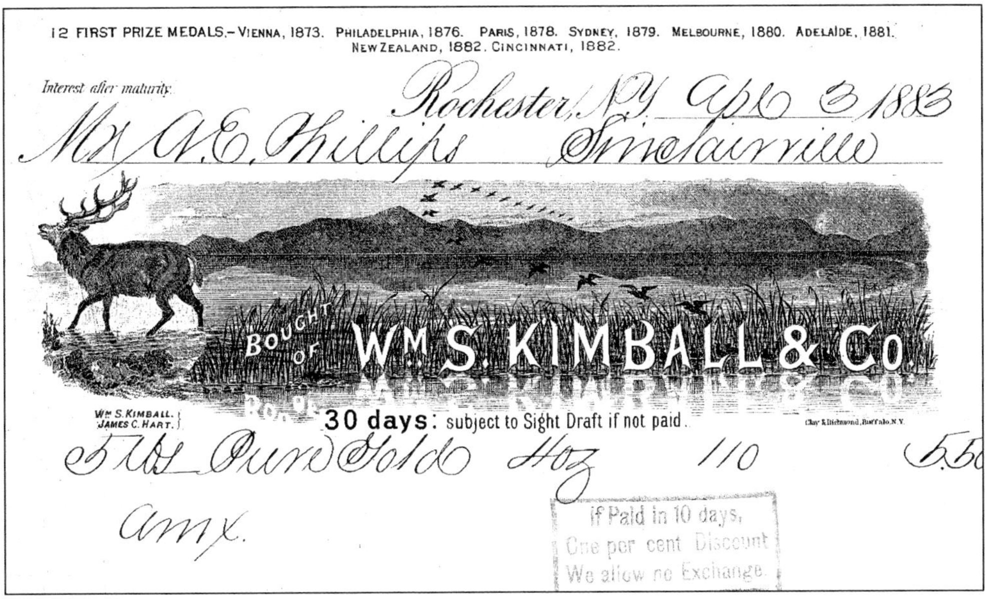
12 FIRST PRIZE MEDALS.–VIENNA, 1873. PHILADELPHIA, 1876. PARIS, 1878. SYDNEY, 1879. MELBOURNE, 1880. ADELAIDE, 1881. NEW ZEALAND, 1882. CINCINNATI, 1882.

Interest after maturity. Rochester, N.Y. Apl 3 1883

Mr A. E. Phillips Sinclairville

BOUGHT OF WM. S. KIMBALL & CO

WM. S. KIMBALL. JAMES C. HART. 30 days: subject to Sight Draft if not paid.

5 lbs Pure Gold 4oz 110 5.50

Amx.

If Paid in 10 days, One per cent Discount We allow no Exchange.

A very masculine-appearing billhead used by William S. Kimball characterizes his personality. The invoice is for five pounds of Pure Gold tobacco. The Peerless Tobacco Company was also the first to produce and ship Old Gold tobacco, in 1883.

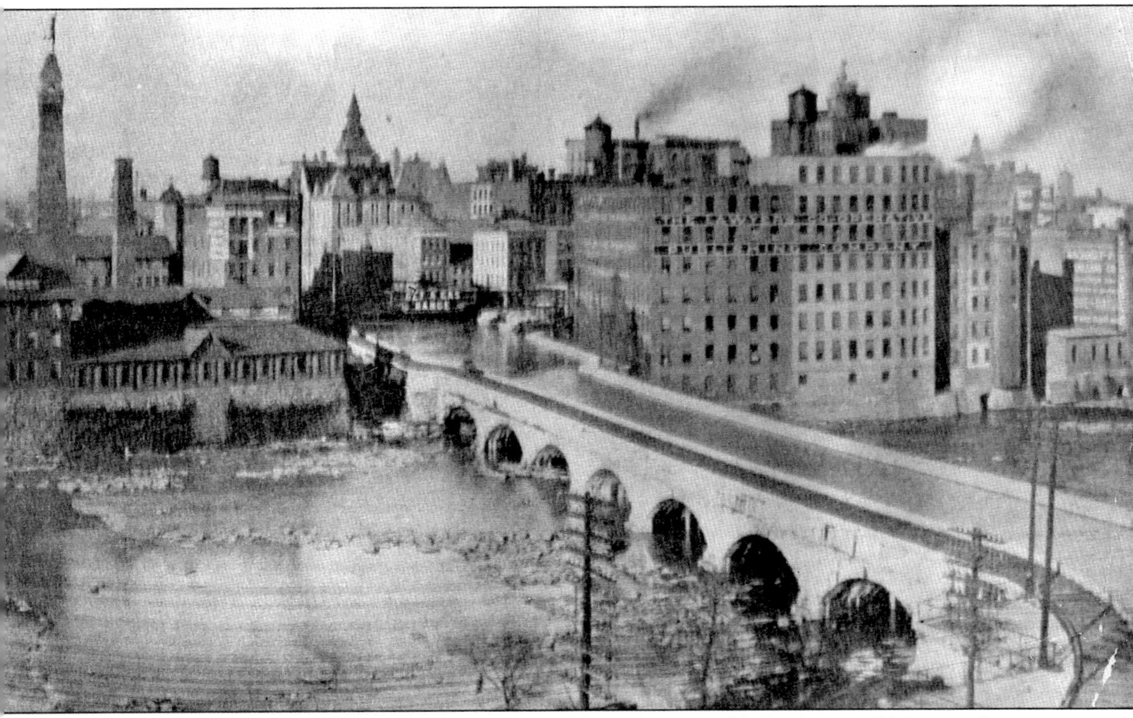

Peerless Tobacco Company's buildings, designed by James Goold Cutler in 1881, was due to their location on a former island in the Genesee River. The river, the aqueduct, and a mill canal produced a peninsula-like site. Access to the Tudor-style factory was from the western end of Court Street.

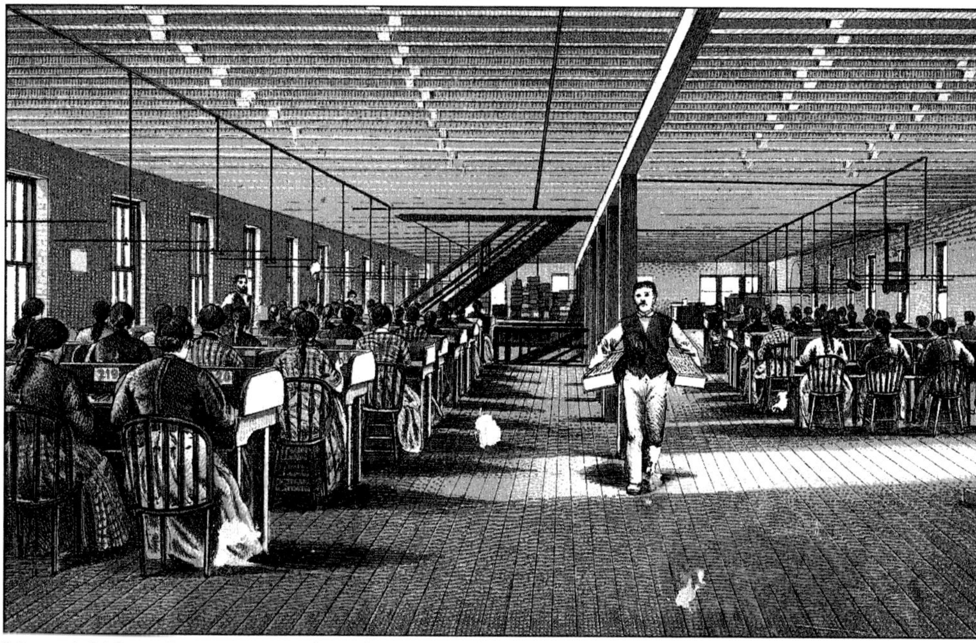

Up to 1,200 workers were employed, many of them young women called "cigarette girls." Sitting at long tables, they rolled the thinly cut tobacco into the small cigarlike forms called "cigarettes." So considerable was the tobacco business, it enjoyed a gross revenue of $2.5 million, paying $300,000 annually for federal tax stamps.

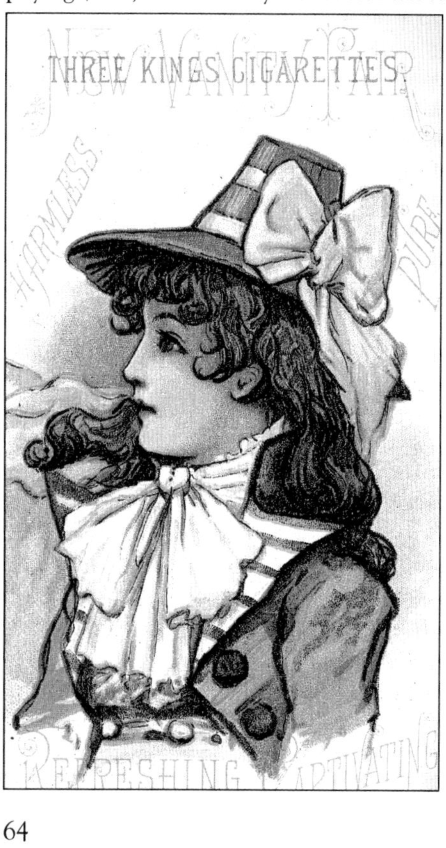

A major promotional method *c.* 1900 was to use colorful advertising cards. In this, William S. Kimball was a wizard. An example is the young woman associated with Three Kings cigarettes. A wide variety of other cards were also distributed. Within early packs, which held 10 cigarettes, were included small pasteboard images of Native American chiefs, baseball players, bathing beauties, actresses, flags, and even playing cards—all to promote a particular brand. In a single year, more than 750 million cigarettes were shipped from Rochester.

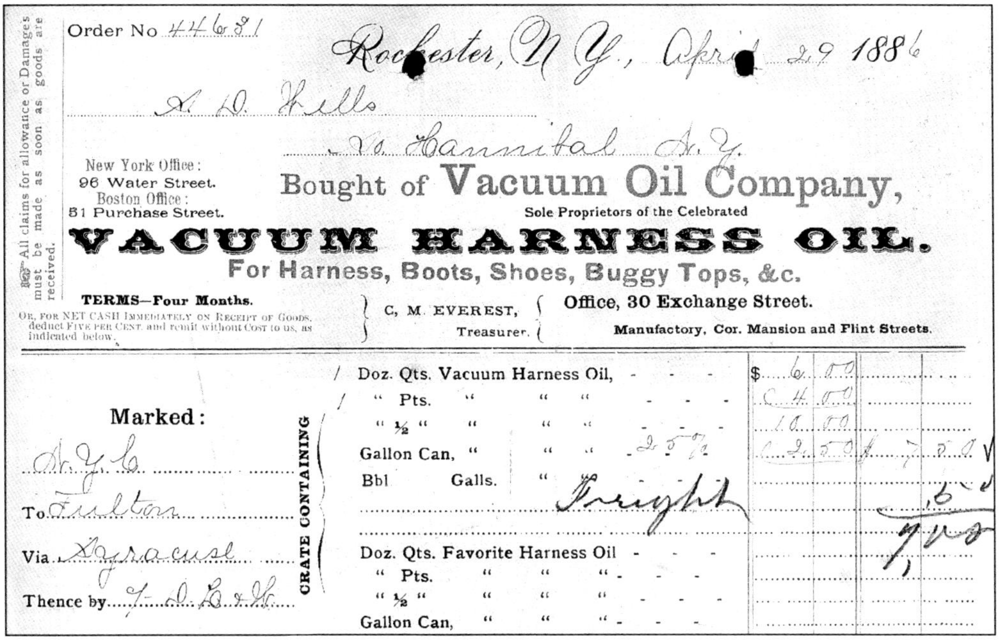

All claims for allowance or Damages must be made as soon as goods are received.

Order No 44631

Rochester, N.Y., April 29 1886

New York Office: 96 Water Street.
Boston Office: 51 Purchase Street.

Bought of Vacuum Oil Company,

Sole Proprietors of the Celebrated

VACUUM HARNESS OIL.

For Harness, Boots, Shoes, Buggy Tops, &c.

TERMS—Four Months.
OR, FOR NET CASH IMMEDIATELY ON RECEIPT OF GOODS, deduct FIVE PER CENT. and remit without COST to us, as indicated below.

C. M. EVEREST, Treasurer.

Office, 30 Exchange Street.
Manufactory, Cor. Mansion and Flint Streets.

Marked:

To

Via

Thence by

CRATE CONTAINING

1	Doz. Qts. Vacuum Harness Oil,	$ 6 00
1	" Pts. " " "	4 00
	" ½ " " " "	
	Gallon Can, " " "	
	Bbl Galls. "	
	Doz. Qts. Favorite Harness Oil	
	" Pts. " " "	
	" ½ " " " "	
	Gallon Can, " " "	

When horses were the principle power source for agriculture and transportation, a good grade of harness oil was essential. To meet that need, Hiram Bond Everest and his son Charles Marvin Everest created an enormous industrial complex on the banks of the Genesee River at the corner of Mansion and Flint Streets in 1868. There, they employed a vacuum distillation process to produce a wide variety of lubricating oils.

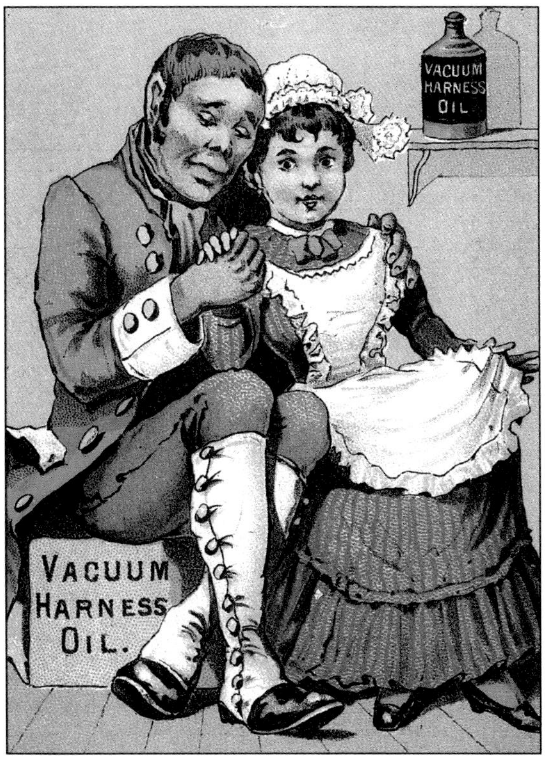

Comical advertising cards promoted the use of Vacuum Harness Oil from the 1870s into the 1900s. Sweet Mistress O'Doyle, obviously a housemaid, is being wooed by a very red-headed gentlemen, perhaps of Irish extraction.

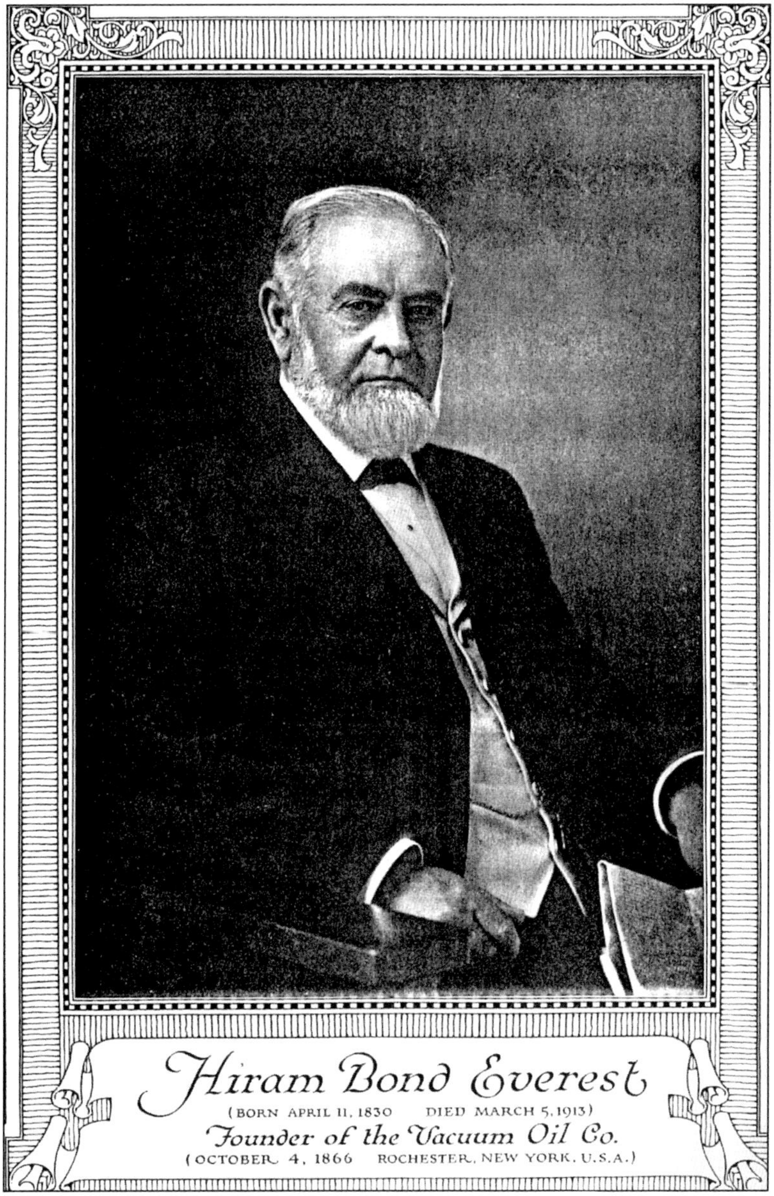

Millionaire Hiram Bond Everest, Rochester's "oil baron," was once called the "world's richest failure." For years, his enterprises ended in disaster by frost or by fire. Then, he bought out the interests of Matthew P. Ewing. In a chicken coop in his yard, at 71 Monroe Avenue, Ewing had mastered a vacuum process to extract kerosene from crude oil. At first, Everest sold the inky, gooey residue of the process as a superior harness oil. Later, he realized the tremendous potential for using the process to extract various grades of lubricating oil. At the time, vegetable oil and animal products were used in the fledgling automobile industry to lubricate horseless carriages. Clouds of smoke and sticky valves resulted. The automobile industry owes a huge debt to Hiram Everest for his early success. Had Everest not developed his Gargoyle 600 Weight Steam Cylinder Oil, viscous enough to withstand the heat and pressure of the crude internal combustion engines, the automobile industry might have turned to electricity or steam. The Vacuum Oil Company sold out becoming Socony-Vacuum, then Mobil, now Exxon-Mobil.

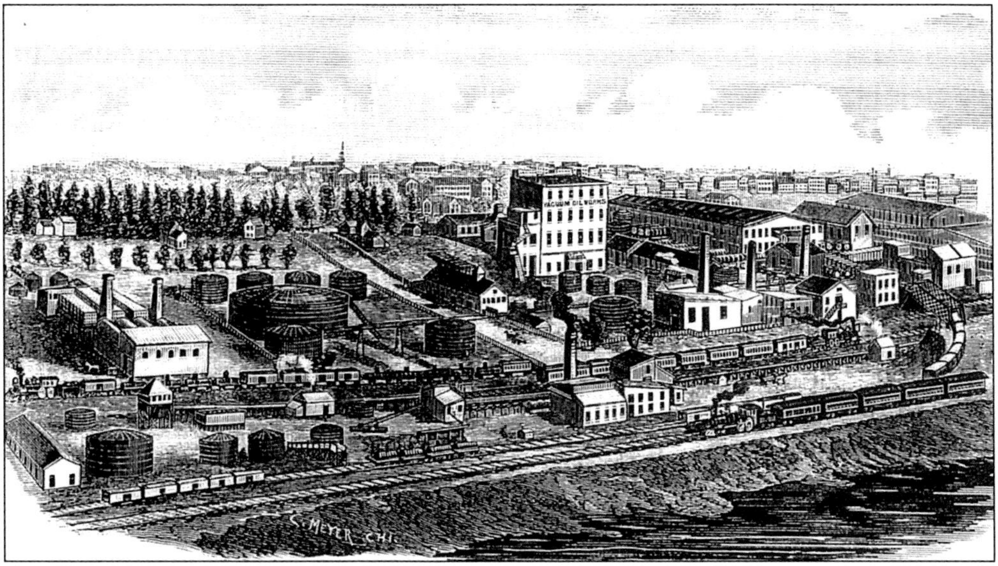

The first tank cars used by the Erie and the Rochester & Genesee Valley Railroad, were wooden tubs fastened to flatcars. After storage in Olean, the tank cars transported a continuous flow of crude oil from Pennsylvania oil fields to Rochester for vacuum distillation.

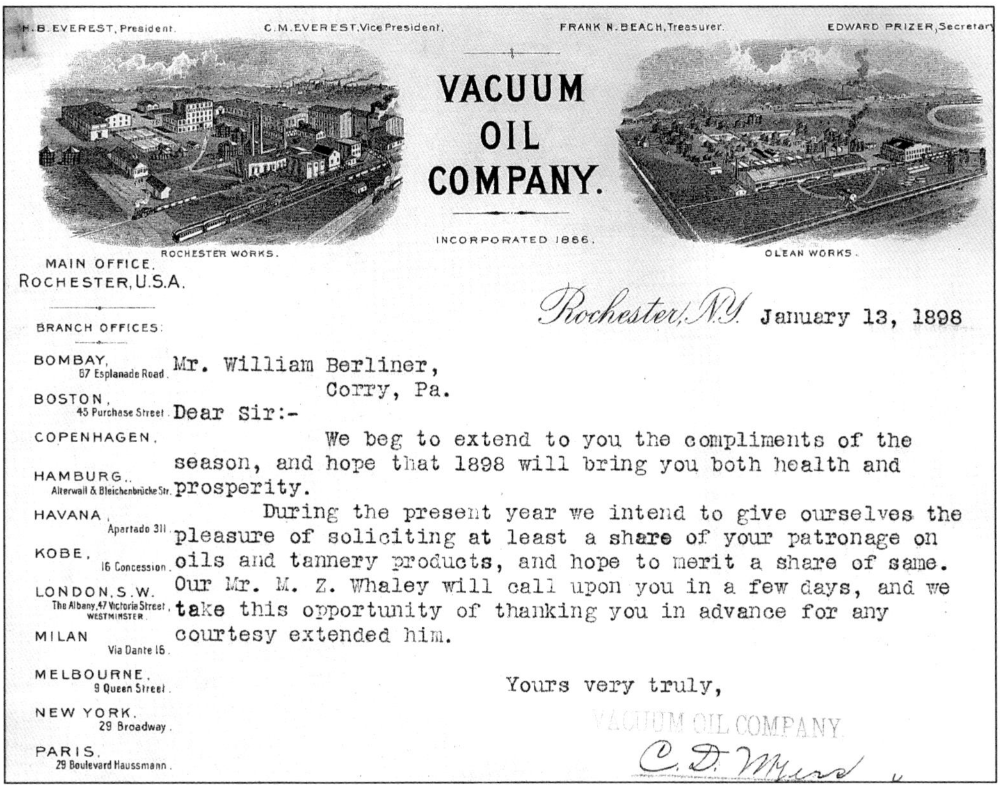

H. B. EVEREST, President. C. M. EVEREST, Vice President. FRANK N. BEACH, Treasurer. EDWARD PRIZER, Secretary.

VACUUM OIL COMPANY.

INCORPORATED 1866.

ROCHESTER WORKS. OLEAN WORKS.

MAIN OFFICE, ROCHESTER, U.S.A.

BRANCH OFFICES:
BOMBAY, 67 Esplanade Road.
BOSTON, 45 Purchase Street.
COPENHAGEN.
HAMBURG, Alterwall & Bleichenbrücke Str.
HAVANA, Apartado 311.
KOBE, 16 Concession.
LONDON, S.W. The Albany, 47 Victoria Street, WESTMINSTER.
MILAN Via Dante 16.
MELBOURNE, 9 Queen Street.
NEW YORK, 29 Broadway.
PARIS, 29 Boulevard Haussmann.

Rochester, N.Y. January 13, 1898

Mr. William Berliner,
Corry, Pa.

Dear Sir:-

We beg to extend to you the compliments of the season, and hope that 1898 will bring you both health and prosperity.

During the present year we intend to give ourselves the pleasure of soliciting at least a share of your patronage on oils and tannery products, and hope to merit a share of same. Our Mr. M. Z. Whaley will call upon you in a few days, and we take this opportunity of thanking you in advance for any courtesy extended him.

Yours very truly,

VACUUM OIL COMPANY

C. D. Myers

Two vignettes at the top of the Vacuum Oil Company billhead draw attention to the sizable oil "works" in both Rochester and Olean. By 1898, Rochester's Vacuum Oil Company was known internationally and had a growing number of offices located around the globe.

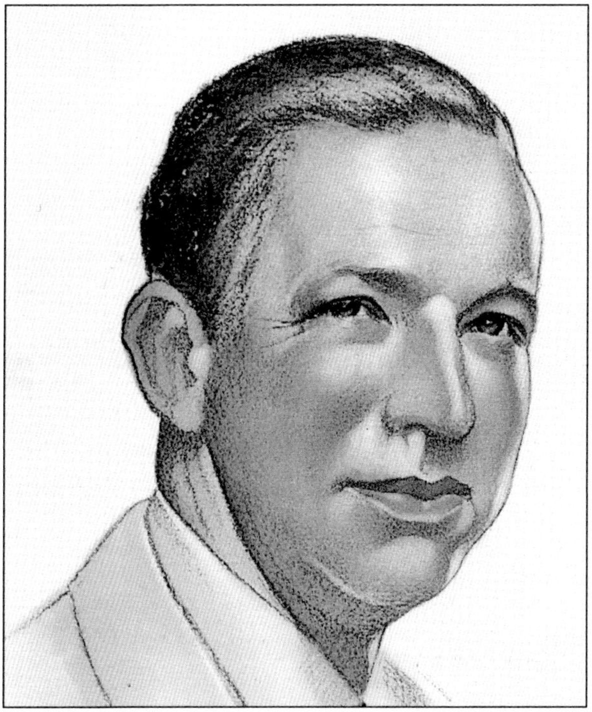

This fine portrait sketch of S. Rae Hickok was executed by Carlo Adriano Garrone. In the late spring of 1912, University of Rochester freshman S. Rae Hickok began using his kitchen oven at home to bake enamel on initialed watch fobs for sale to his classmates. His next project was ornate metal monograms for women's handbags. Next, it was enameled, initialed belt buckles. Thus was born a new Rochester industry. The Hickok plant, located at 850 St. Paul Street, was within a stone's throw of the Genesee River.

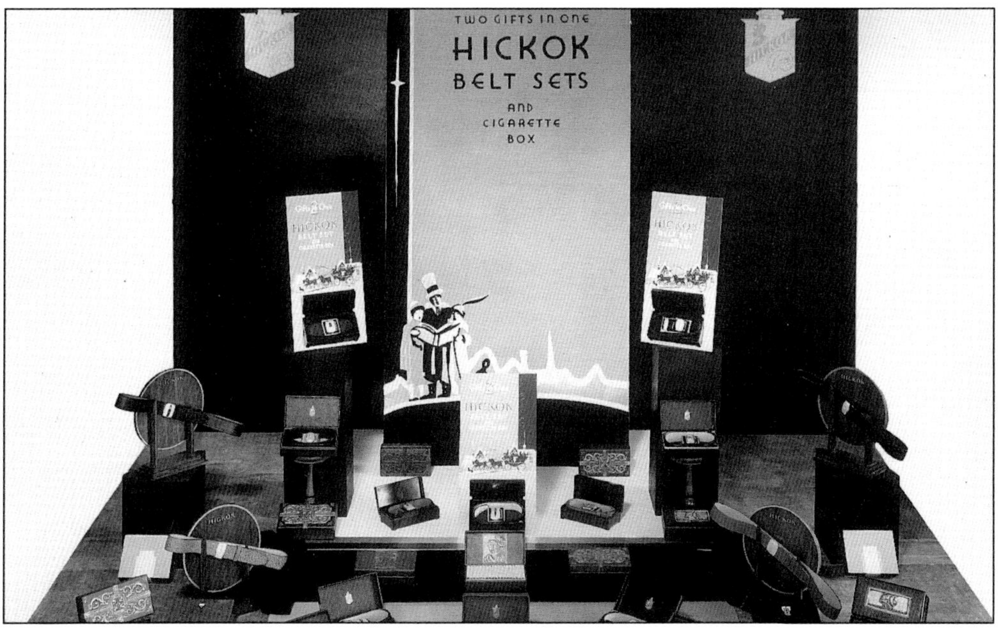

Under many a Christmas tree, dad, son, or granddad discovered that Santa had left a Hickok belt or a handsome, initialed Hickok belt buckle. The boxes holding the items were quite attractive, becoming collector's items today. Other products manufactured at Hickok included men's leather braces, garters, and wallets, men's jewelry, and automotive safety belts. The company was later purchased by the Tandy Company and moved to Texas. An expensive, bejeweled Hickok belt was awarded to a deserving American athlete at the annual Rochester sports banquet.

Four

Exposition Park

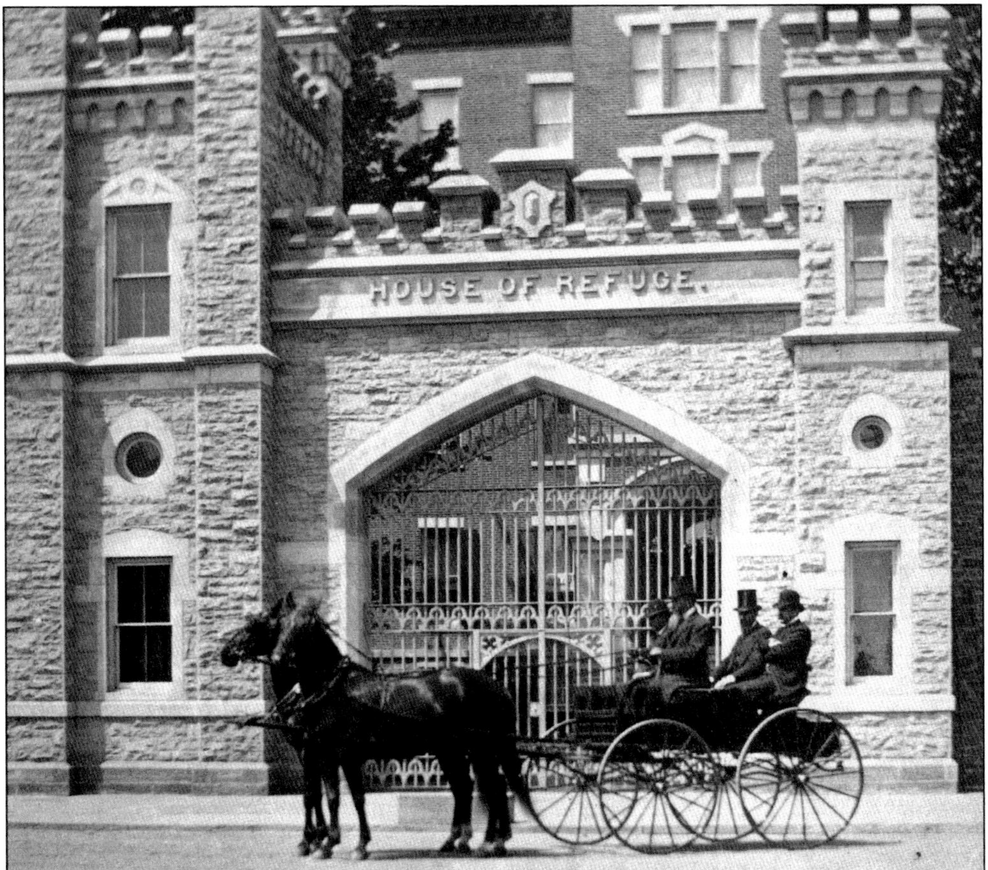

The impressive entrance to the Western House of Refuge looms over the carriage holding the trustees of the establishment built to hold wayward young people. Most inmates were boys ages 8 to 18. When the Erie Canal closed during the winter months, many young boys (mule drivers, or "hogees") were left destitute in Rochester. They were rounded up and incarcerated in this institution. The image is from an 1870s stereograph.

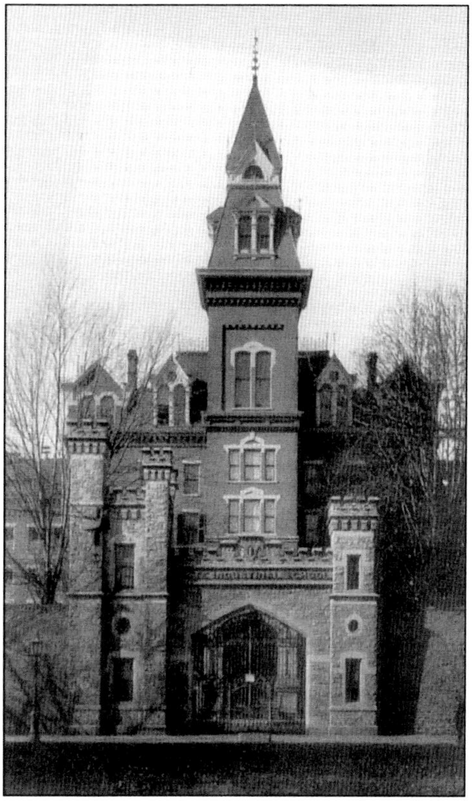

Seen here is the seven-story tower of the State Industrial School. Located between Emerson Street and Dewey, Backus, and Bloss Avenues, the institution was known as the Western House of Refuge until the 1890s. Opened on May 8, 1846, it was only the second such walled institution of its kind in the United States. After 1890, efforts were made to humanize the facility by changing its name and recommending that its massive walls be removed.

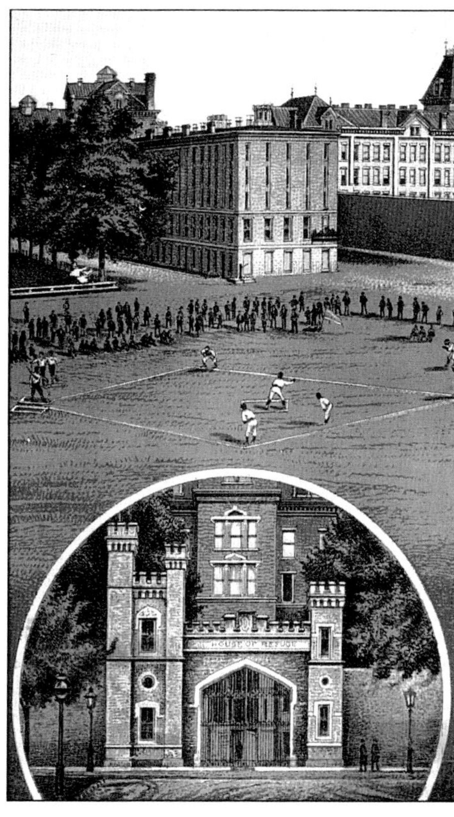

Within the 20-foot-high stone walls surrounding six and a half acres of the Western House of Refuge for Juvenile Delinquents was a farm, a tailor and shoe shop, a chair-caning shop, and a baseball diamond. One suspects that the opportunity to play baseball while in the facility was very limited.

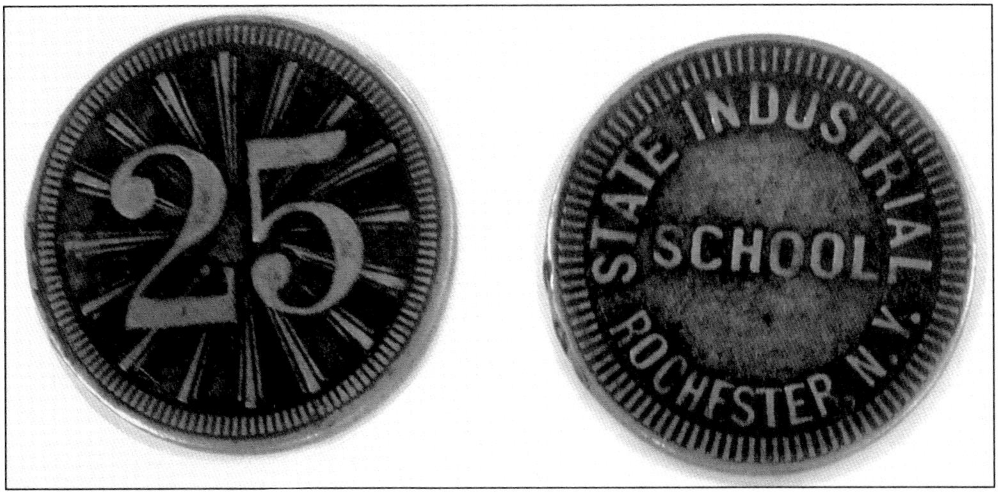

The nimble fingers of many of the State Industrial School inmates were turned to productive use. Some of the boys were employed by the Robinson Chair Company to weave the caning in the firm's chairs. Their "reward" was a metal token bearing the establishment's name on the obverse and a "25" on the reverse. No indication of its value to the boys has been found. (Courtesy Gerry Muhl.)

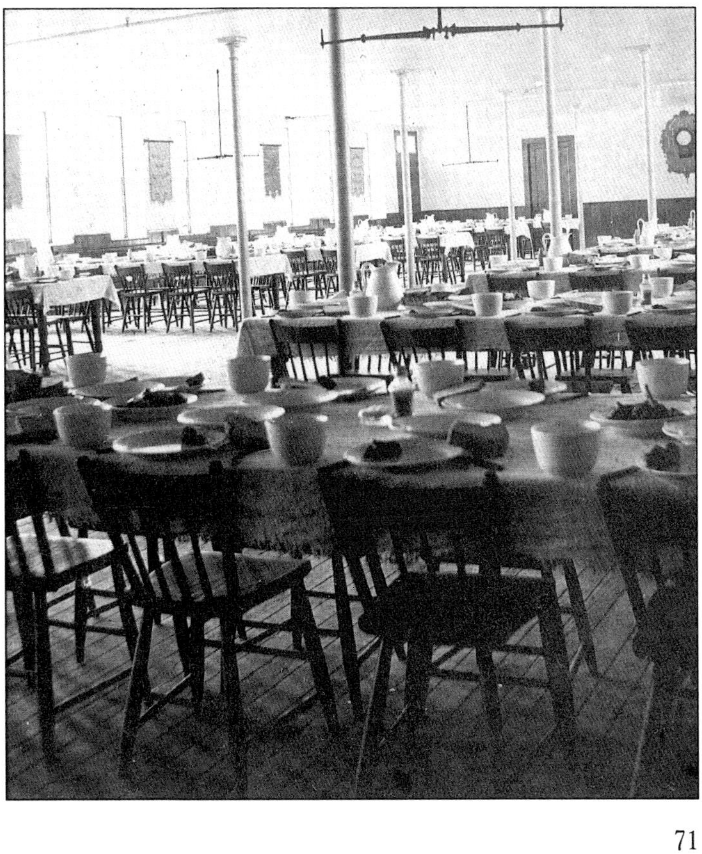

The photograph of the dining hall for the Western House of Refuge provides one with an idea of how many inmates the place held (379 boys in 1869). Meals that year consisted mainly of coffee, pork, boiled rice, molasses, bread, and soup. (Courtesy Jack Kemp.)

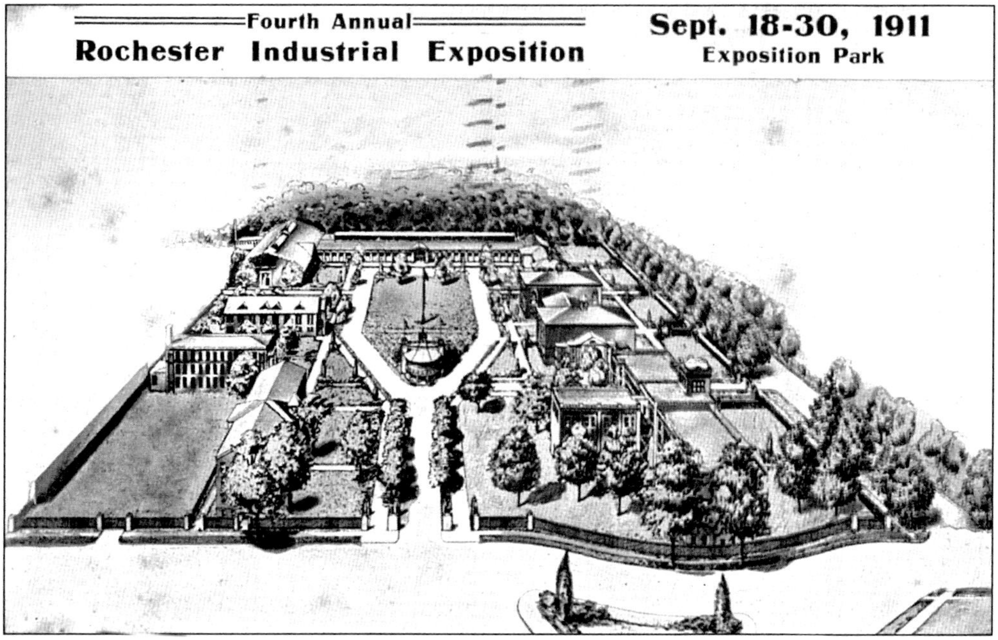

It was with vast pride that Mayor Hiram H. Edgerton opened Rochester's newest civic venture on September 18, 1911. Standing as one of Rochester's greatest public endeavors, the former State Industrial School grounds were transformed into a wonderful complex called Exposition Park. Conceived by the mayor, a contractor prior to his election, he designed the park to be a center for public exhibitions, horse shows, sporting events, and cultural pursuits.

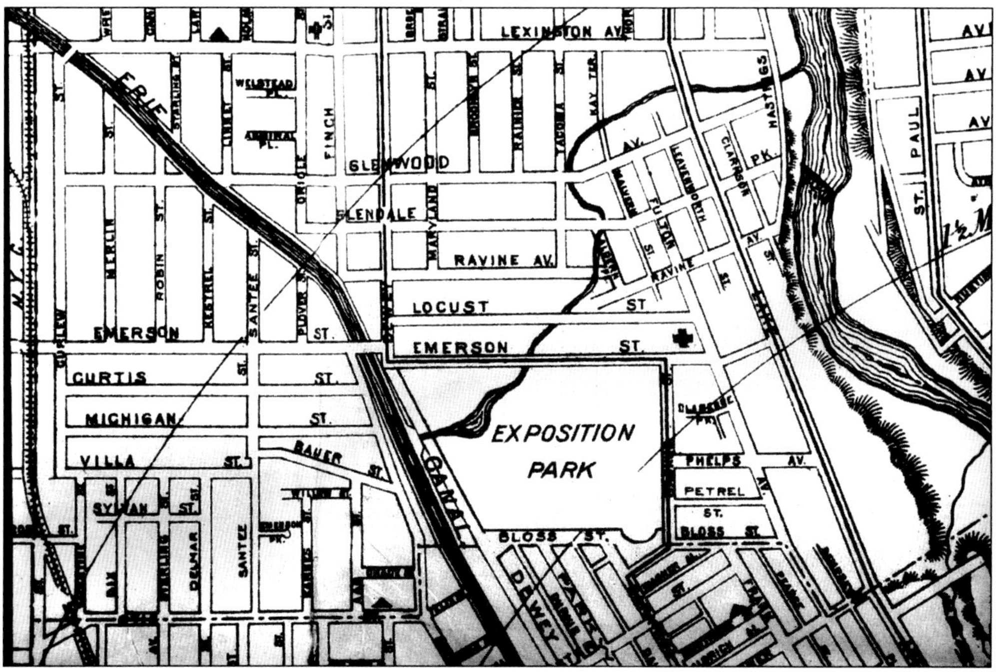

The exposition grounds took up a prominent section of Rochester's west side between the Genesee River and the Erie Canal. The Deep Hollow tributary, leading from the Erie Canal to the Genesee River, once flowed through the park.

Mayor Hiram H. Edgerton served in office from 1907 to 1921. For his city, he held "a vision of a smiling, clean-scrubbed happy metropolis in which certain business leaders exercised an oligarchic rule, and the public rejoiced in pleasant homes on tree-shaded streets. . . . His hopes and philosophy found their fullest expression in what came to be known as Edgerton Park."

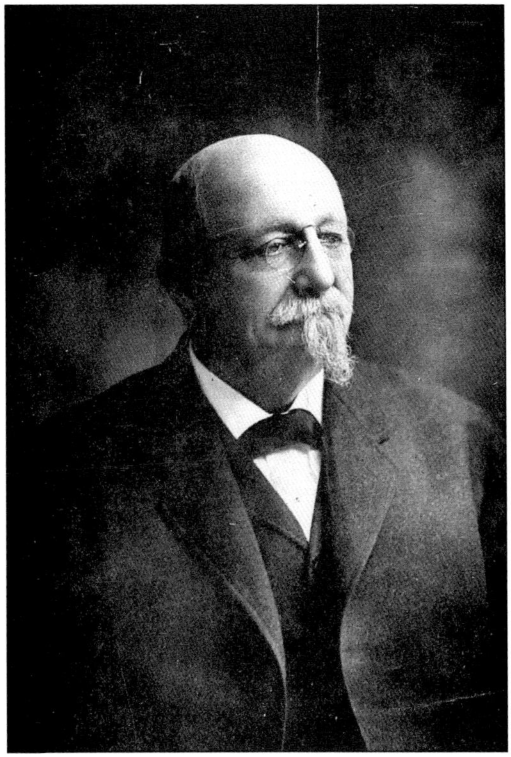

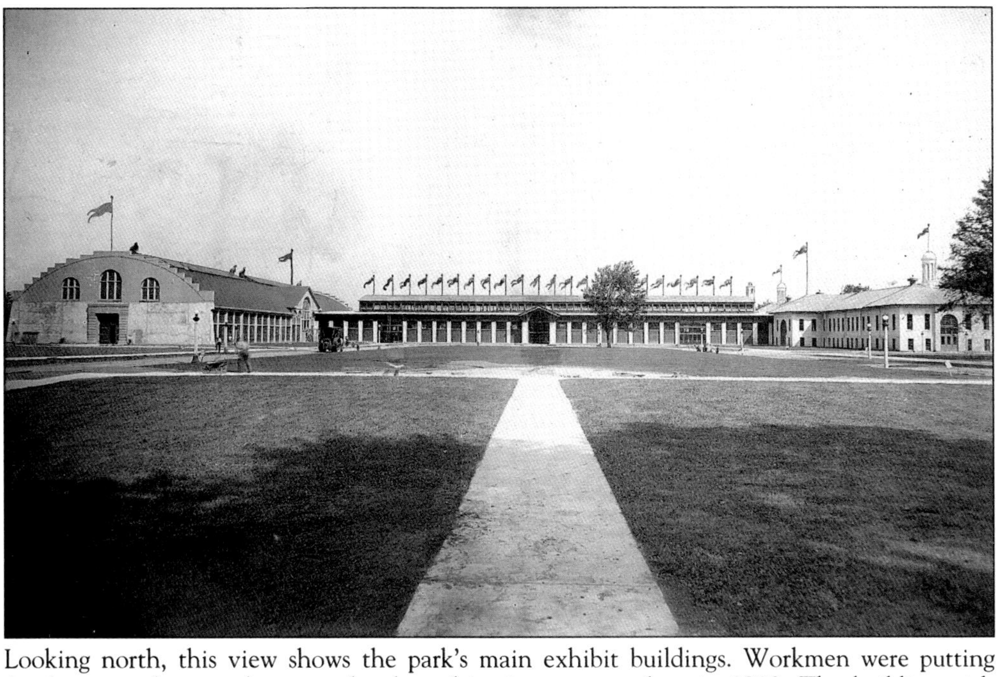

Looking north, this view shows the park's main exhibit buildings. Workmen were putting finishing touches on the grounds when this picture was taken in 1910. The building with the curved roof at left later became the home of the Rochester Royals basketball team. The professional players never finished below second place in their division. From 1911 until Mayor Hiram H. Edgerton passed away in 1921, the site was known as Exposition Park.

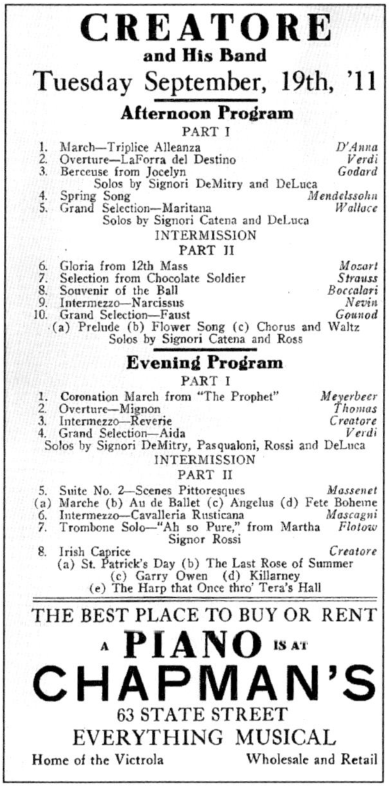

CREATORE
and His Band
Tuesday September, 19th, '11

Afternoon Program

PART I

1. March—Triplice Alleanza — *D'Anna*
2. Overture—LaForra del Destino — *Verdi*
3. Berceuse from Jocelyn — *Godard*
   Solos by Signori DeMitry and DeLuca
4. Spring Song — *Mendelssohn*
5. Grand Selection—Maritana — *Wallace*
   Solos by Signori Catena and DeLuca

INTERMISSION

PART II

6. Gloria from 12th Mass — *Mozart*
7. Selection from Chocolate Soldier — *Strauss*
8. Souvenir of the Ball — *Boccalari*
9. Intermezzo—Narcissus — *Nevin*
10. Grand Selection—Faust — *Gounod*
   (a) Prelude (b) Flower Song (c) Chorus and Waltz
   Solos by Signori Catena and Ross

Evening Program

PART I

1. Coronation March from "The Prophet" — *Meyerbeer*
2. Overture—Mignon — *Thomas*
3. Intermezzo—Reverie — *Creatore*
4. Grand Selection—Aida — *Verdi*
   Solos by Signori DeMitry, Pasqualoni, Rossi and DeLuca

INTERMISSION

PART II

5. Suite No. 2—Scenes Pittoresques — *Massenet*
   (a) Marche (b) Au de Ballet (c) Angelus (d) Fete Boheme
6. Intermezzo—Cavalleria Rusticana — *Mascagni*
7. Trombone Solo—"Ah so Pure," from Martha — *Flotow*
   Signor Rossi
8. Irish Caprice — *Creatore*
   (a) St. Patrick's Day (b) The Last Rose of Summer
   (c) Garry Owen (d) Killarney
   (e) The Harp that Once thro' Tera's Hall

THE BEST PLACE TO BUY OR RENT
A **PIANO** IS AT
CHAPMAN'S
63 STATE STREET
EVERYTHING MUSICAL
Home of the Victrola — Wholesale and Retail

This original program was carefully preserved by someone who enjoyed the stirring music of "Giuseppe Creatore and His Band" on September 19, 1911. Exposition Park audiences also thrilled to the rousing music of Arthur Pryor's American Band. The Pryor Band gave its concerts in September 1912.

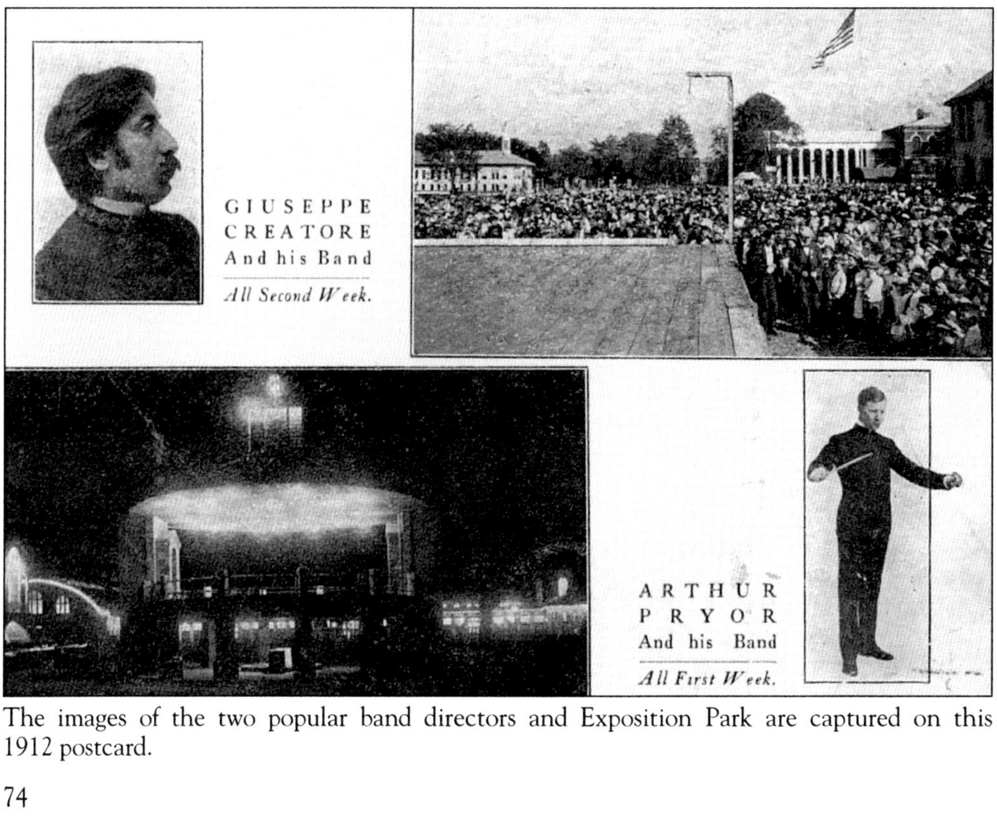

The images of the two popular band directors and Exposition Park are captured on this 1912 postcard.

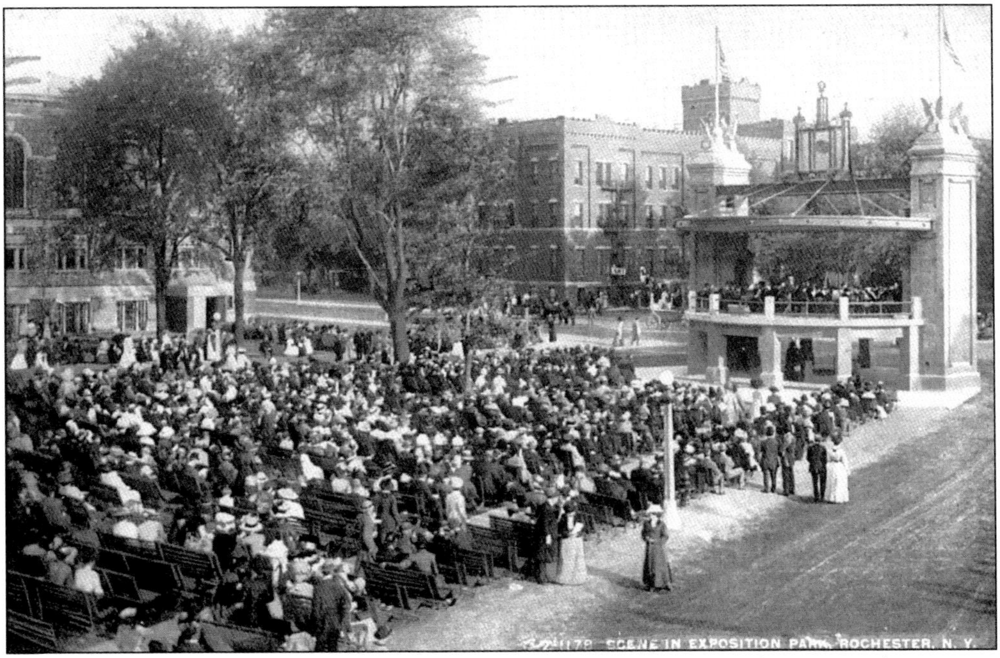

An impressive two-story bandstand, bracketed by flying eagles atop the main columns, was constructed as a focal point for those entering the Exposition Park grounds from Phelps Avenue. Mayor Hiram H. Edgerton was eager to enhance the culture of Rochesterians through outdoor band and choral concerts, popular during the period from 1910 to 1920.

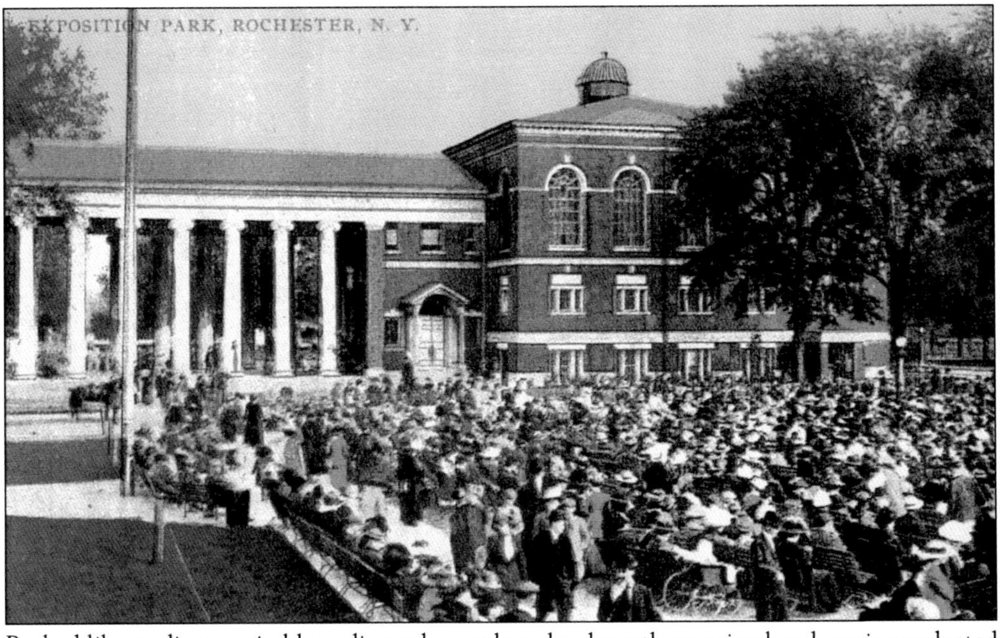

Packed like sardines, a sizable audience has gathered to hear the rousing band music conducted by the nationally famous director Giuseppe Creatore. The concert was performed in September 1912 for the Rochester Industrial Exposition. Seen in the background are the graceful Ionic columns of the Peristyle, leading to Exposition Park's Convention Hall.

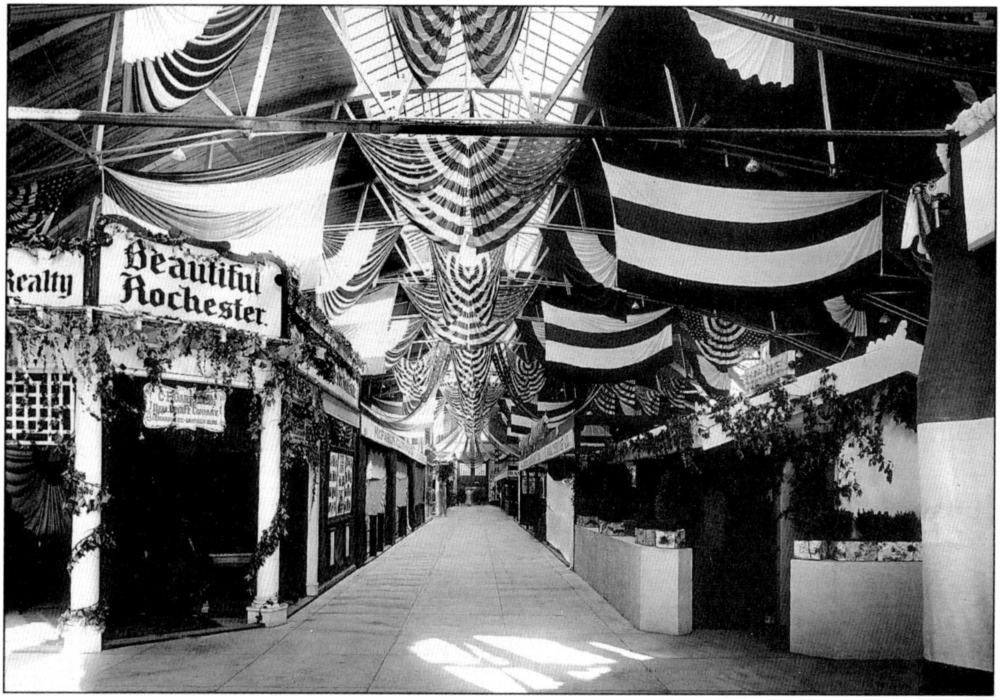

Taken in 1912, this photograph shows the interior of Building No. 5, whose main aisles were draped in a host of patriotic flags, banners, and bunting. Booths on the left promoted city real estate and McFarlans Clothing Store. On the right are booths for a carriage company, the Bastian Brothers Jewelry exhibit, and the specimens of Ward's Natural Science Establishment.

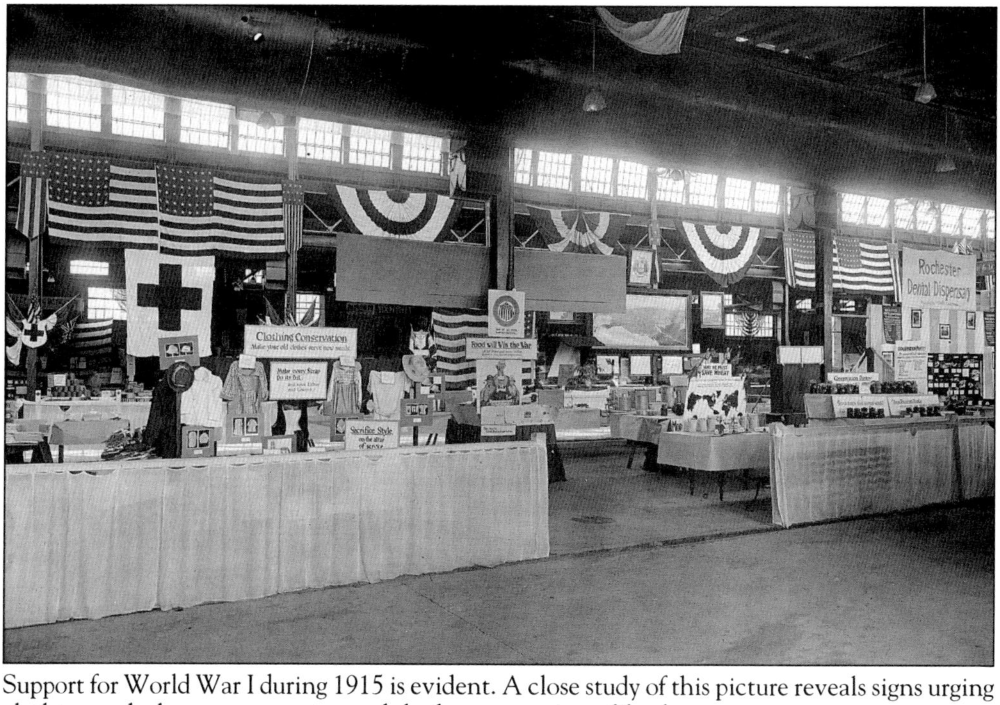

Support for World War I during 1915 is evident. A close study of this picture reveals signs urging clothing and wheat conservation and the home canning of food.

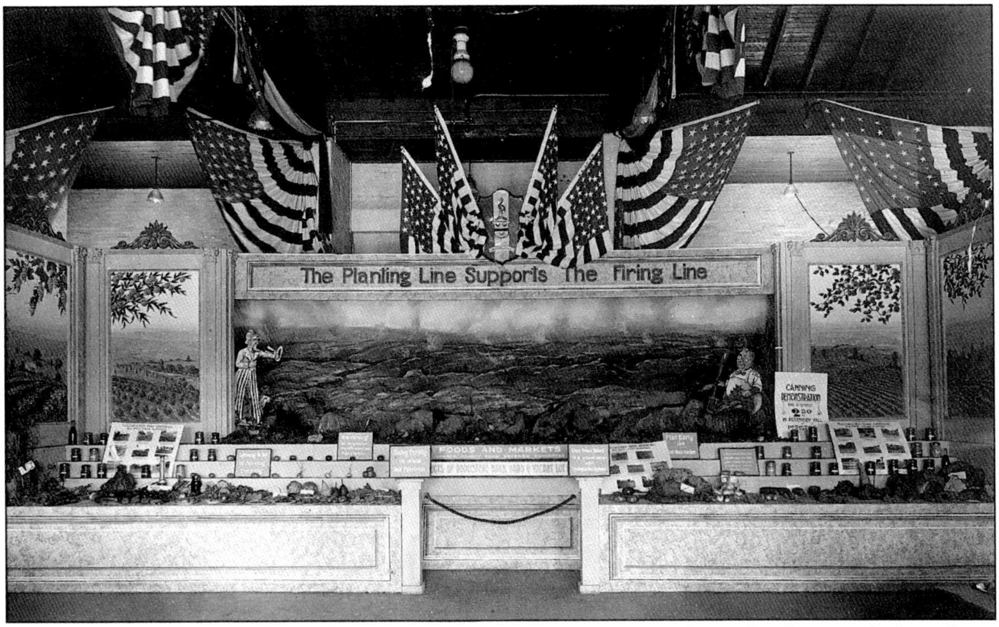

All varieties of canned and raw fruits and vegetables are exhibited in a display entitled Products of Rochester's Back Yard & Vacant Lot. Victory gardens were widely promoted during World War I. The city's crest is seen in the center between the flags at the top of the display.

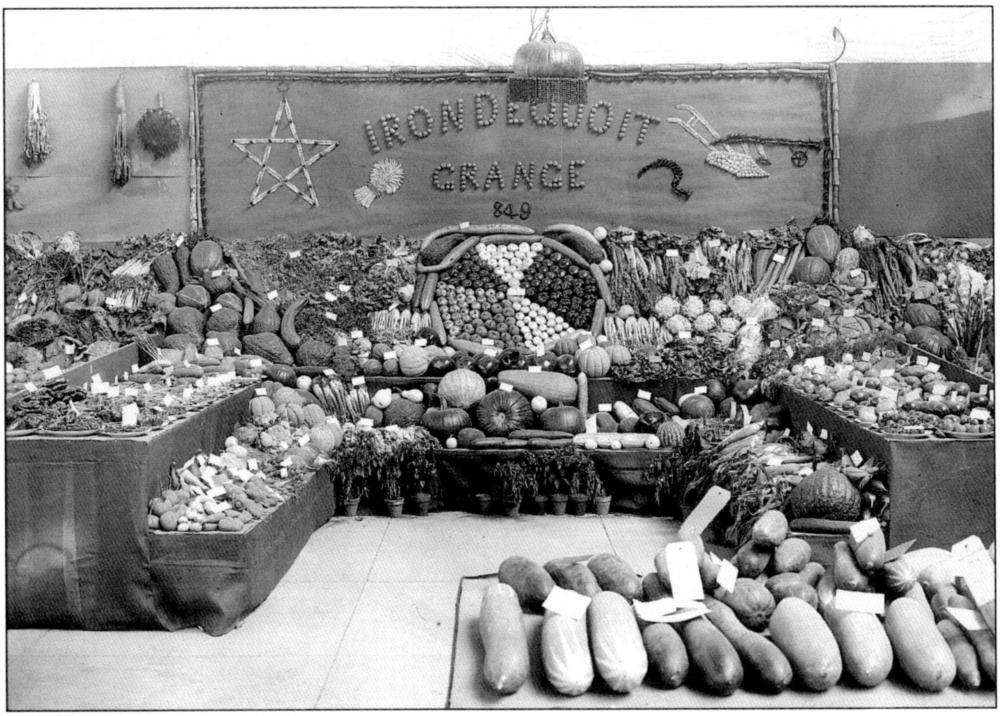

The winner of the many agricultural exhibits entered in the Products of a Rich Gardening category had to have been the Irondequoit Grange. The display, full of color, was a spectacular eye-catcher and included many wonderfully sweet Irondequoit melons. Notice that the shade over the light above the vegetable exhibit is a hollowed-out pumpkin.

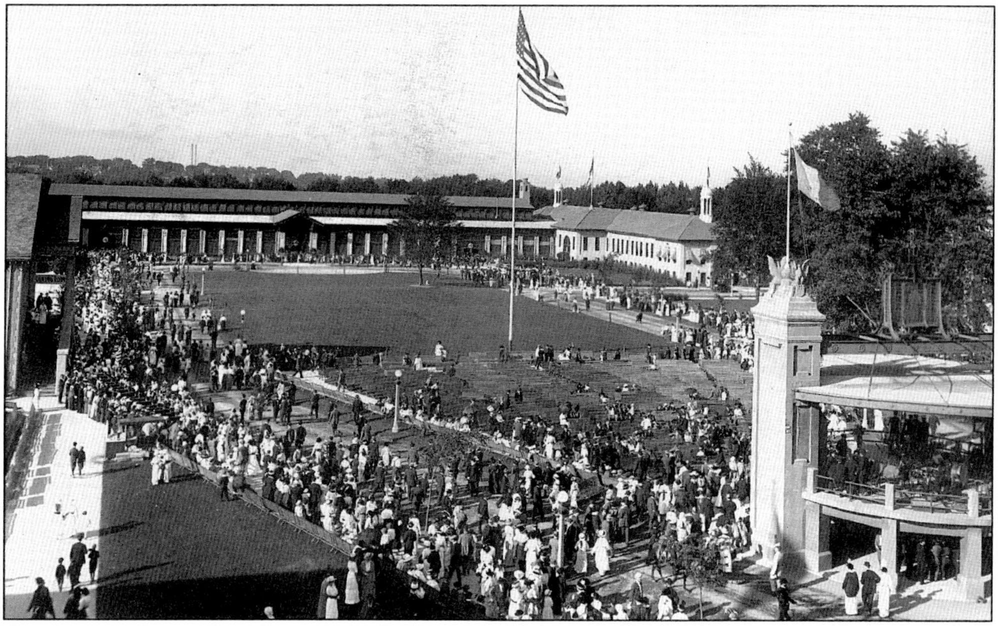

On a warm September day in 1915, throngs of eager citizens crowd the broad walkways of Exposition Park to see the latest industrial and agricultural displays in the exposition halls. The park, just five years old at the time, featured new buildings and attractive grounds, which are visible in this aerial view.

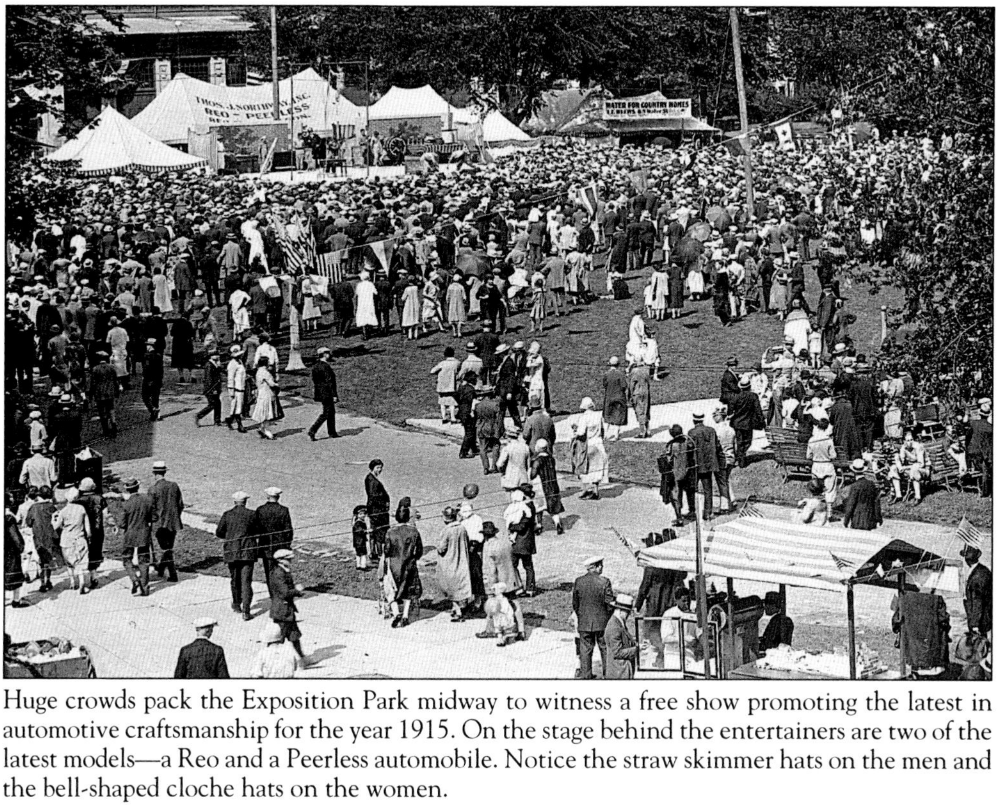

Huge crowds pack the Exposition Park midway to witness a free show promoting the latest in automotive craftsmanship for the year 1915. On the stage behind the entertainers are two of the latest models—a Reo and a Peerless automobile. Notice the straw skimmer hats on the men and the bell-shaped cloche hats on the women.

Five

EDGERTON PARK

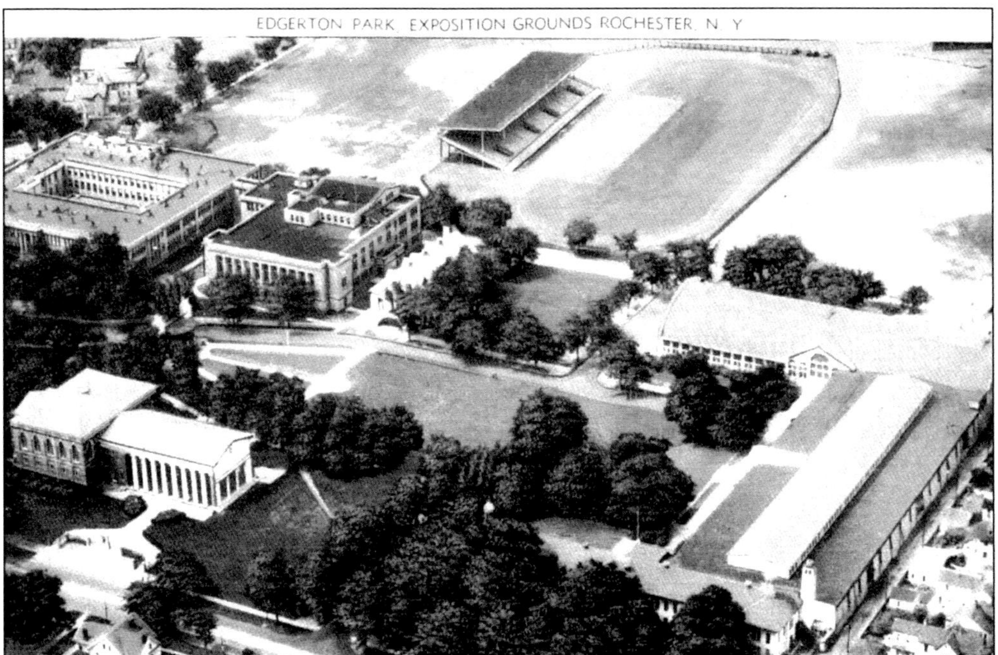

This aerial photograph of Exposition-Edgerton Park was taken in the late 1930s. It shows Jefferson Junior High School at the upper left, many mature trees, and a large grandstand built for the Rochester centennial celebration in 1934.

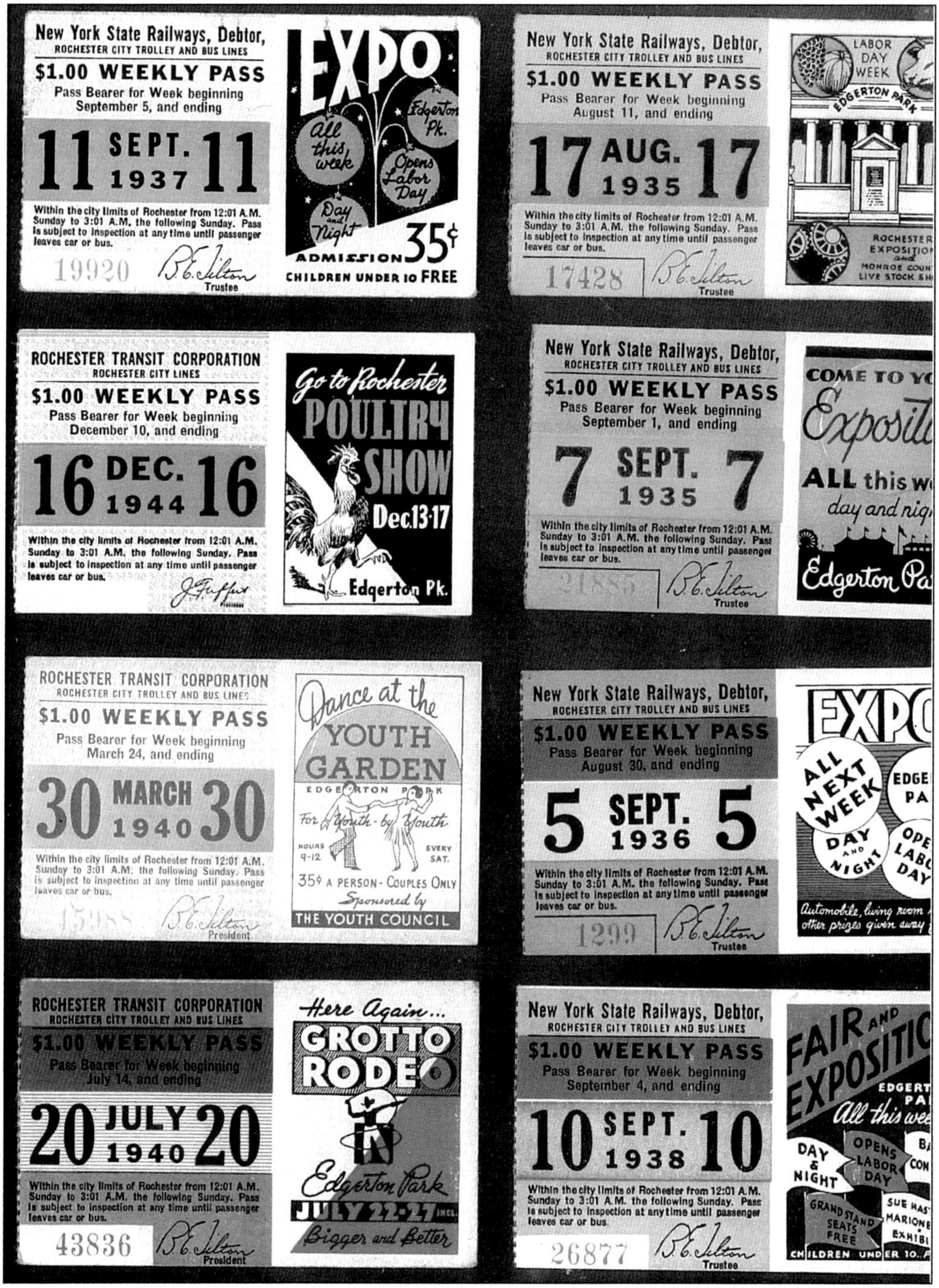

Once upon a time, weekly paper passes were issued to bus riders. Many advertised local events or social concerns. These advertise events to be held at the Edgerton Park.

Over the years, Exposition-Edgerton Park has been host to many venues. The pins and the badge are tangible memories of those wonderful bygone years.

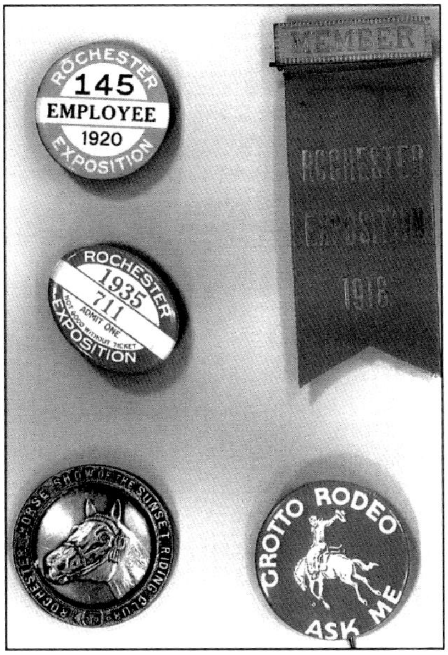

ROCHESTER HOME BUREAU
REGISTRATION OFFICE
RED CROSS TENT
REST ROOMS
RELAY RACES
REFORESTRATION

SCHOLARSHIP CONTESTS
SOLOISTS
SPECIALTY SHOW
STAGE SHOWS
SINGING
STATE EXHIBITS
SPECIAL TRAINS IN ALL DIRECTIONS
SPRINTING

TROLLEY CARS PASS GROUNDS
TUBERCULOSIS AND HEALTH ASSOCIATION
TRANSPORTATION DEPT.
THRILLING ENTERTAINMENT
TRAINS AT ALL HOURS
TRACTOR SHOW
TELEPHONE and TELEGRAPH OFFICE
TICKETS (See footnote)
THEATRICAL ATTRACTIONS
TOILETS PLENTIFUL

U. S. GOVERNMENT SHOW
UNUSUAL SHOW (Specialties)

VAUDEVILLE ACTS
VEGETABLE SHOW
VISITING NURSE

WOMEN'S BLDG.
WORK HORSE SHOW

XTRA FEATURES UNANNOUNCED

YOUNG PEOPLE'S DEPARTMENTS

ZEALOUS POLICE PATROL
ZOO
ZYMURGICAL BEVERAGES VOLSTEDIZED
& THEN SOME

For further details address

Rochester Exposition Association

307-309 Powers Bldg. Rochester, N. Y.

William B. Boothby, Gen. Mgr. Main 1697

Apply there for additional copies of this folder

Rochester Exposition and Horse Show

SEPT. 1 to 6

Six Days "Opens Labor Day" Six Nights

— 1930 —

"COME"

MONDAY:	Labor Day Kiwanis Club Day
TUESDAY:	American Legion Day Children's Day Rotary Club Day
WEDNESDAY:	Governor's Day
THURSDAY:	Manufacturers' Day Press Day Ad Club Day High School Day
FRIDAY:	Grange Day Chamber of Commerce Day Lions Club Day
SATURDAY:	Rochester Day Automobile Day Commercial Travelers' Day Gyro Club Day

1910—1930

"Twenty Years of Progress"

This small brochure is not only an invitation to attend the Rochester Exposition and Horse Show but also a list (left column) of just a few of the many amenities and other attractions available at Edgerton Park. The last one listed is a gem. The annual horse show became one of Rochester's premier social events.

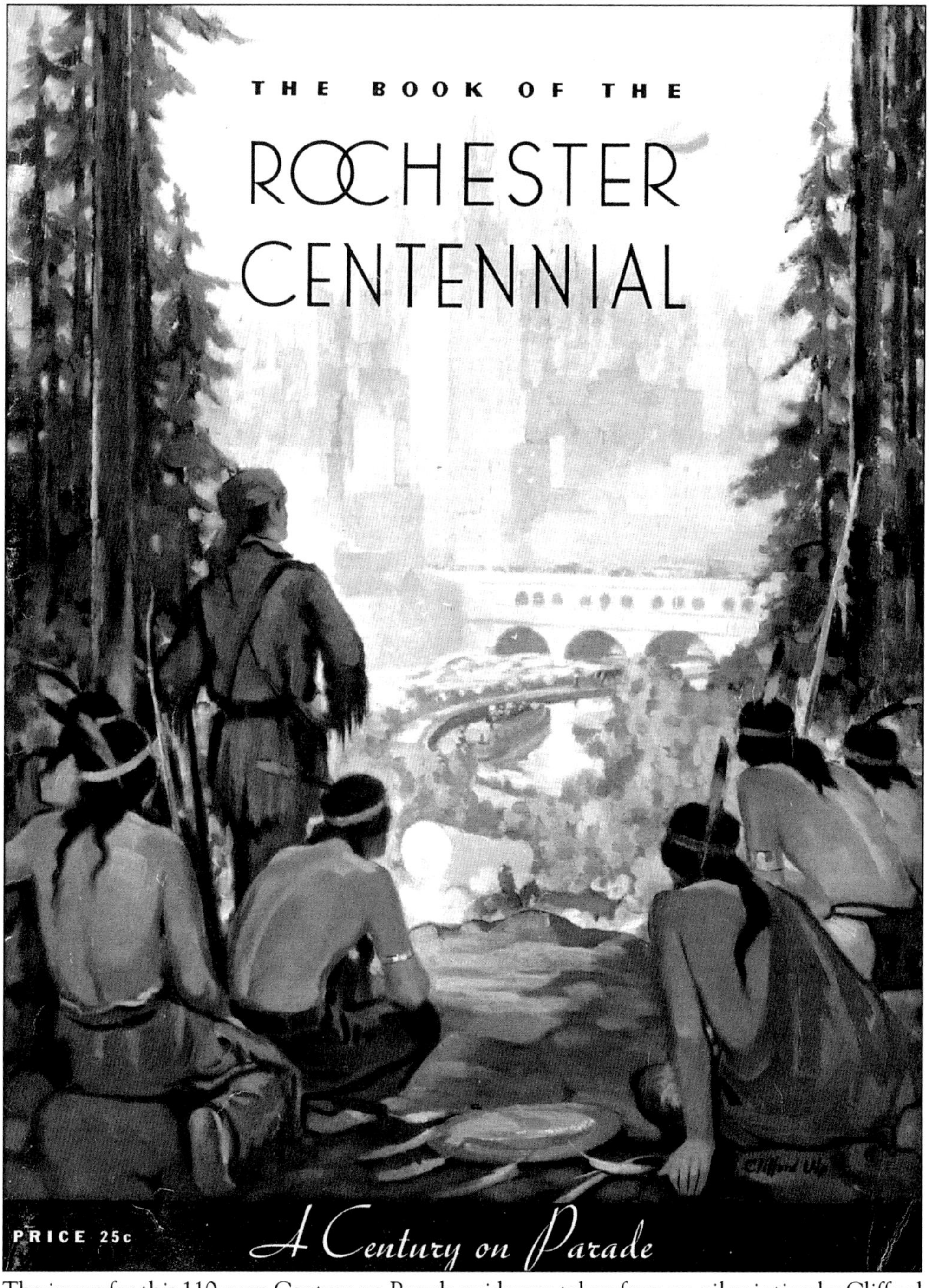

The image for this 110-page Century on Parade guide was taken from an oil painting by Clifford M. Ulp, an instructor at the Rochester Institute of Technology. Filled with brief accounts of Rochester's history, the guide became a treasured souvenir for many who attended Rochester's 100th birthday party.

This advertisement is an invitation for the entire nation to come see Rochester's "national exhibition and historical dramatic spectacle."

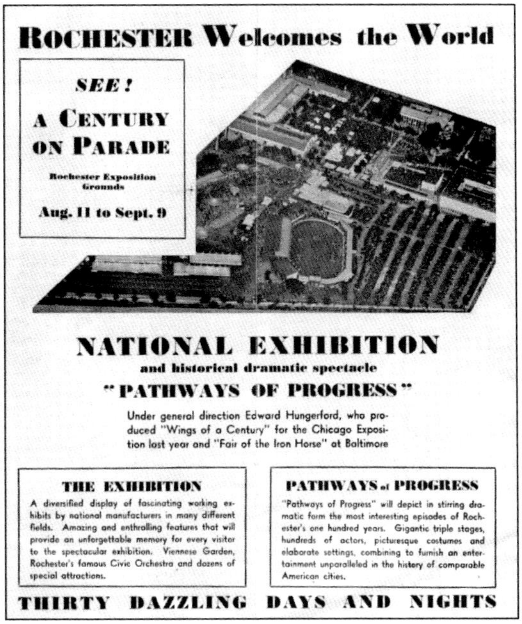

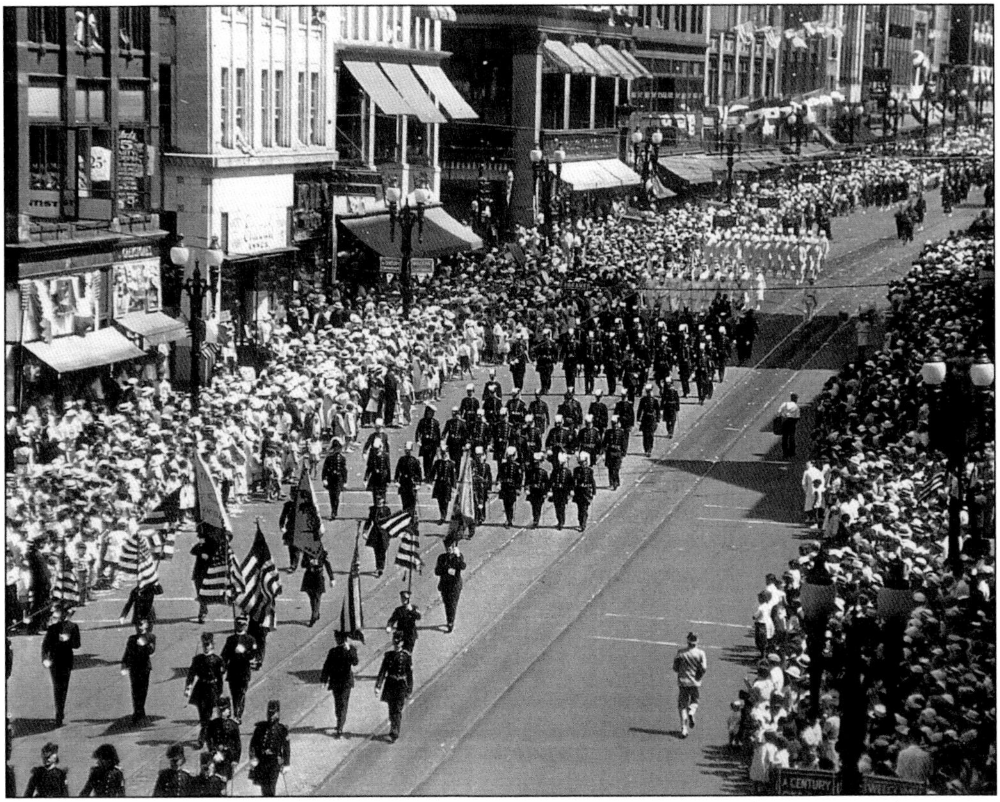

Main Street was packed up to 10 deep as some 7,000 marchers passed in review. There were civic and military units parading by, flags flying, bands bursting with music, bunting-bedecked floats, and a host of dignitaries waving their hats in greeting to the applauding multitudes. (Courtesy History Division, Rochester Public Library.)

THE ROCHESTER CENTENNIAL

Officers

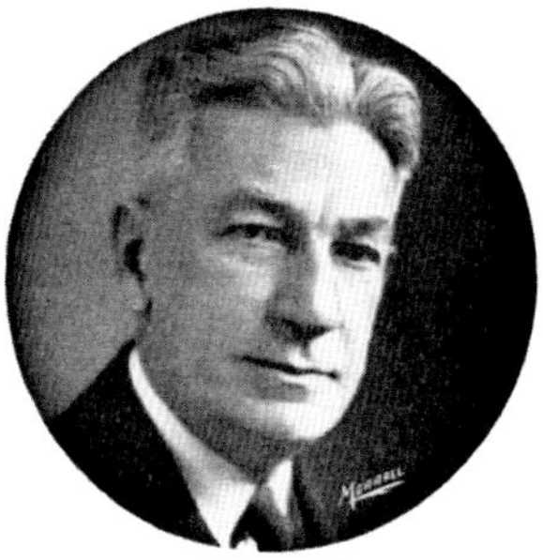

MAYOR CHARLES STANTON
Honorary Chairman

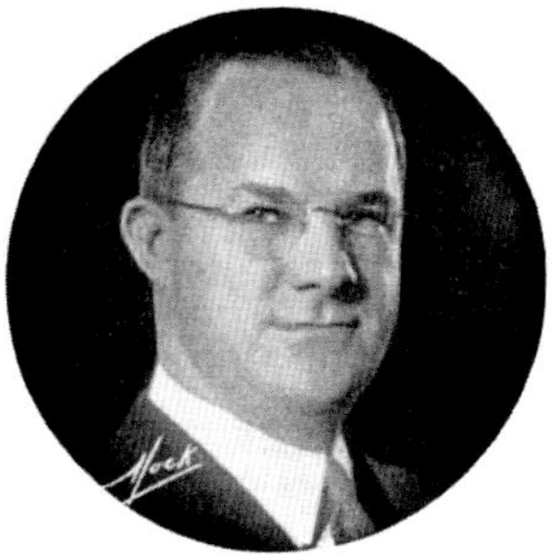

CARL S. HALLAUER
General Chairman

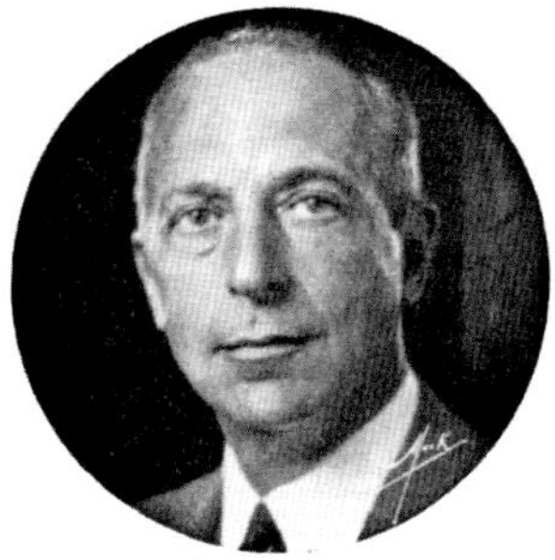

HARPER SIBLEY
President

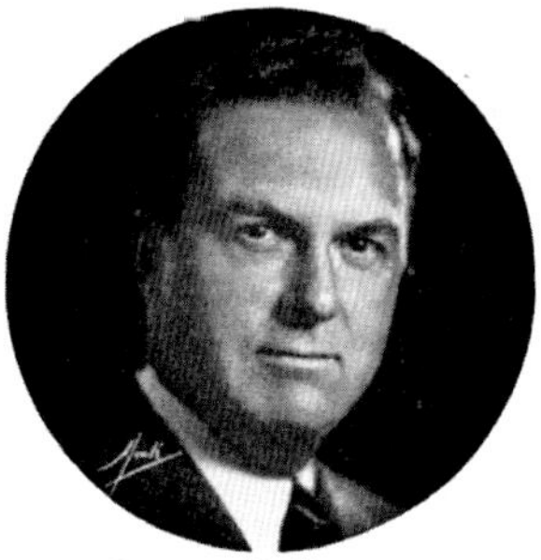

BERNARD E. FINUCANE
Vice-Chairman

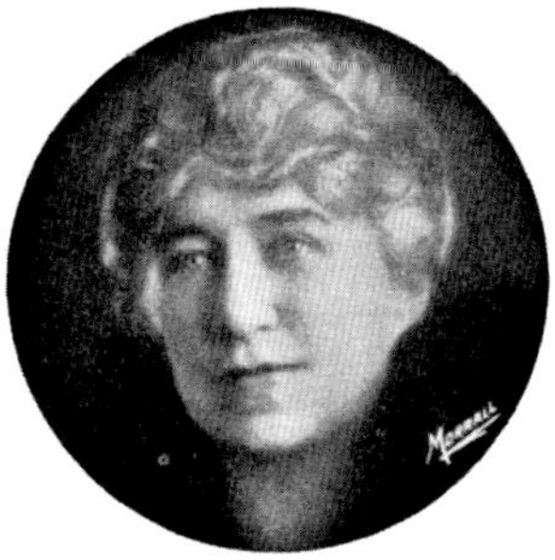

MRS. RICHARD T. FORD
Vice-Chairman

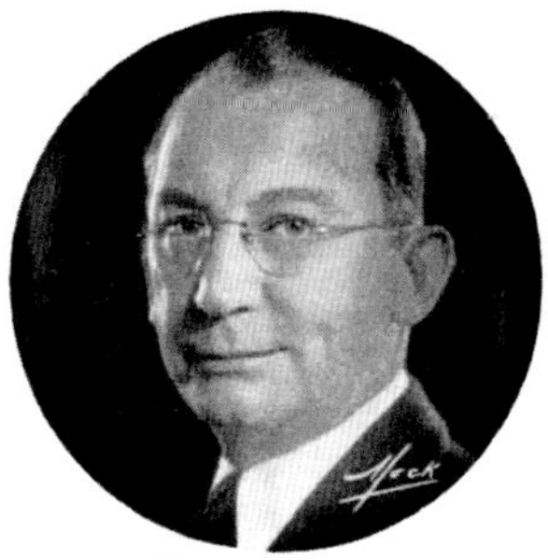

FRANK J. SMITH
Vice-Chairman

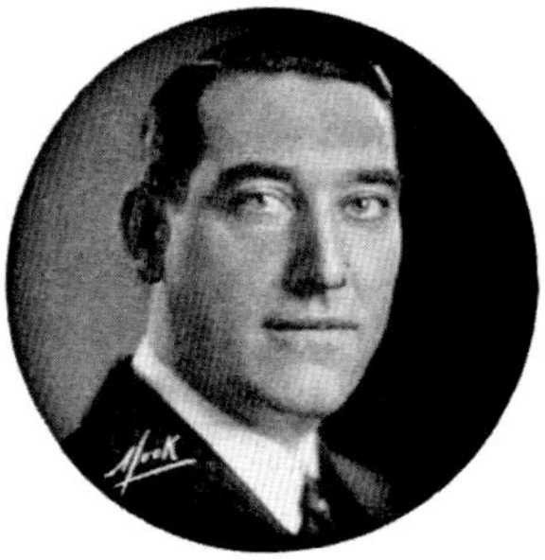

JOHN A. MURRAY
Treasurer

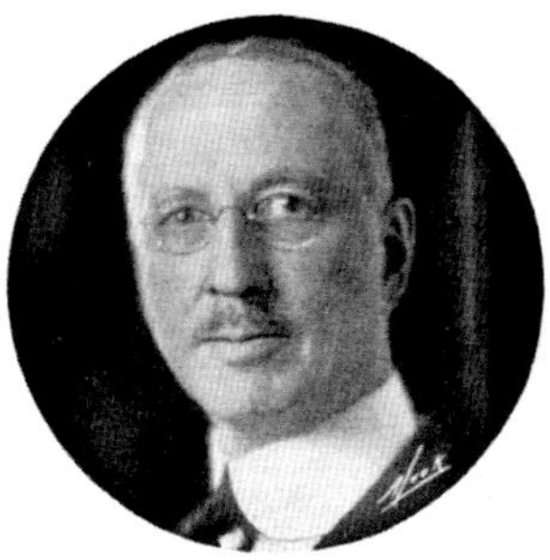

EDWARD R. FOREMAN
Secretary

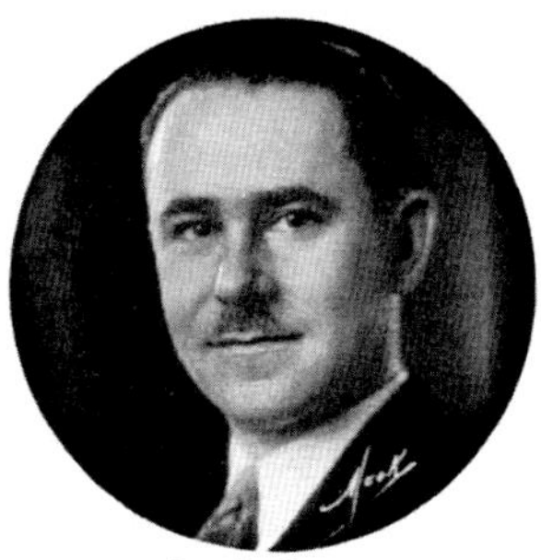

ROY R. RUMPFF
Executive Secretary

The nine members of the executive committee for Rochester's centennial represented some of the city's leading citizens. All were people of importance who wished to show the nation and the local citizens the historic and economic stature the city had achieved during its first 100 years.

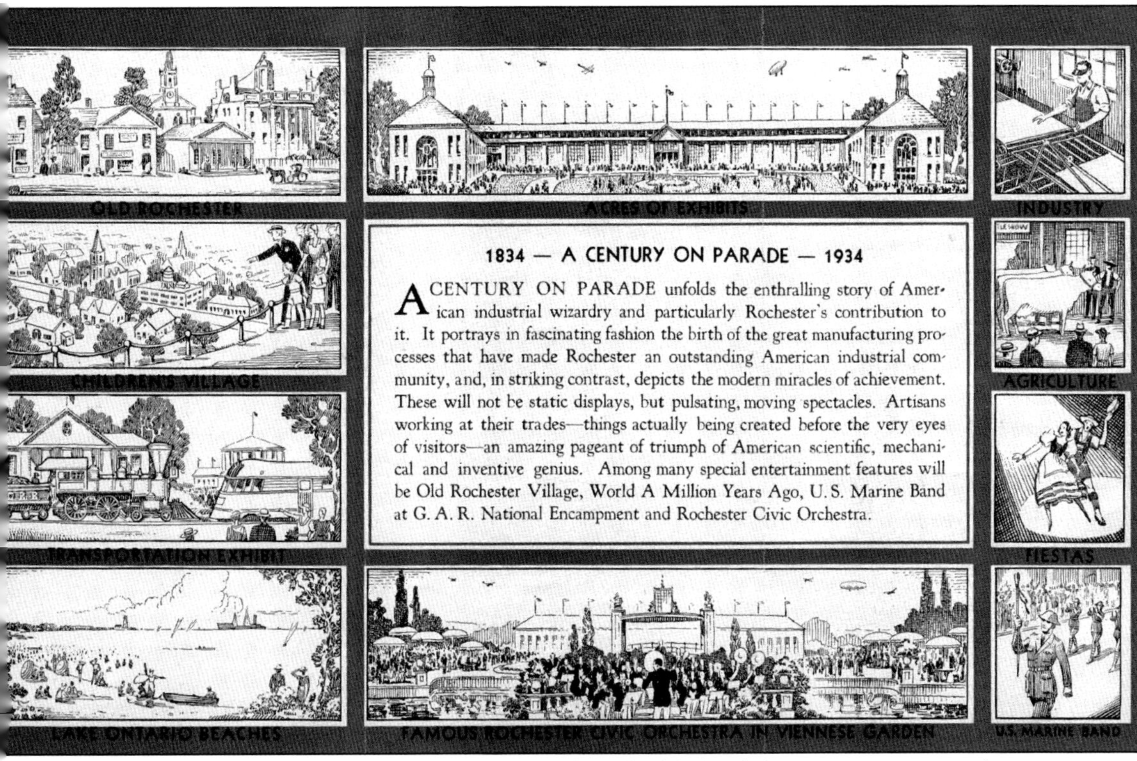

To promote the Century on Parade event, a brochure highlighted the many attractions during the event. The text sketches the purpose and philosophy behind the exhibits to create "an amazing pageant of the triumph of American scientific, mechanical and inventive genius."

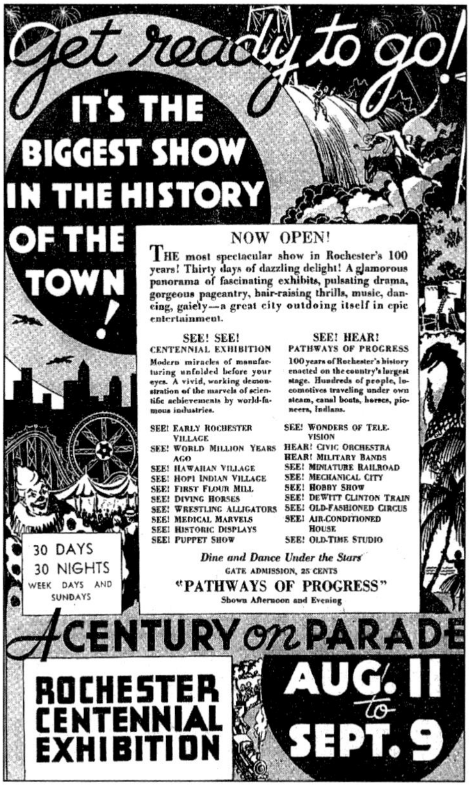

This advertisement details many of the attractions to be enjoyed at Rochester's "Biggest Show in the History of the Town." Among the sights were alligator wrestling, diving horses, and the "Wonders of Television." (Courtesy *Democrat & Chronicle*.)

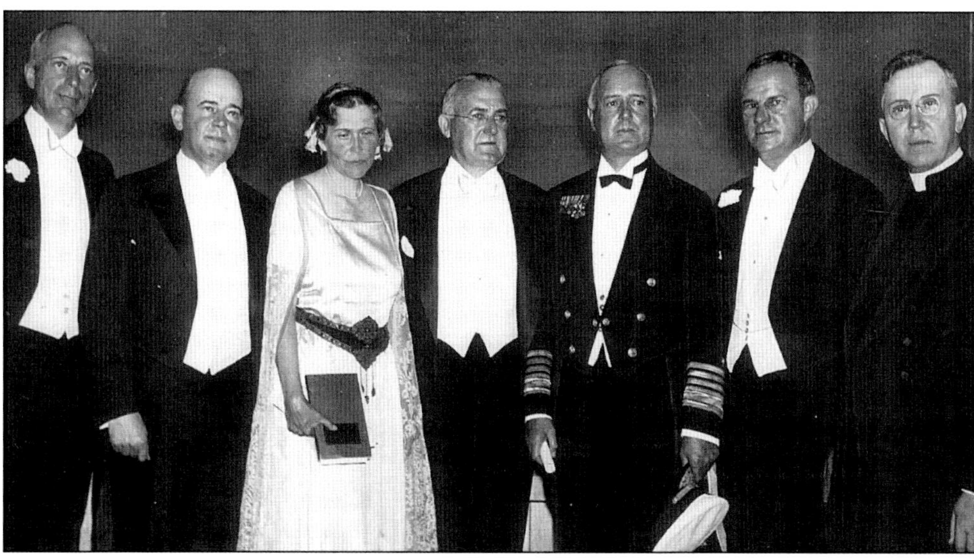

Sunday, June 10, 1934, was proclaimed Civic Day, a part of the centennial celebration. Among the dignitaries taking part in the Civic Day celebration at the Eastman Theatre are, from left to right, the Most Reverend Edward Mooney, D.D., Carl S. Hallauer, Adm. David Foote Sellers, Frank E. Gannett, Elizabeth Hollister Frost, Thomas G. Spencer, and Harper Sibley. (Courtesy History Division, Rochester Public Library.)

Displayed at the centennial pageant was a replica of the locomotive *DeWitt Clinton*. When it pulled a pair of stagecoach-like cars on August 9, 1831, between Albany and Schenectady, it became New York State's first railroad train.

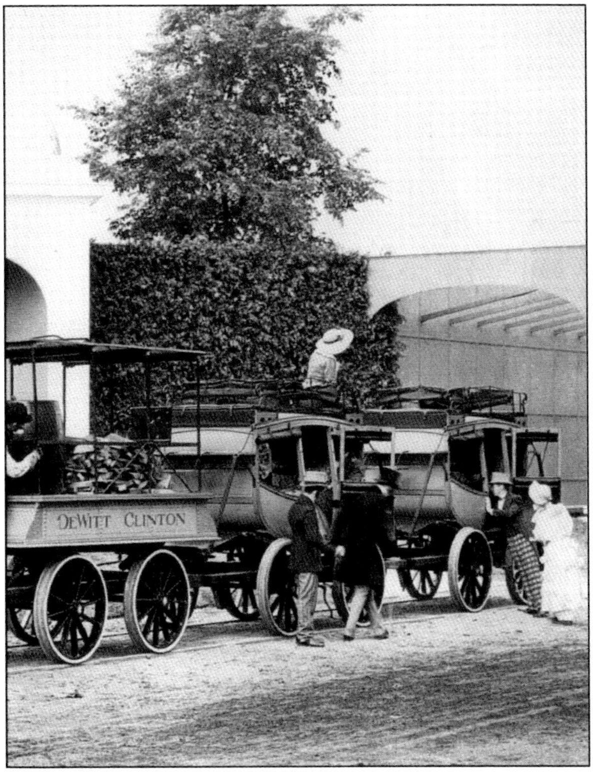

A CENTURY ON PARADE

Edgerton Park, Rochester, N. Y.

Schedule of Events, Saturday, Aug. 25, 1934

NORTHERN NEW YORK DAY

Ed Wynn, Radio and Stage Star, Guest of Honor

1:00 P.M.	Proske's Bengal Tigers—Front of Building 6
1:00 P.M.	Horse Shoe Pitching—The Stadium
1:45 P.M.	The Puppet Show—Early Rochester
2:00 P.M.	Ed. Wynn Arrives at Park
2:30 P.M.	Dramatic Spectacle, "Pathways of Progress"
2:30 P.M.	Wild Animal Circus—The Midway
3:00 P.M.	Concert—Rochester Park Band—Viennese Garden
4:00 P.M.	Ed Wynn Leads Parade Through Park
4;00 P.M.	Western New York Athletic Championships
4:00 P.M.	The Puppet Show—Early Rochester
4:30 P.M.	Ed Wynn Made Honorary Chief—Rochester Fire Department
5:30 P.M.	The Diving Horse—The Midway
5:45 P.M.	Wild Animal Circus—The Midway
6:30 P.M.	Proske's Bengal Tigers—Front of Building 6
6:45 P.M.	Concert—Rochester Civic Orchestra—Viennese Garden
7:00 P.M.	The Puppet Show—Early Rochester
7:00 P.M.	Horse Shoe Pitching—The Stadium
7:15 P.M.	Wild Animal Circus—The Midway
8:15 P.M.	Dramatic Spectacle, "Pathways of Progress"
9:00 P.M.	The Puppet Show—Early Rochester
9:30 P.M.	Concert—Rochester Civic Orchestra—Viennese Garden
9:30 P.M.	Wild Animal Circus—The Midway
10:00 P.M.	The Puppet Show—Early Rochester
11:00 P.M.	The Diving Horse—The Midway

Industrial Show, Hobby Show, Early Rochester Village Television Show and other Features Continuous

Each day of the 30-day celebration was dedicated to a specific group or region. Ed Wynn was the guest of honor on Northern New York Day, Saturday, August 25, 1934.

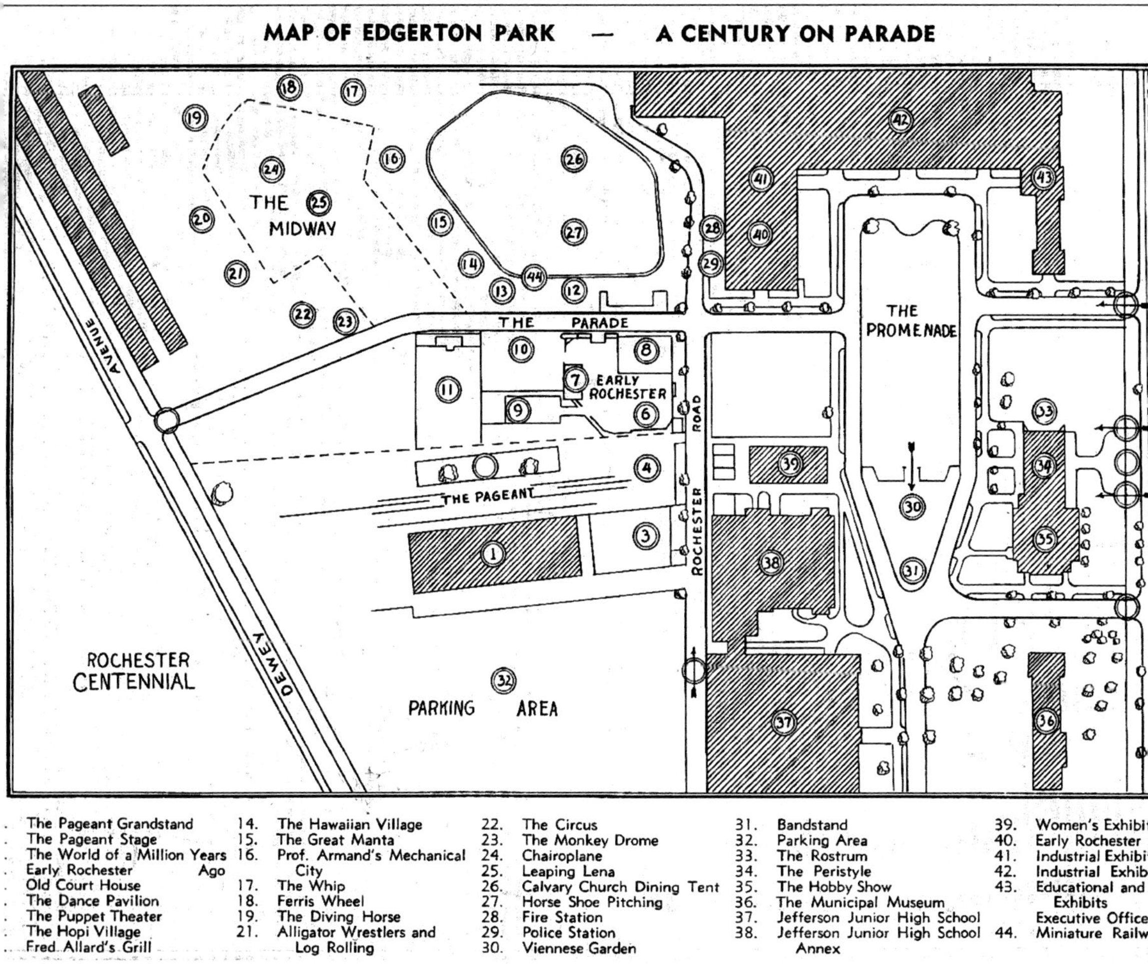

A detailed map of Edgerton Park shows how elaborate the preparations were for this spectacular 100th-year birthday event.

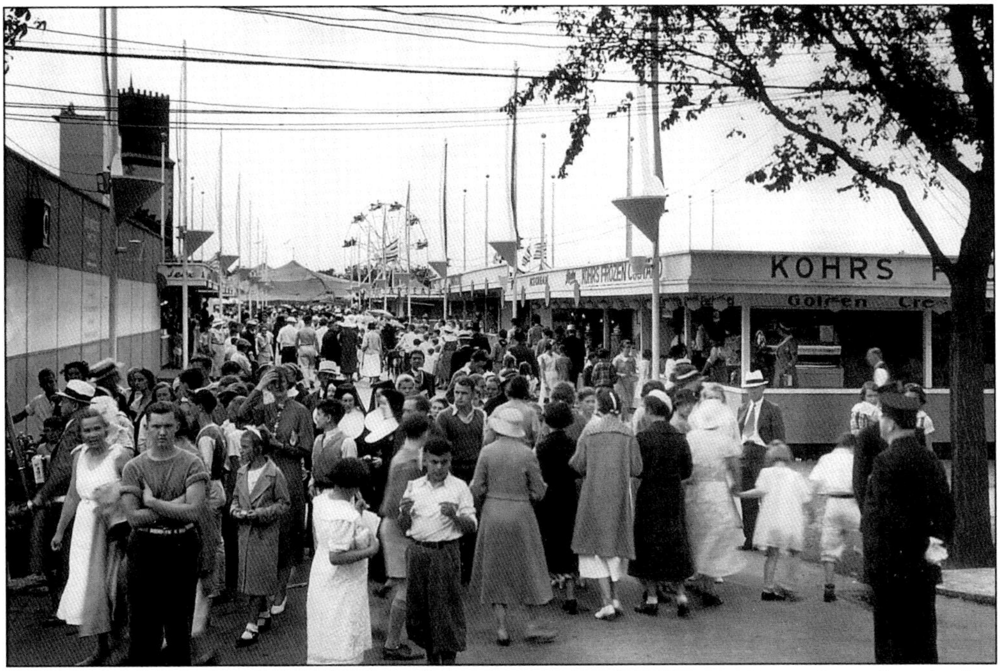

En route to the midway, crowds of Rochesterians pass Kohr's Frozen Custard stand and other refreshment booths. At the right, an officer is surveying the throngs. Also visible is one man with a custard cone. (Courtesy History Division, Rochester Public Library.)

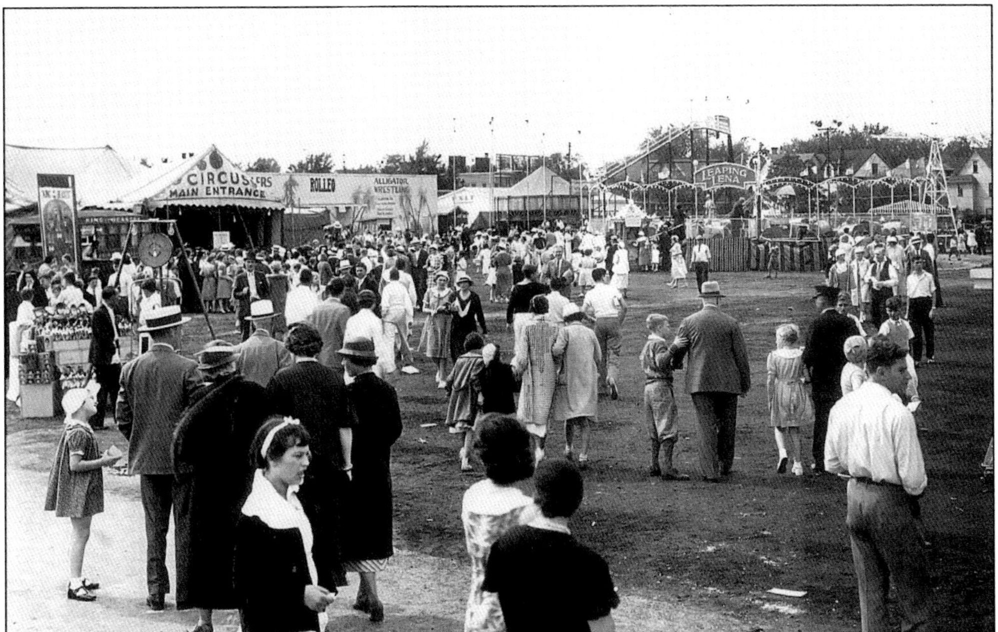

Midway rides included the Chairoplane, Leaping Lena, Ferris wheel, and the Whip. The Rolleo featured world-champion logrollers, and Alligator Tex wrestled his reptiles at two daily shows. Vendors sold cotton candy, popcorn, and peanuts to those attending the circus. (Courtesy History Division, Rochester Public Library.)

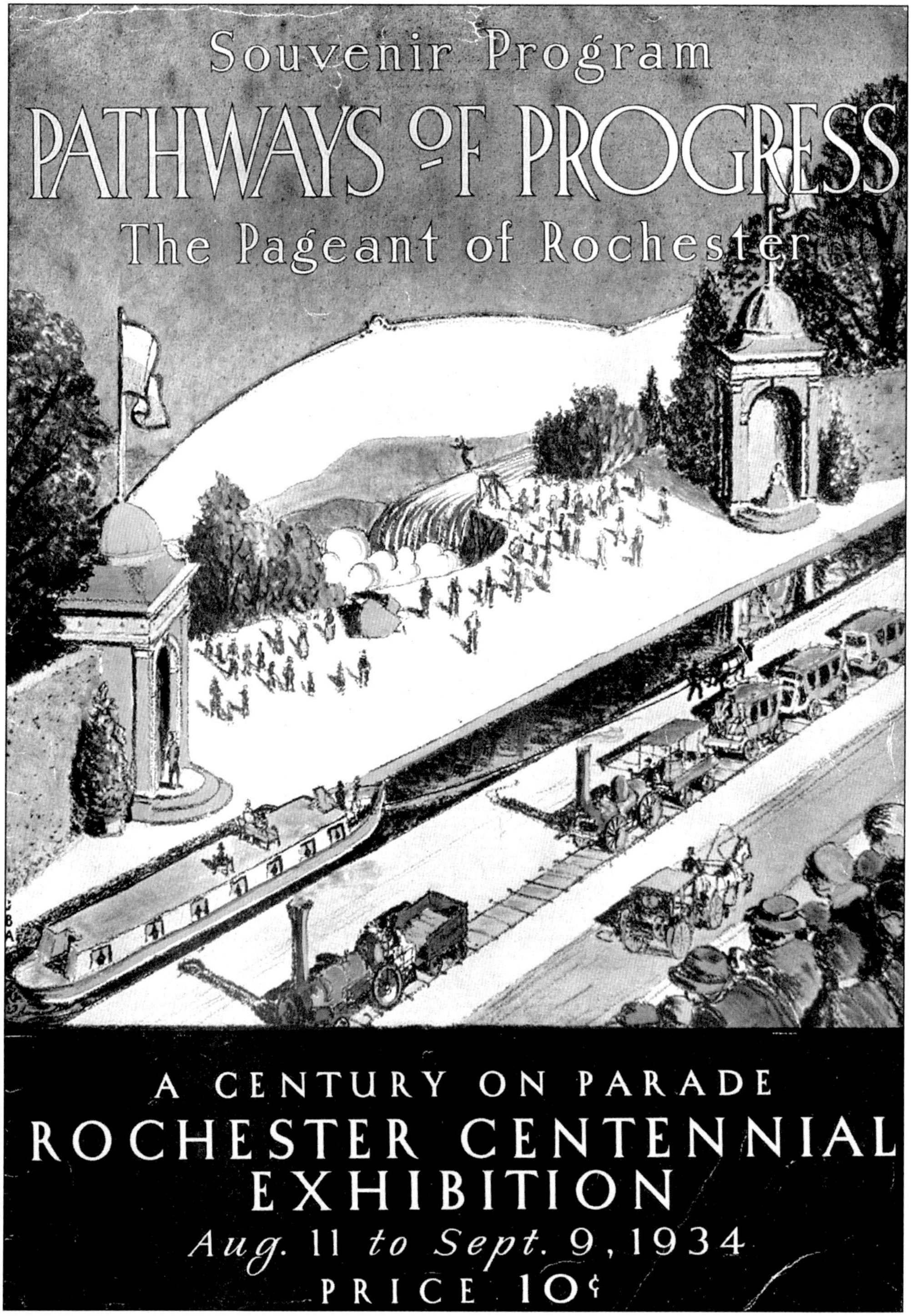

A colorful souvenir program of the Pathways to Progress pageant provided the audience with information on the scenes, the cast members, and the exhibits within the main exhibition buildings.

The Pathways to Progress pageant was created by Edward Hungerford, who in 1933 had produced Chicago's Wings of a Century pageant. The Rochester pageant featured 10 scenes depicting the city's remarkable progress from 1823 to 1934. Each scene was introduced and narrated by Roberta Beatty and Walter F. Folmer.

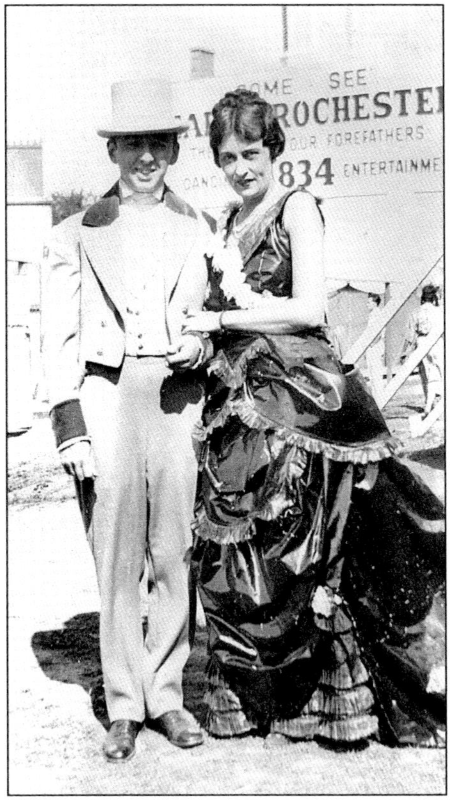

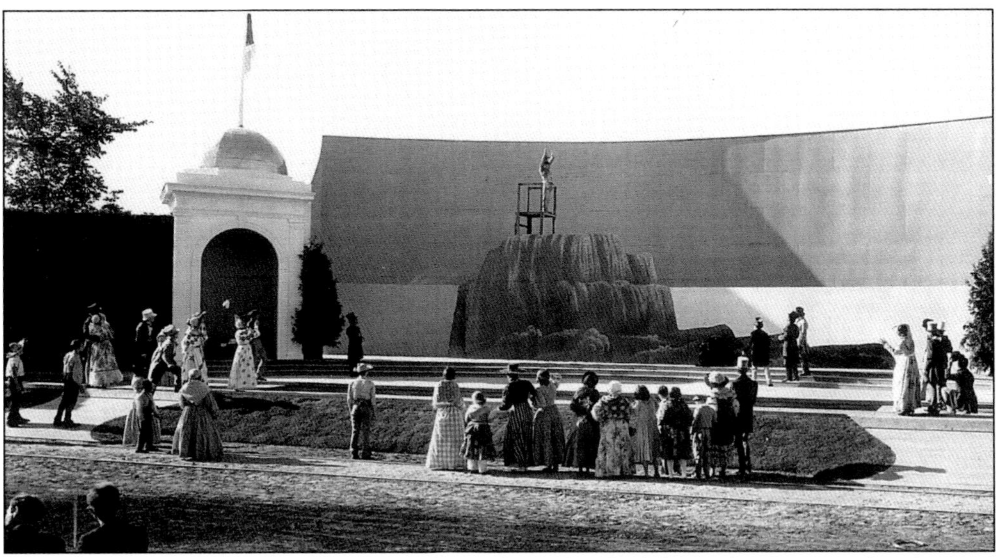

Scene 3 actor Marty Vogt, as Sam Patch, performs his fatal leap of 1829 over the churning waters of the Genesee River's High Falls. It was a crowd pleaser. (Courtesy History Division, Rochester Public Library.)

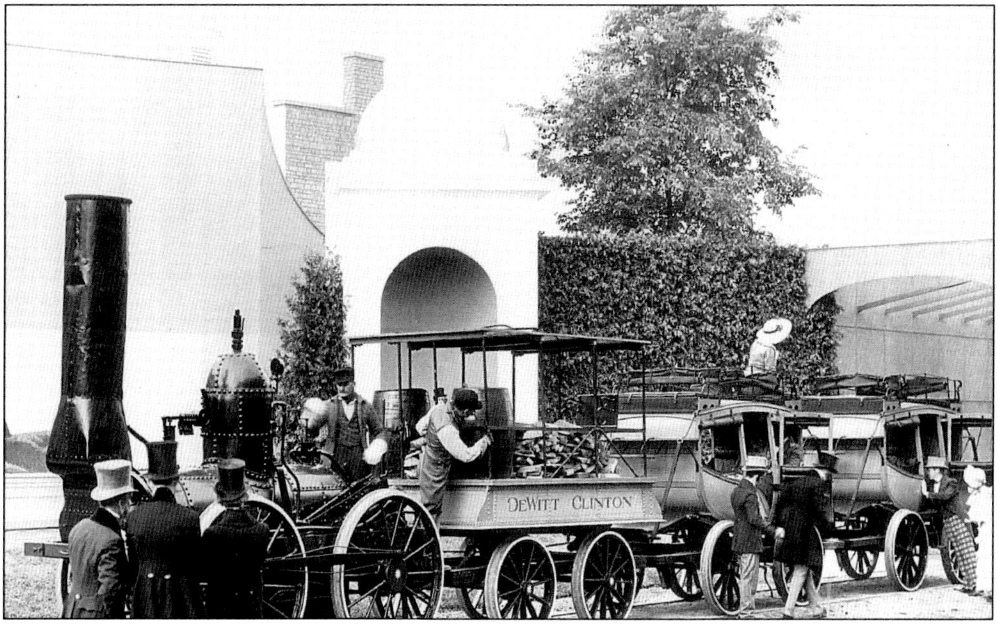

Another dramatic moment in the Pathways to Progress pageant occurs when a replica of New York State's first locomotive, the *De Witt Clinton*, rolls onto the stage, pulling its string of two "coaches." (Courtesy History Division, Rochester Public Library.)

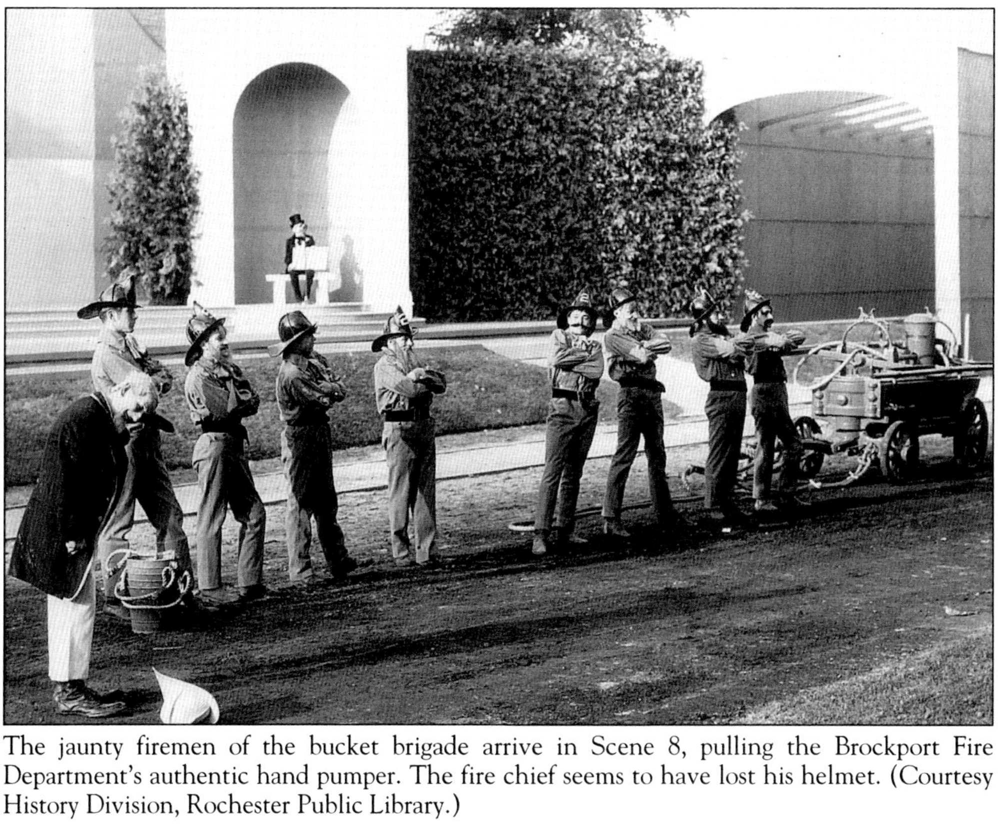

The jaunty firemen of the bucket brigade arrive in Scene 8, pulling the Brockport Fire Department's authentic hand pumper. The fire chief seems to have lost his helmet. (Courtesy History Division, Rochester Public Library.)

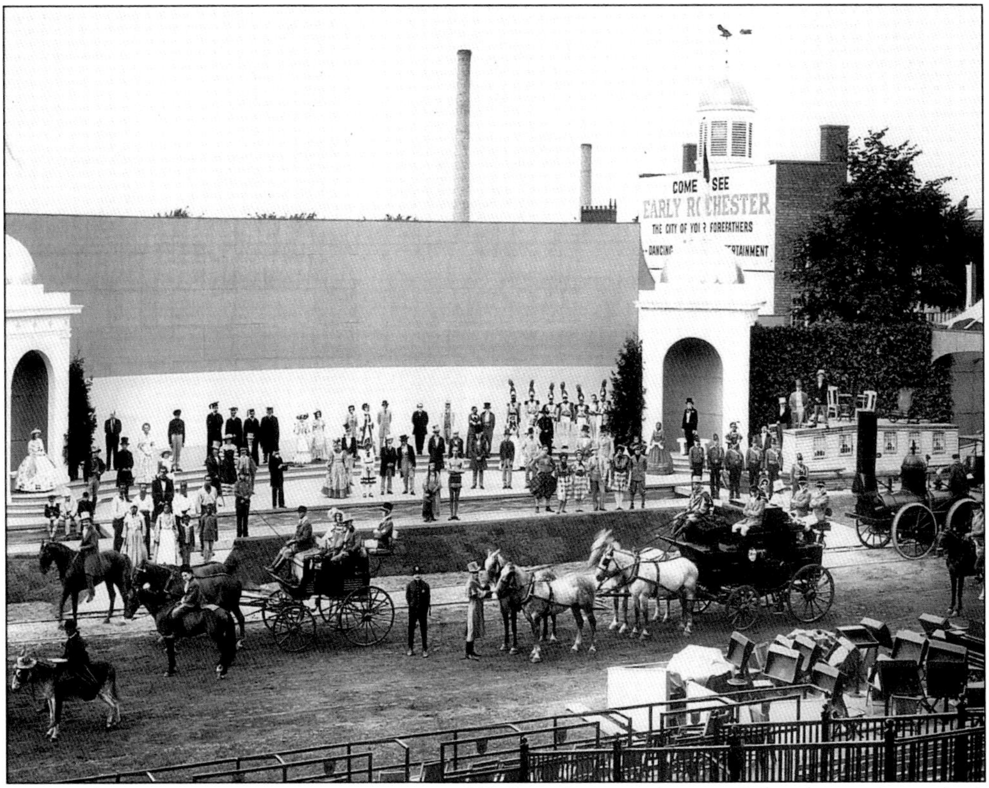

The Pathways to Progress pageant stage is filled at the completion of the dress rehearsal. A permanent, covered grandstand was constructed for pageant audiences. To the right of the stage, an Erie Canal packet boat appears. (Courtesy History Division, Rochester Public Library.)

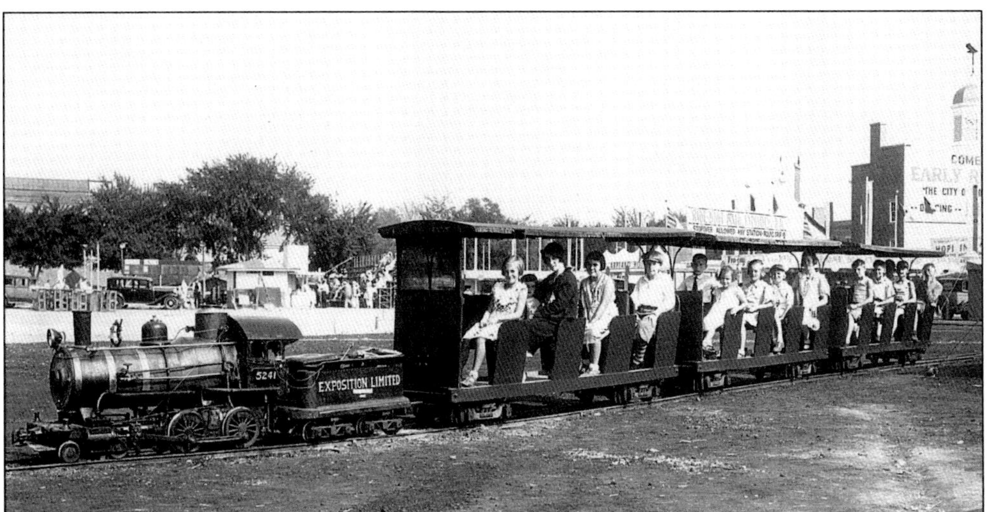

Another highlight of the centennial celebration was a miniature railway circling the exhibition grounds. Holding 24 passengers, the *Exhibition Express* provided a great way to view the park ground's many attractions. (Courtesy History Division, Rochester Public Library.)

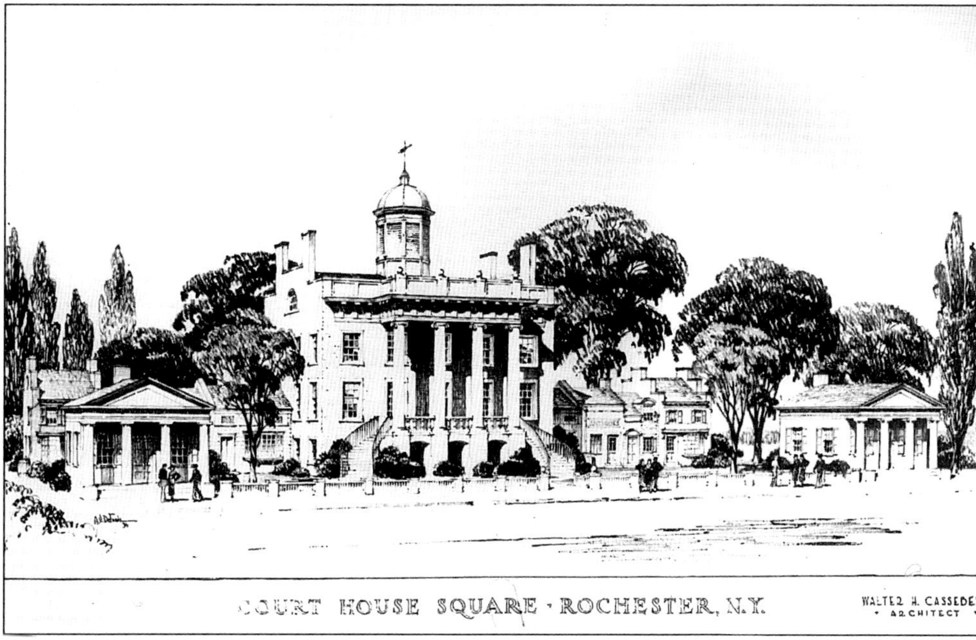

Immense effort went into the preparation for the centennial celebration. An example was the construction of replicas of Rochester's earliest Main Street buildings. This sketch, done by Walter H. Cassebeer, a distinguished local architect, helped in the design and construction of a likeness of Court House Square as it looked in 1834.

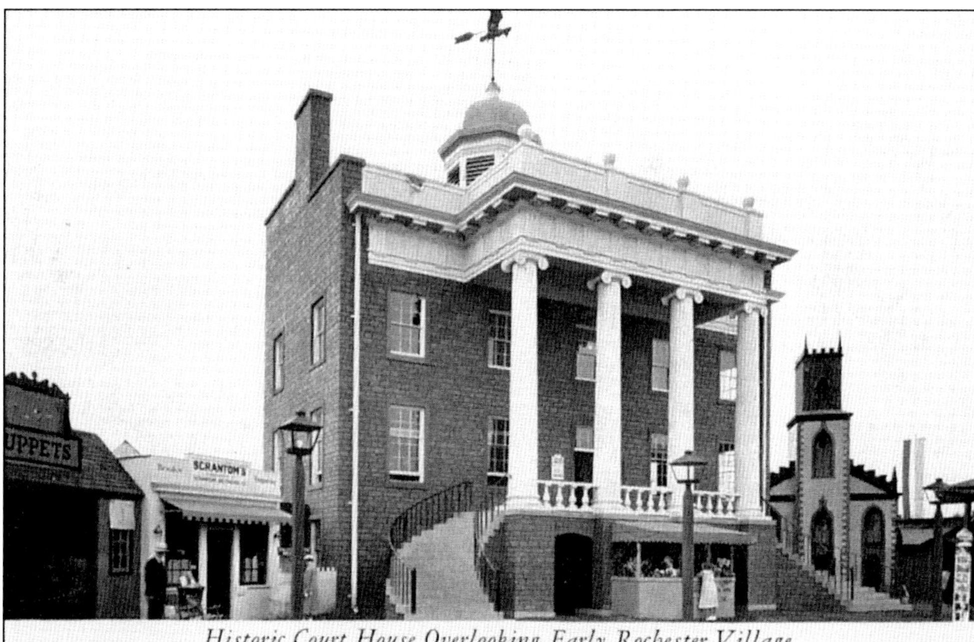

The completed Court House Square, a part of the Early Rochester exhibit, included not only a three-story replica of the first courthouse but also replicas of St. Luke's Episcopal Church and other associated buildings.

Six

Night Life in the Gay 1890s

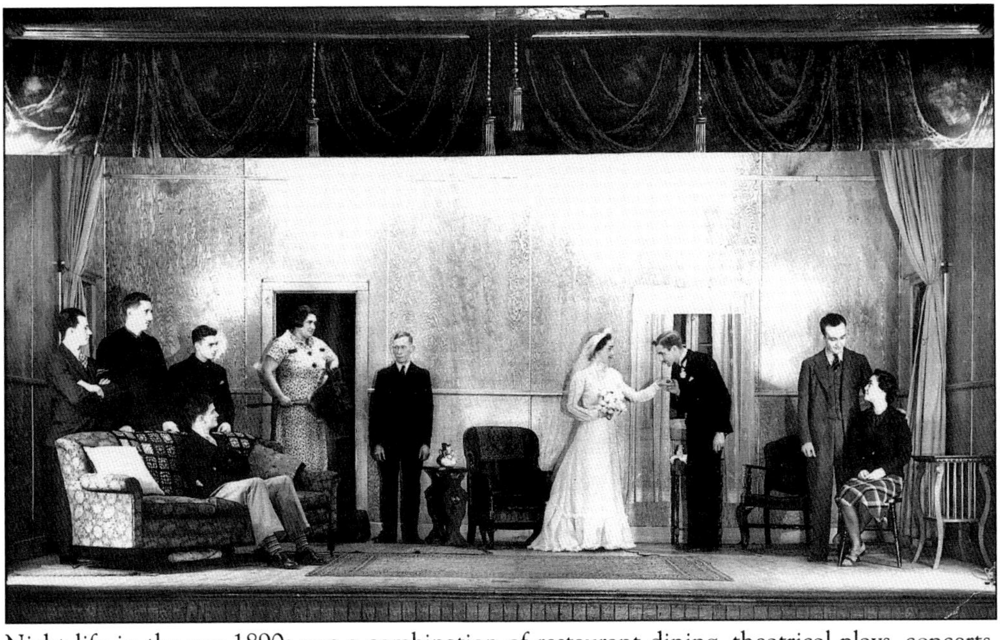

Night life in the gay 1890s was a combination of restaurant dining, theatrical plays, concerts, vaudeville, and minstrel shows. A drama contest brought the thespians from the West Henrietta Baptist Church Dramatic Club to Rochester for their entry. The one-act play *Old Lady of Lynbrook* was written and directed by George Caswell, who also acted in the production. Other cast members were Regina Schillinger, Earl McConnel, Gale Howlett, Mary Early Sloman, Harvey Page, Charles Nelson, John Gaylord Lowe, Everett Quackenbush, and Charles White.

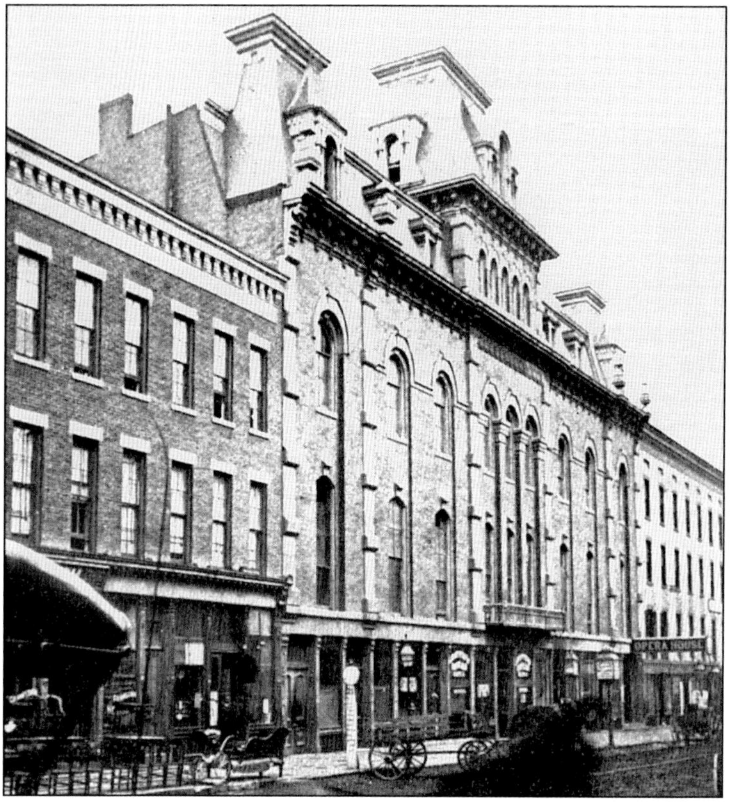

The Grand Opera House on South St. Paul Street (South Avenue) drew world-famous actors and actresses. During 1876 and again in 1881, Sarah Bernhardt performed at this Rochester theater.

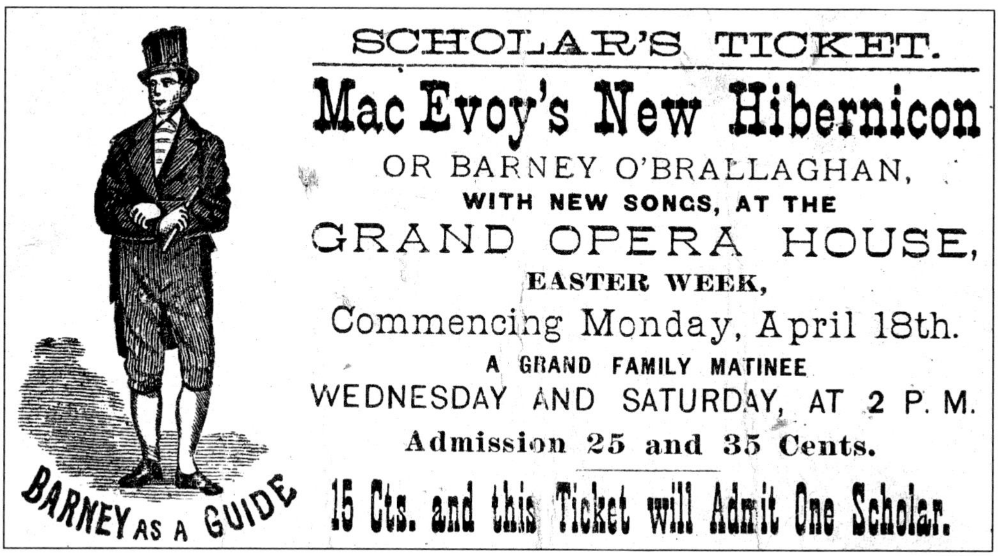

The "scholar's ticket" admits one to see Mac Evoy's *New Hibernicon* at the Grand Opera House. This modest memento of yesterday has slipped through the funnel of time, surviving for at least 125 years.

The Academy of Music program lists the play as *Enemies for Life*. It called the dramatic presentation a "realistic melo-dramatic success." The Academy of Music was located on Corinthian Street between State and Mill Streets.

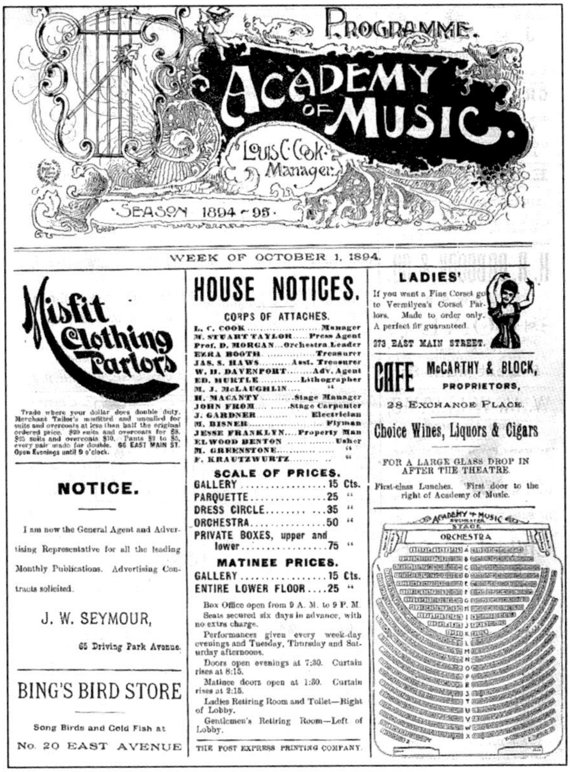

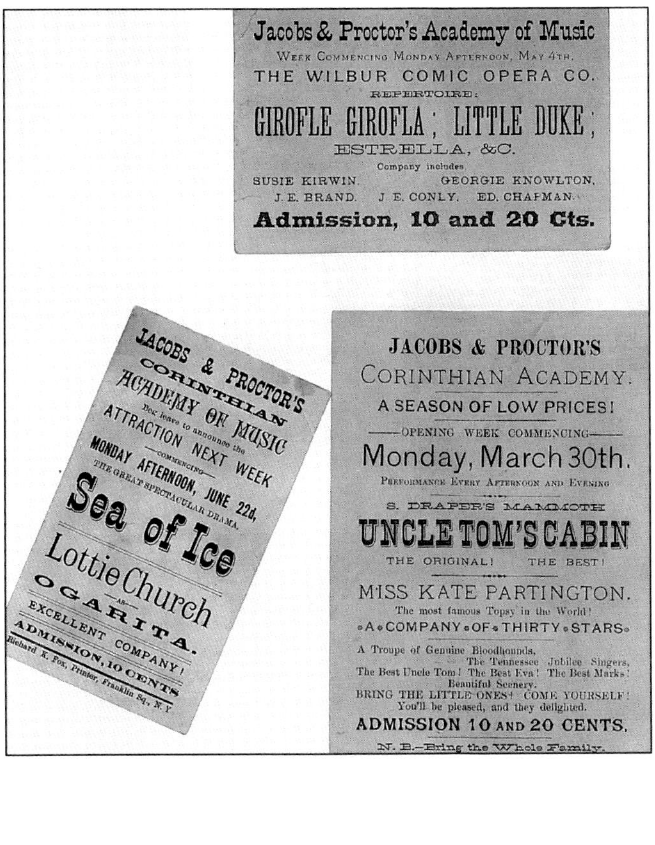

The small advertising cards used by the Academy of Music and Corinthian Academy offered the best in legitimate theater to evening playgoers c. 1900.

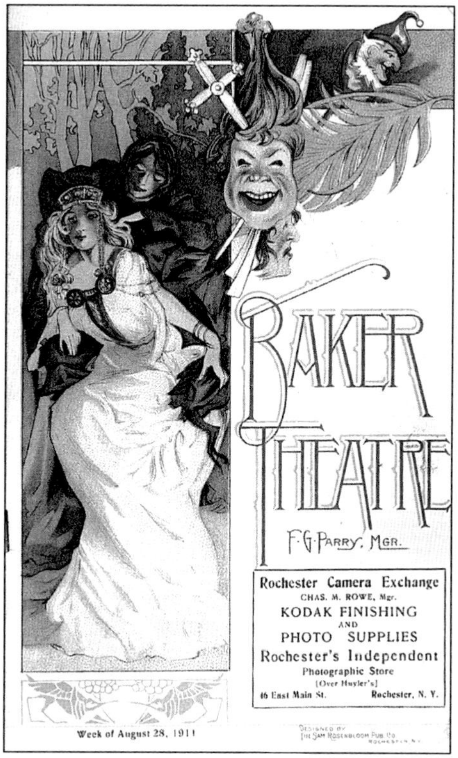

On August 30, 1909, Rochester night-lifers enjoyed the Baker Theatre's leading man, Bert Lytell, in a three-act German farce. The theater was located at 20 North Fitzhugh Street.

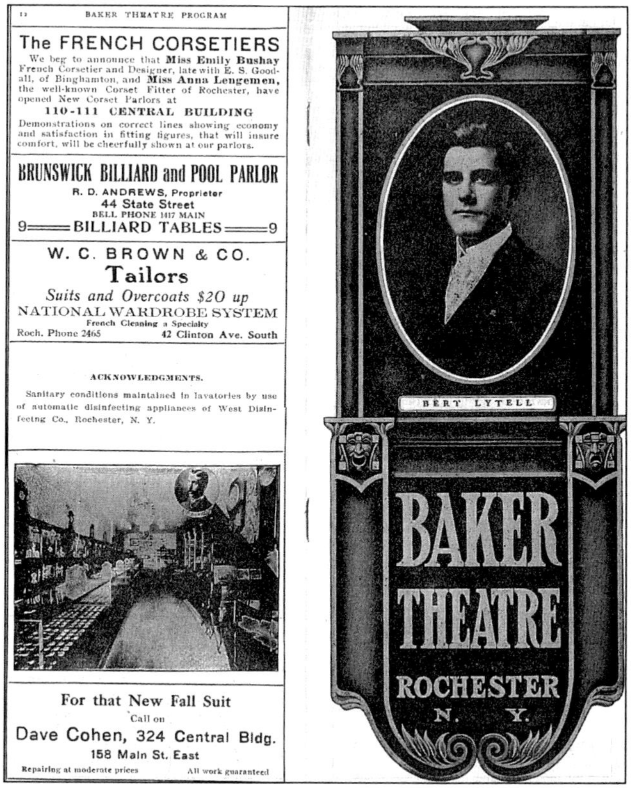
12 BAKER THEATRE PROGRAM

The FRENCH CORSETIERS

We beg to announce that **Miss Emily Bushay** French Corsetier and Designer, late with E. S. Goodall, of Binghamton, and **Miss Anna Lengemen,** the well-known Corset Fitter of Rochester, have opened New Corset Parlors at

110-111 CENTRAL BUILDING

Demonstrations on correct lines showing economy and satisfaction in fitting figures, that will insure comfort, will be cheerfully shown at our parlors.

BRUNSWICK BILLIARD and POOL PARLOR
R. D. ANDREWS, Proprietor
44 State Street
BELL PHONE 1417 MAIN
9 BILLIARD TABLES 9

W. C. BROWN & CO.
Tailors
Suits and Overcoats $20 up
NATIONAL WARDROBE SYSTEM
French Cleaning a Specialty
Roch. Phone 2465 42 Clinton Ave. South

ACKNOWLEDGMENTS.

Sanitary conditions maintained in lavatories by use of automatic disinfecting appliances of West Disinfecting Co., Rochester, N. Y.

For that New Fall Suit
Call on
Dave Cohen, 324 Central Bldg.
158 Main St. East
Repairing at moderate prices All work guaranteed

BERT LYTELL
BAKER THEATRE
ROCHESTER
N. Y.

The handsome playbill for 1911 was for the four-act play *Brewster's Millions*. The playbill boasts that the Baker Theatre's show will be a "big scenic production." The Baker Theatre became a burlesque house called the Gayety in the 1920s.

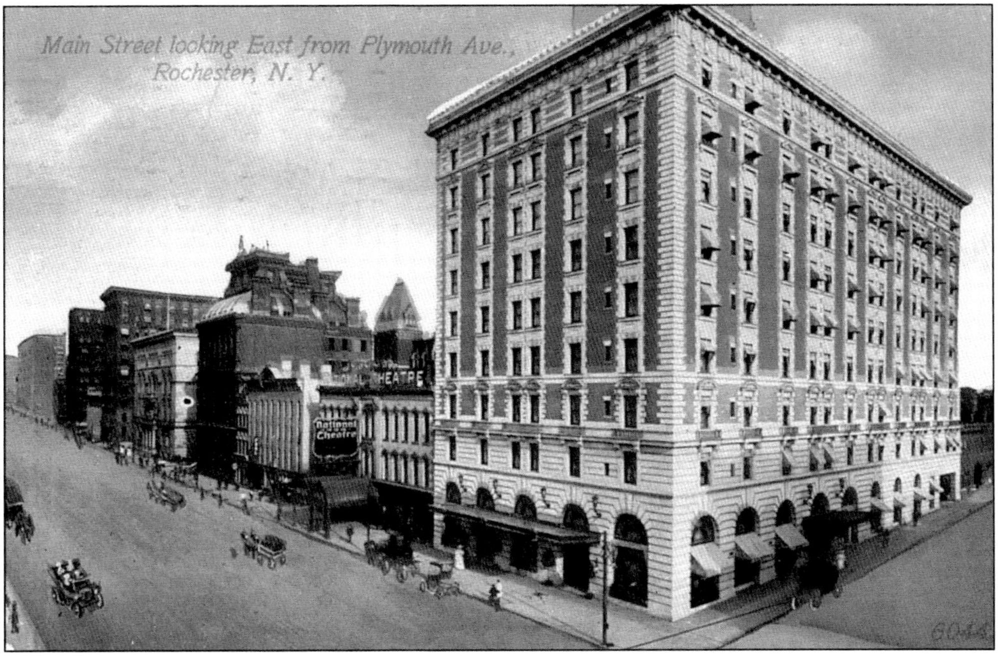

This 1912 postcard locates the National Theatre (later, the Sam S. Shubert Theatre). The 700-seat theater opened in May 1903 at 75 West Main Street, next to the National Hotel (after 1907, the Hotel Rochester). The theater's proximity to the hotel enabled patrons to dine in the hotel's splendid Crystal Dining Room before or after performances.

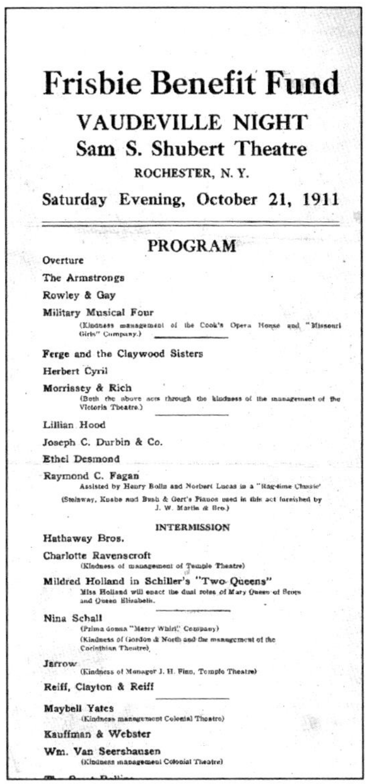

Frisbie Benefit Fund

VAUDEVILLE NIGHT

Sam S. Shubert Theatre

ROCHESTER, N. Y.

Saturday Evening, October 21, 1911

PROGRAM

Overture

The Armstrongs

Rowley & Gay

Military Musical Four

(Kindness management of the Cook's Opera House and "Missouri Girls" Company.)

Ferge and the Claywood Sisters

Herbert Cyril

Morrissey & Rich

(Both the above acts through the kindness of the management of the Victoria Theatre.)

Lillian Hood

Joseph C. Durbin & Co.

Ethel Desmond

Raymond C. Fagan

Assisted by Henry Bolln and Norbert Lucas in a "Rag-time Classic"

(Steinway, Knabe and Bush & Gert's Pianos used in this act furnished by J. W. Martin & Bro.)

INTERMISSION

Hathaway Bros.

Charlotte Ravenscroft

(Kindness of management of Temple Theatre)

Mildred Holland in Schiller's "Two Queens"

Miss Holland will enact the dual roles of Mary Queen of Scots and Queen Elizabeth.

Nina Schall

(Prima donna "Merry Whirl" Company)

(Kindness of Gordon & North and the management of the Corinthian Theatre).

Jarrow

(Kindness of Manager J. H. Finn, Temple Theatre)

Reiff, Clayton & Reiff

Maybell Yates

(Kindness management Colonial Theatre)

Kauffman & Webster

Wm. Van Seershausen

(Kindness management Colonial Theatre)

Capt. John J. Frisbie, a local aviator, gained a wide following with his aeronautical skill. On September 1, 1911, he became the first to fly his two-cycle engine Curtiss biplane over the city. While performing an aerial stunt, he was killed in a crash in Norton, Kansas. A benefit show for his widow and children was held by the Sam S. Shubert Theatre (formerly the National). Five other Rochester vaudeville houses supplied performers for the benefit.

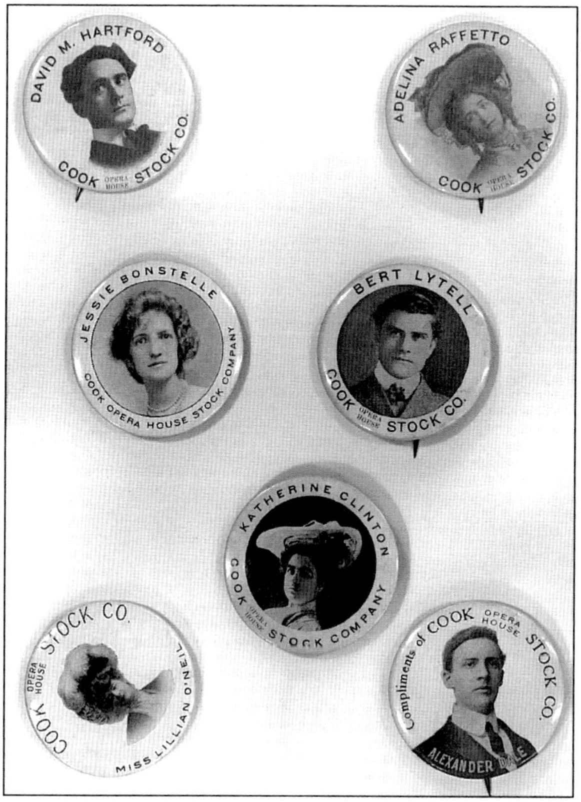

Rarer than early playbills are these pin-backed photograph buttons of the Cook Opera House Stock Company. These trivial trinkets of the past were highly prized when they became available to Rochester's enthusiastic followers of the stock company's actors and actresses. The Frederick Cook Opera House opened in the 1880s.

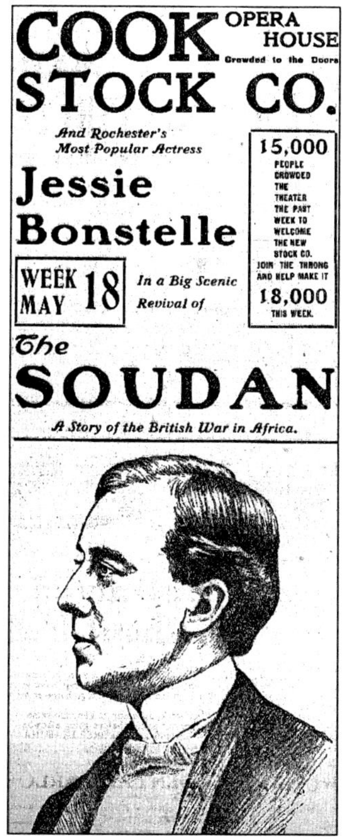

Soudan was the name of the play, but it was Rochester's own Jessie Bonstelle who drew the overflowing crowds. Born to the Bonesteel family of the neighboring town of Greece, she changed her last name to the more romantic-sounding "Bonstelle" after seeing it misspelled one evening on a theater marquee. Her photograph is seen among the buttons in the previous image.

First-nighters to the new Temple Theatre were given this souvenir playbill tied with a ribbon. The theater, located at 37 South Clinton Avenue, opened as a "house of refined vaudeville" on December 6, 1909.

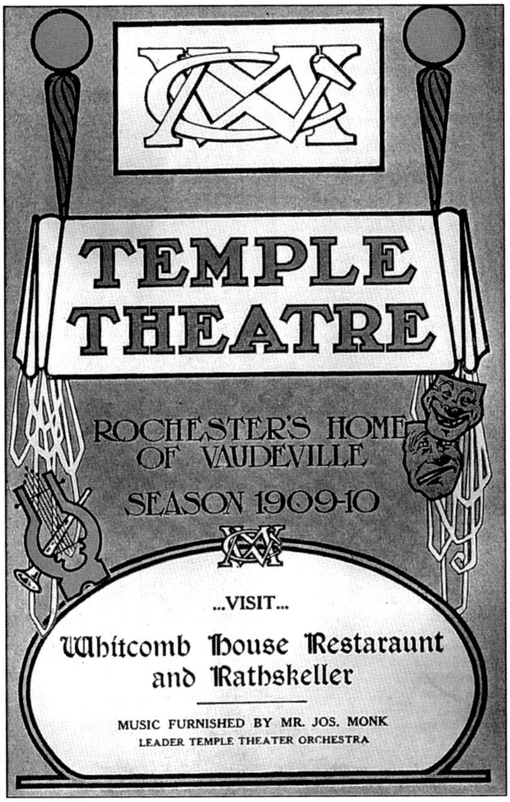

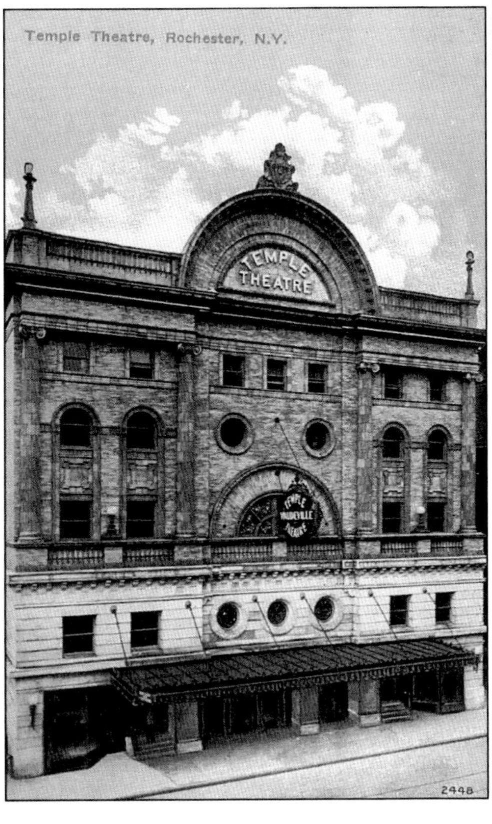

The Temple Theatre was at first part of the B.F. Keith-Albee chain of vaudeville houses. Detroit had a duplicate theater. Later, it became associated with the Cukor-Kondoff Vaudeville circuit. Again, it changed in 1941, becoming the RKO Temple Theatre. It closed in April 1951.

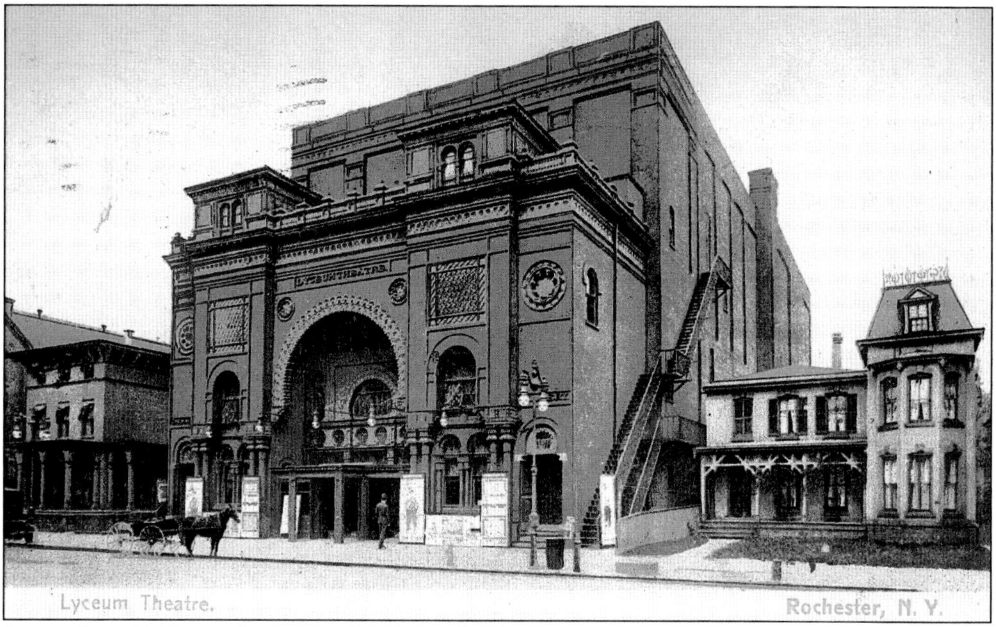

Opened in 1888 on the east side of South Clinton Avenue, the Lyceum Theatre was an eclectic mix of styles. Its arches were Roman, but it had a distinctively Moorish feeling to its decorative facade. Private homes were still the principal structures along South Clinton when this photograph was taken in 1907.

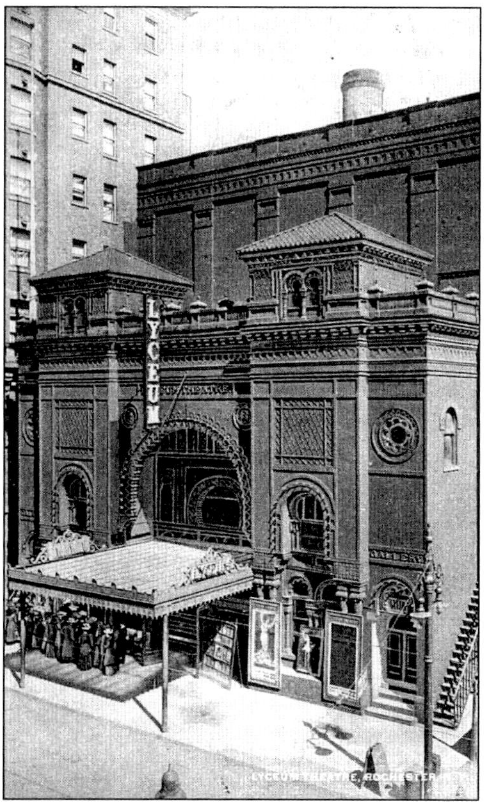

By 1910, a huge hotel, the Seneca, had risen north of the Lyceum Theatre. An elaborate porte-cochere was added to the facade for first-nighters stepping out of their carriages.

Of the half-dozen Rochester playhouses, none was more highly regarded by the public than the Lyceum Theatre. The performing arts theater was established by a group of east side business leaders. It opened on October 8, 1888, and it closed on May 19, 1934.

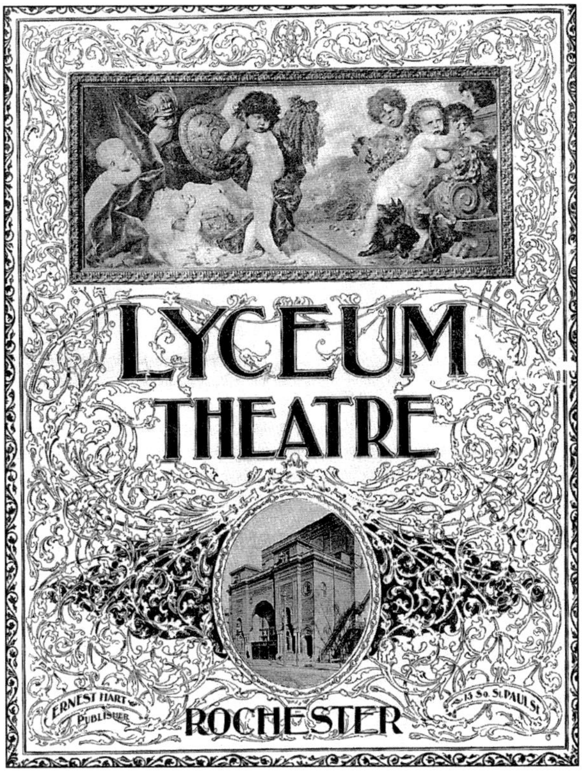

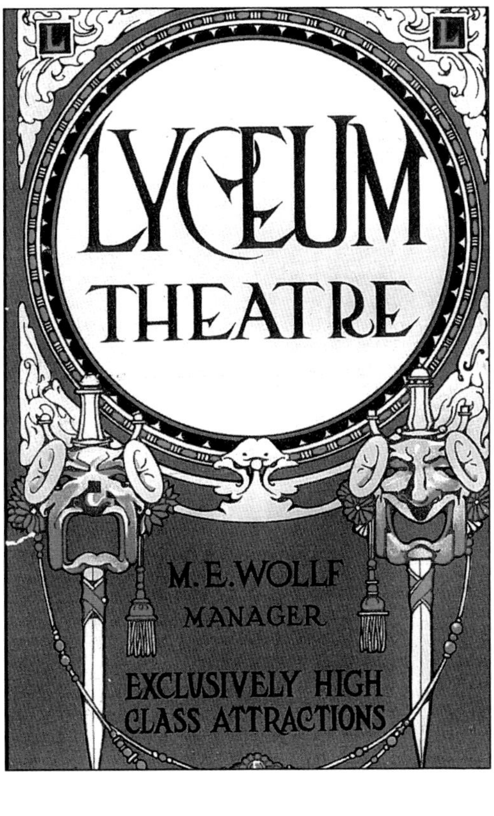

Great actors and actresses graced the Lyceum's stage. In 1900–1901, Frohman "sent twelve of his 24 New York successes that year to Rochester." Fourteen Shakespearian plays topped all seasons in 1914. Spectacles such as *Ben Hur*, *Jeanne D'Arc*, and *Uncle Tom's Cabin* attracted early-morning lines a block long into South Clinton Avenue hours before ticket sales had begun.

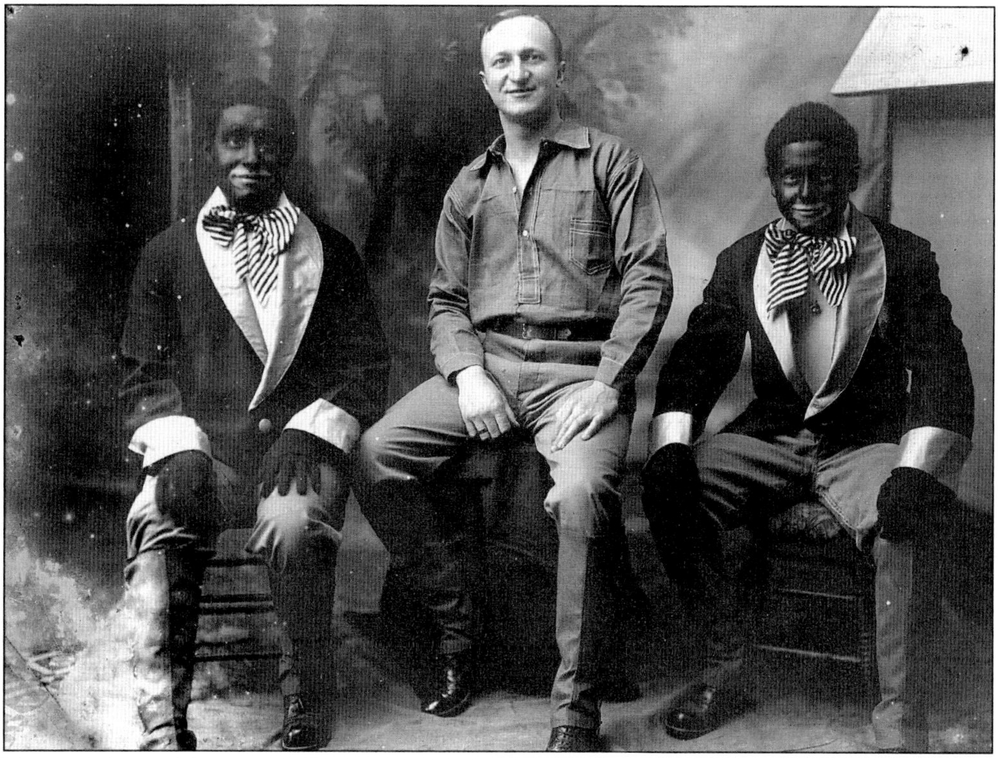

Minstrel shows, like vaudeville, were an integral part of yesterday's entertainment. Frederick Wagner, shown with his end men, produced dozens of minstrel shows for church, social, and other community groups. As "Mr. Interlocutor," Wagner exchanged quips with his end men, sang Steven Foster ballads with a chorus of local talent, and poked fun at local dignitaries.

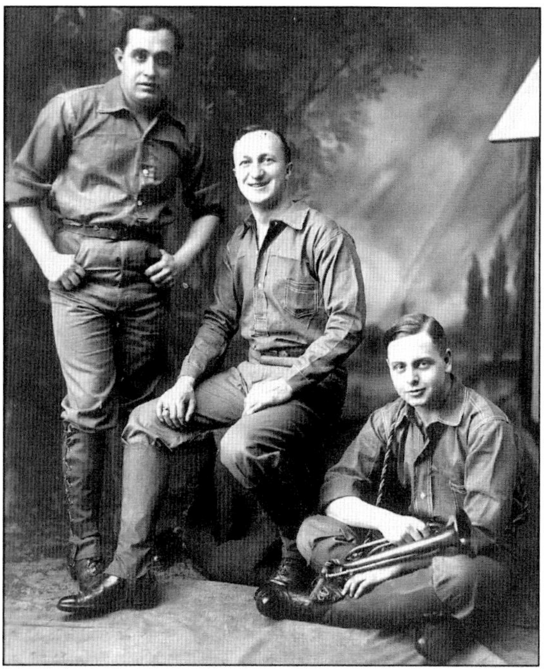

Fred Wagner's Novelty Minstrels are shown dressed for a skit poking fun at the Civilian Conservation Corp that was formed for men needing work in the 1930s.

Seven

Downtown's Entertainment Centers

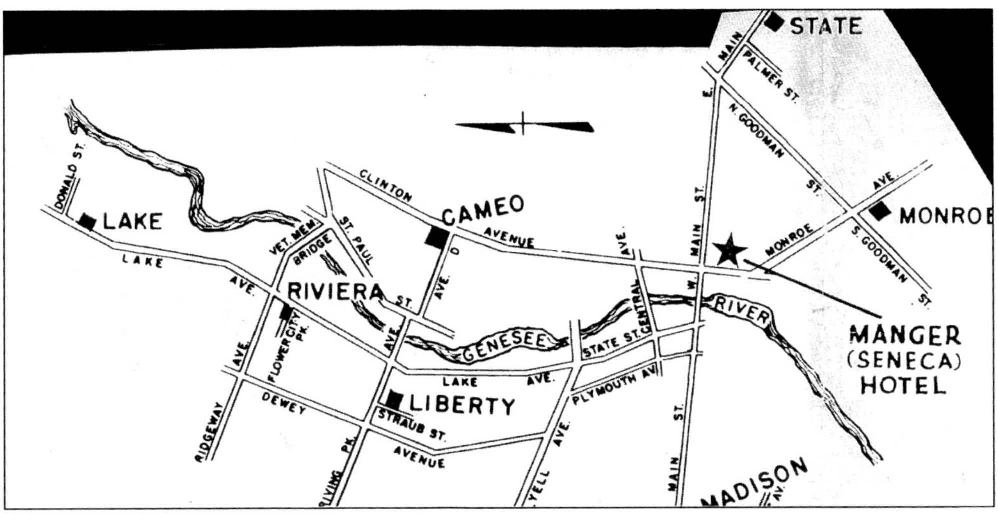

Neatly located on the map are eight of Rochester's many neighborhood theaters that were still playing into the 1950s, creating a storehouse of memories. They were the place to go to see the cowboy heroes and bad guys, the cliff-hanging serials, the outrageous cartoons, the awesome newsreels, and the marvelous Little Rascals short features.

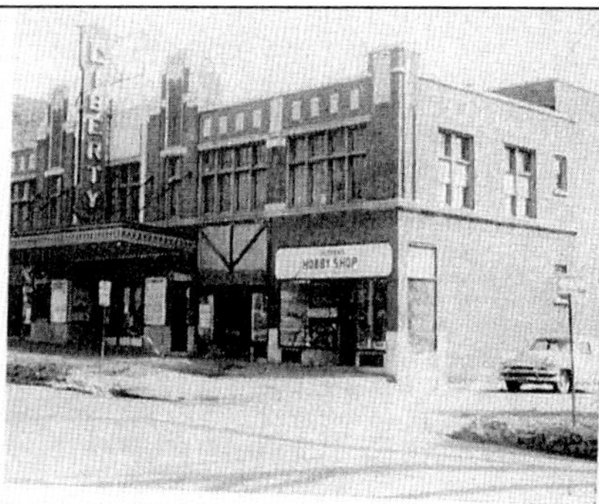

LIBERTY THEATRE*
nown as 275 Driving Park Ave.)
Corner of Driving Park Ave.
& Straub St.

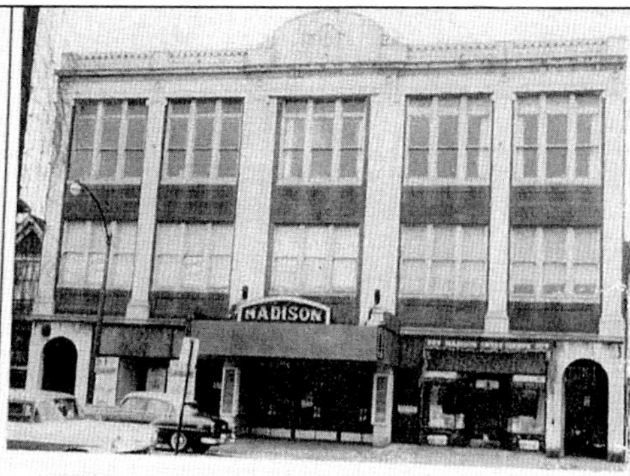

2 MADISON THEATRE*
(known as 300 Genesee St.)

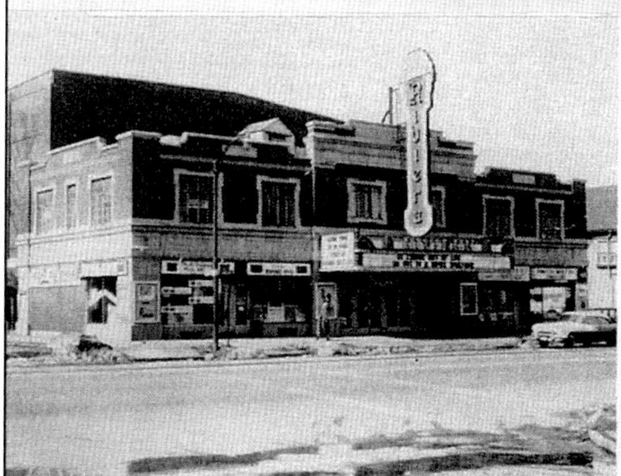

3 RIVIERA THEATRE*
(known as 1451 Lake Ave.)
Northwest corner of Lake Ave.
& Flower City Park St.

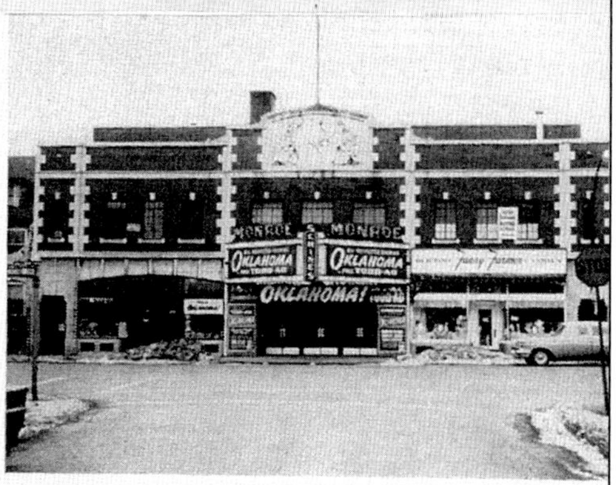

4 MONROE THEATRE*
585-91 Monroe Street

A "movie" usually meant two feature-length films, a newsreel, cartoons, a serial, and coming attractions. In addition, there was "dish night," cartoon matinees, and movie bingo.

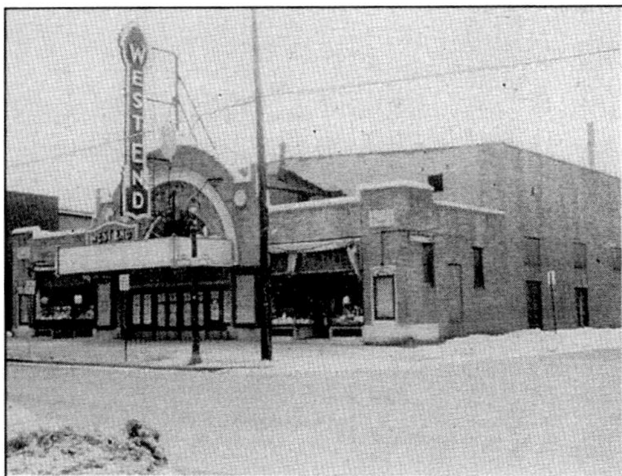

5 **WEST END THEATRE**

(known as 555 Thurston Road)

S.W. Corner of Thurston Road & Midvale Terrace

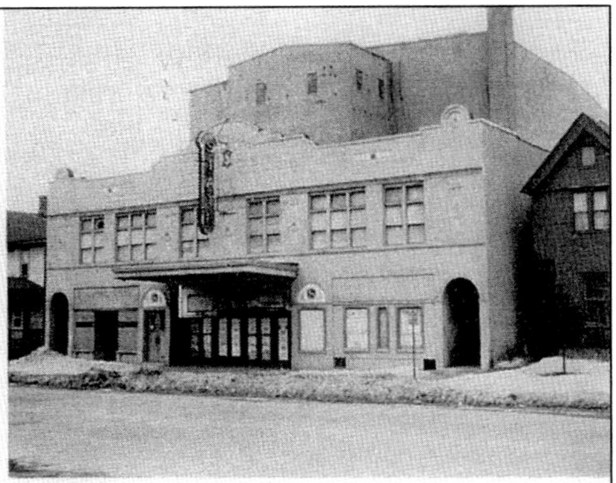

6 **STATE THEATRE**

1335-9 East Main St.

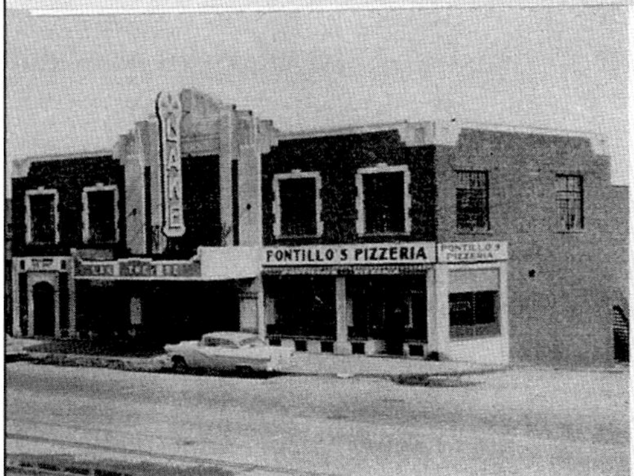

7 **LAKE THEATRE**

3190-4 Lake Ave.; cor. of Boxart St.

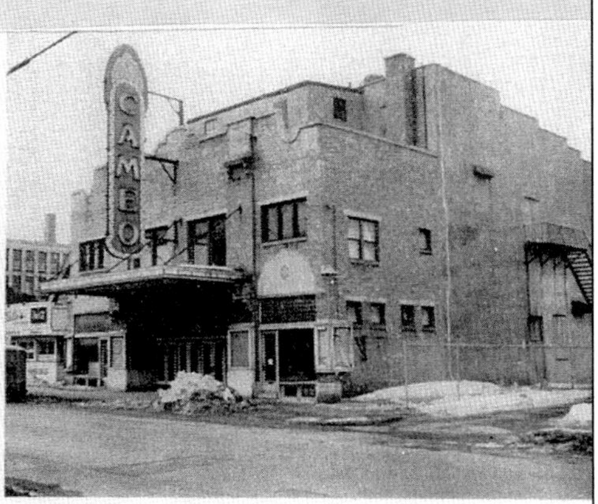

8 **CAMEO THEATRE**

1195 to 1199 North Clinton Ave.

In that heady era before television, this was grand entertainment for many city families.

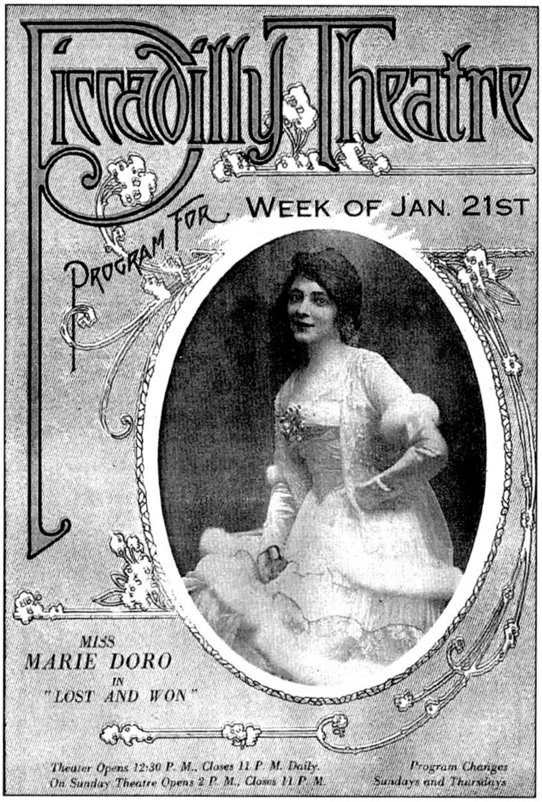

The Piccadilly Theatre opened in 1916 as a photo-playhouse. Owned by the Clinton-Mortimer Corporation, it was located at the corner of Clinton and Mortimer Streets. The theater became the Century Theatre from 1932 to 1948. Finally, it became the Paramount in 1949 until closing on January 13, 1974. The Century Sweet Shop was a popular after-movie stop.

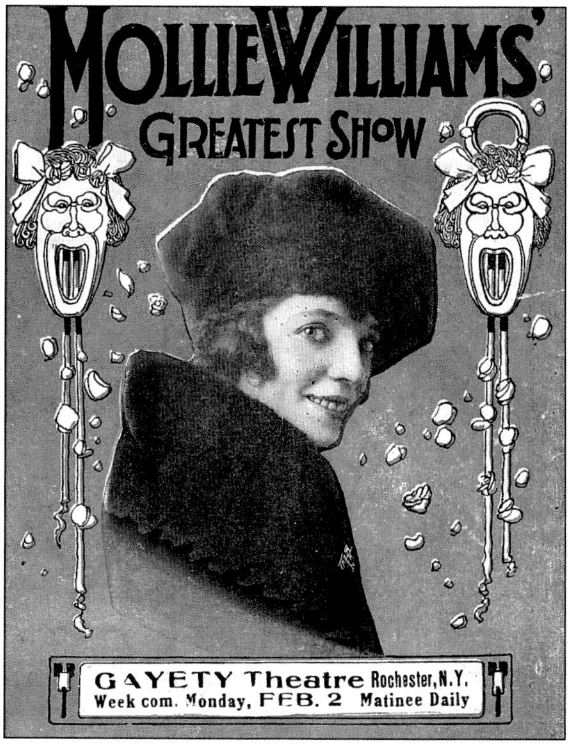

As tastes changed following World War I, the Baker Theatre changed from vaudeville to burlesque. It became the Gayety Theatre, part of the Columbia Amusement Company. Attractions included "A Perfect 36," "High Hat Revue," and "Bare Facts."

Patrons were welcomed to the new Rochester Theatre in 1928, when it opened with Ronald Colman and Vilma Banky in *The Magic Flame*. Located in a building complex at 120 South Clinton Avenue and Court Street, the "air cooled" theater drew huge audiences to its silver screen. Its manager was Albert A. Fenyvessy.

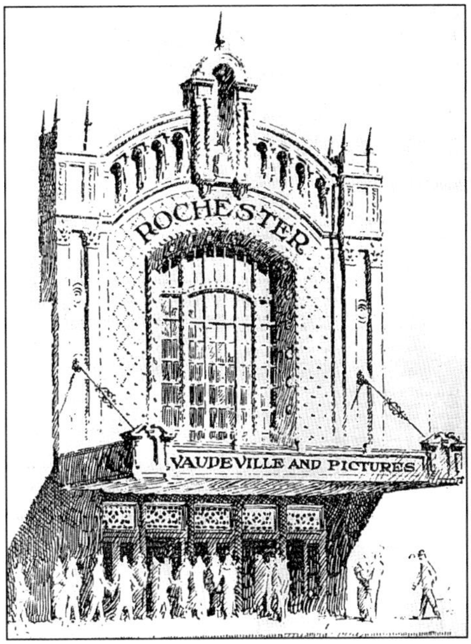

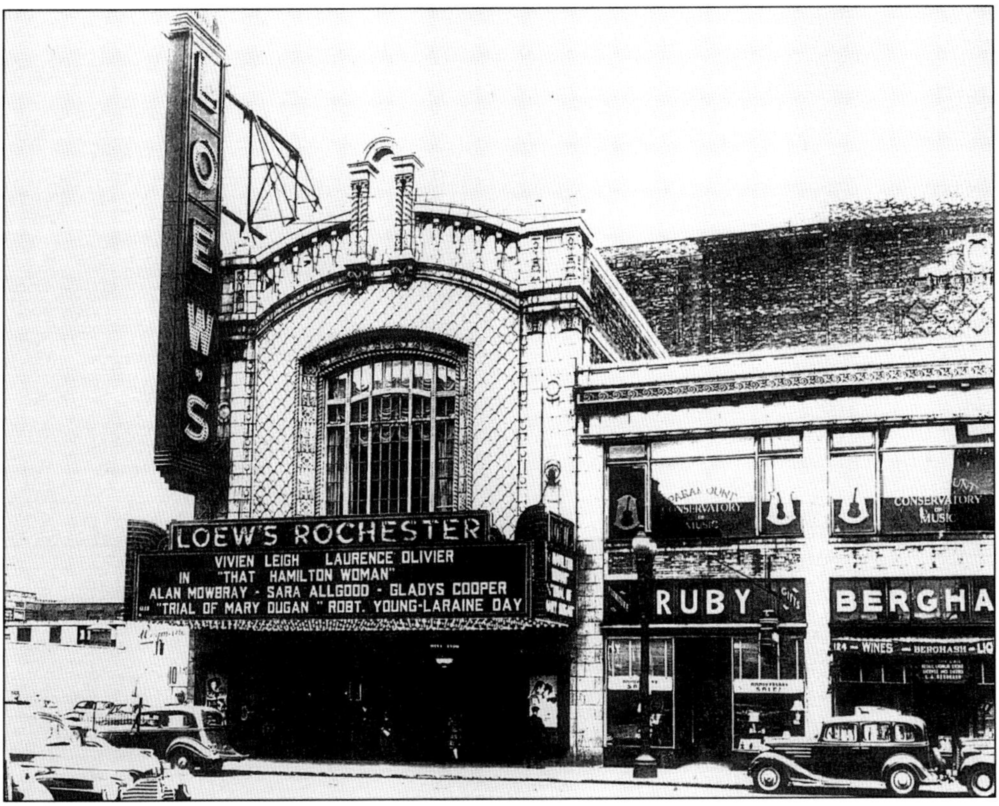

Marcus Loew purchased the Rochester Theatre on January 19, 1930, renaming it Loew's Rochester. Loew's had 4,000 seats and a Walgreen's drugstore on the corner. The curtain closed on the last film in October 1964. Subsequently, a skyscraper for the company named Xerox was built on the site.

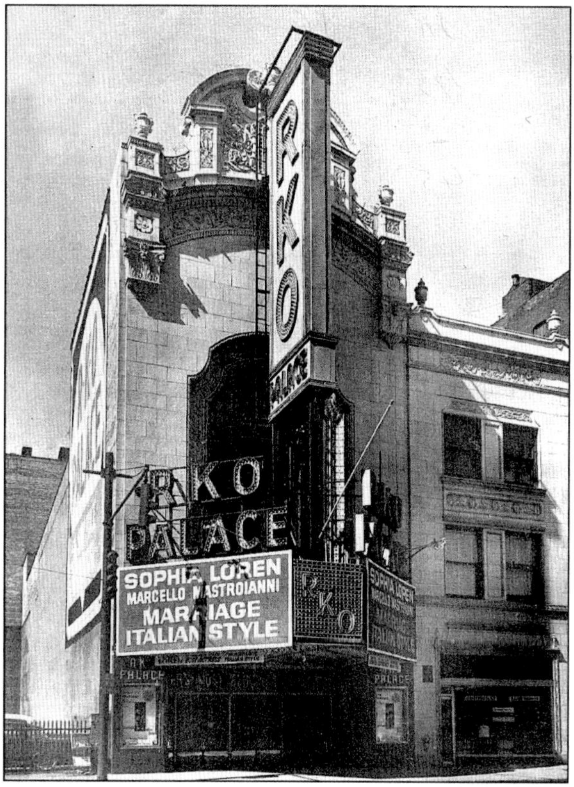

To this day, there has never been a motion picture theater in Rochester equal in opulence to the RKO Palace. The Palace opened on Christmas Day of 1928, at 71 North Clinton Avenue. Its interior was created to impress the masses, which it surely did.

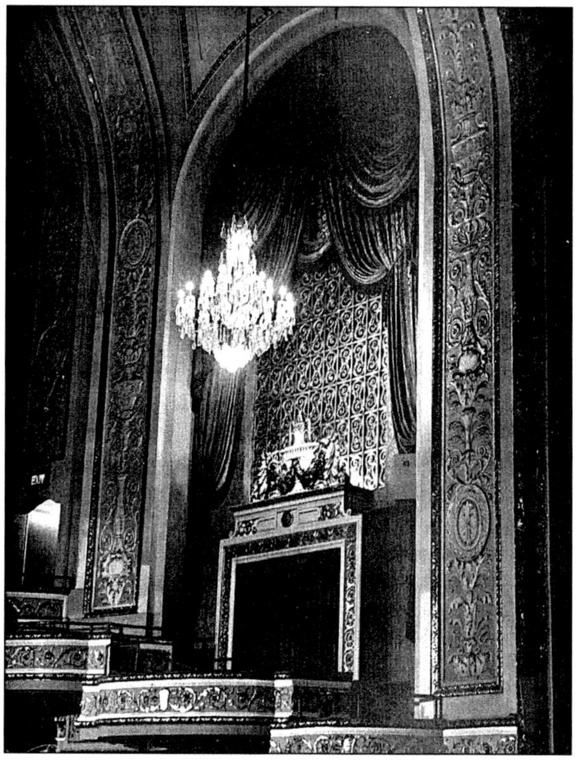

The splendor within was proclaimed by the loge area, the golden grillwork in front of the organ chambers, the purple velvet draperies, and the great crystal chandeliers.

The outer lobby was a commodious area, where long lines of patrons gathered prior to buying tickets. The lobby was resplendent with mirrors, a frescoed ceiling, and a terrazzo floor.

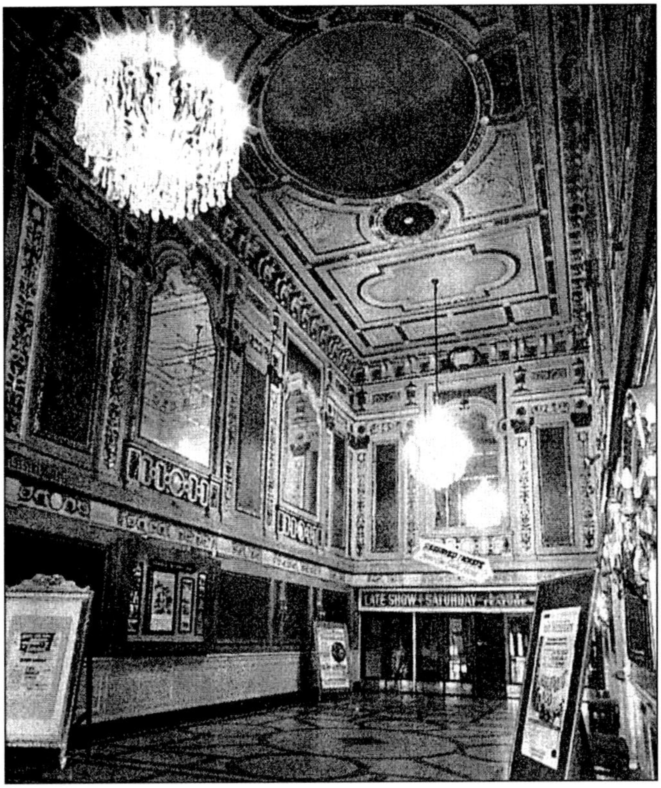

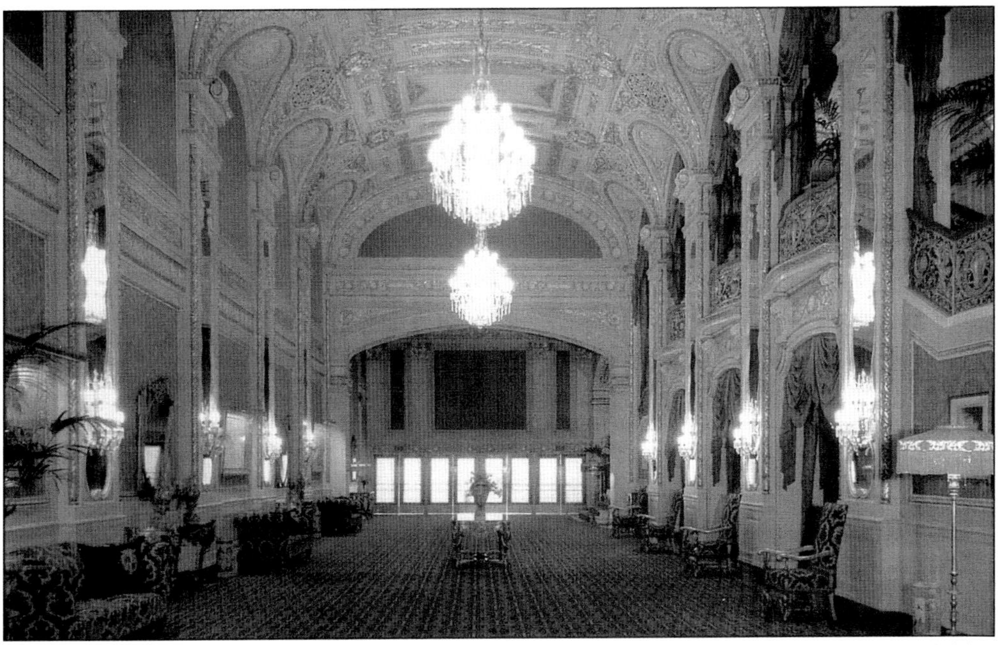

Once through the outer lobby, patrons entered an even more dazzling realm: the inner lobby. Here, the beautifully carpeted floor, majestic chandeliers, and ornate arched ceiling led into the enchanted domain of the silver screen. It was a glorious theater, the pride of downtown. (Courtesy Rochester Historical Society.)

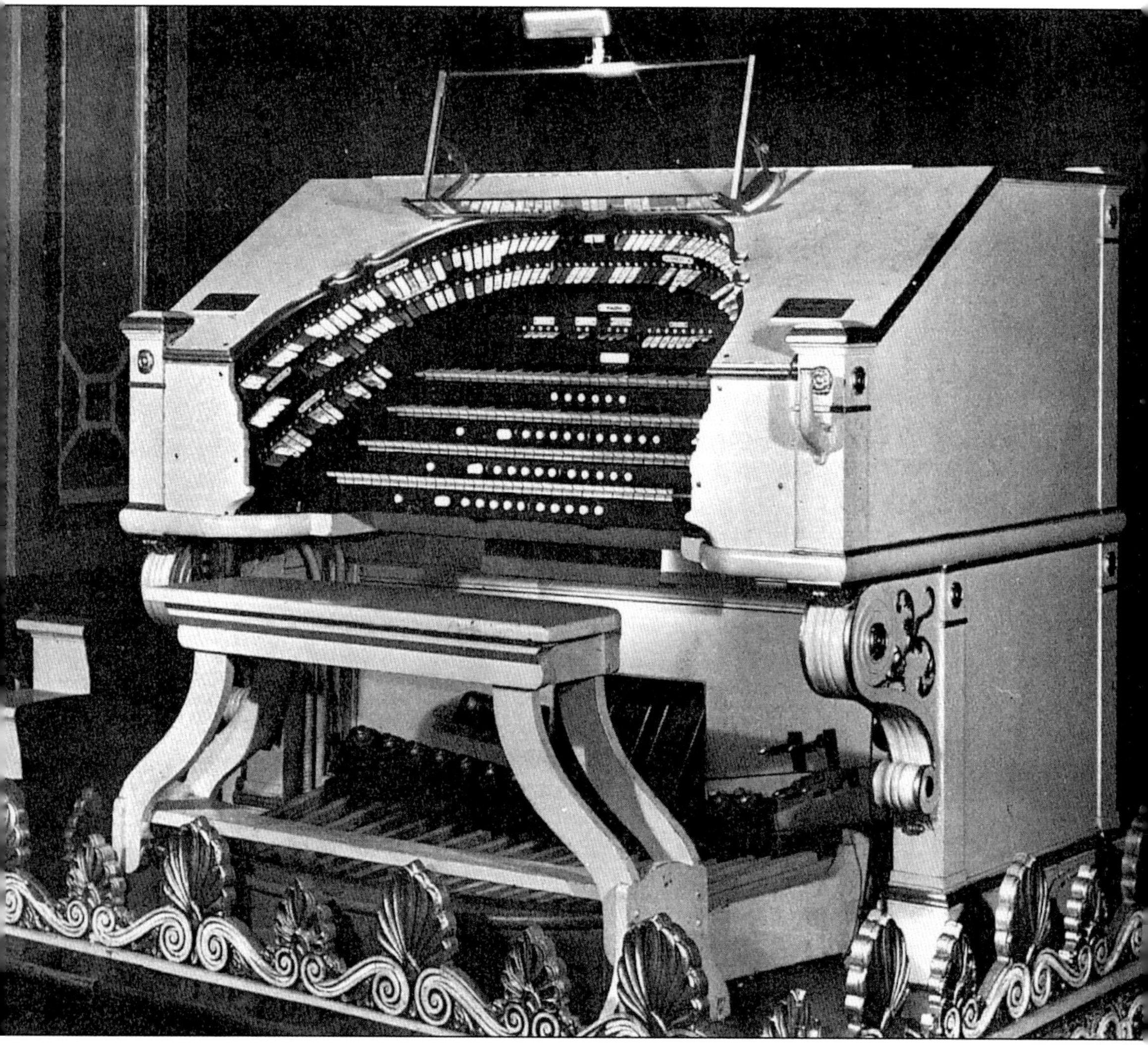

Patrons attended the RKO Palace not only to enjoy the film but also to hear the theater's mighty Wurlitzer organ. As the stage curtains parted, the magnificent organ console rose majestically from the orchestra pit, where a spotlight illuminated organist Tom Grierson. It was a rare and magical experience. Built in North Tonawanda, the organ cost $75,000 in 1928 and is possibly the finest ever constructed there. The theater pipe organ boasts 1,495 pipes, with the 20-foot pipes weighing 400 pounds. Sounds can be made to resemble strings, brass, and woodwinds. Additionally, genuine percussion instruments are built into the organ, including drums, cymbals, glockenspiel, and chimes. The magnificent instrument can also produce such sounds as a bird whistle and car horn. When the RKO Palace closed in 1965, the Rochester Theatre Organ Society rescued the prized organ. Concerts can be enjoyed in the theater organ's current home, at the Rochester Auditorium Center.

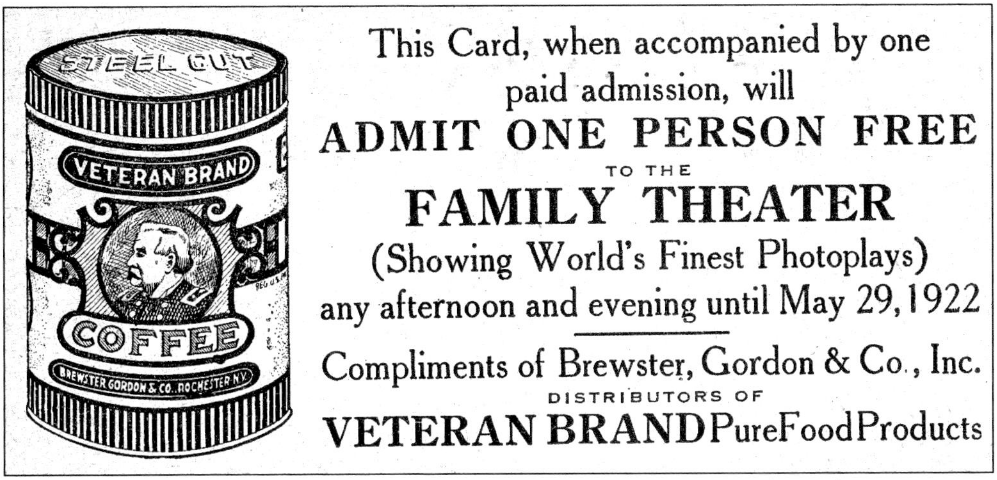

When the final curtain closed on the Cook Opera House in 1913, a new form of entertainment took its place. J.H.W. Fenyvessy opened the Family Theater in the era of silent films, shown on silver screens. The pass is dated 1922.

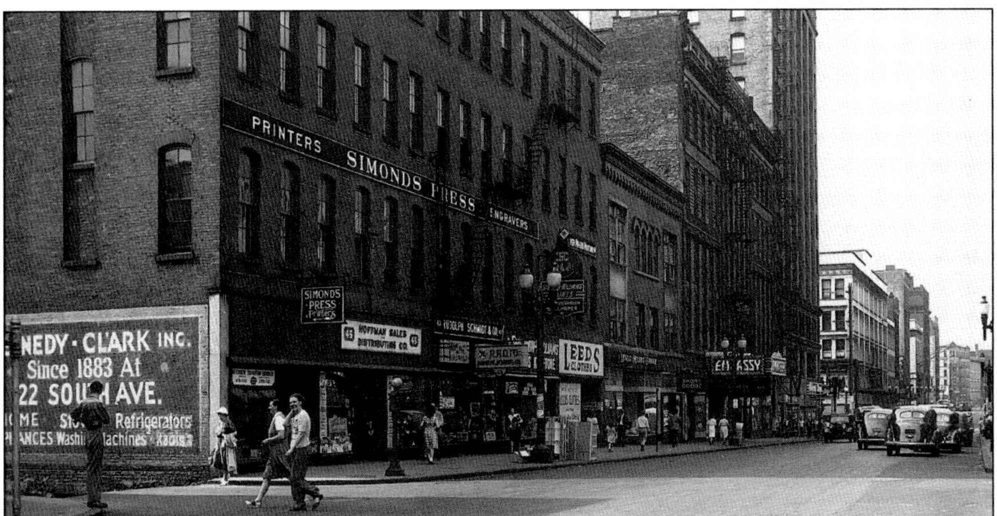

Following World War I, attitudes changed. The Roaring Twenties gave rise to burlesque theaters. Rochester's Embassy was one of them, replacing the Family Theater in 1937 with an entirely different kind of entertainment. The Embassy marquee is seen at the right.

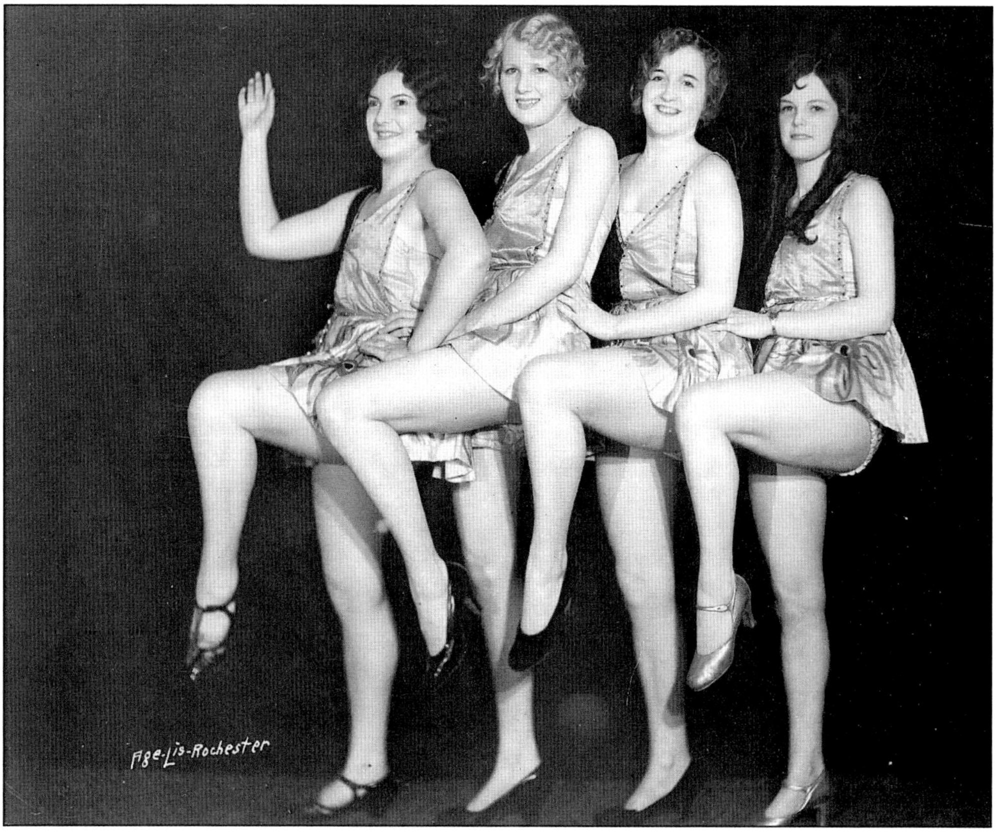

This group known as the "chorus line" of "cuties" was part of the Embassy show in the 1930s. Note the provocative hairdos.

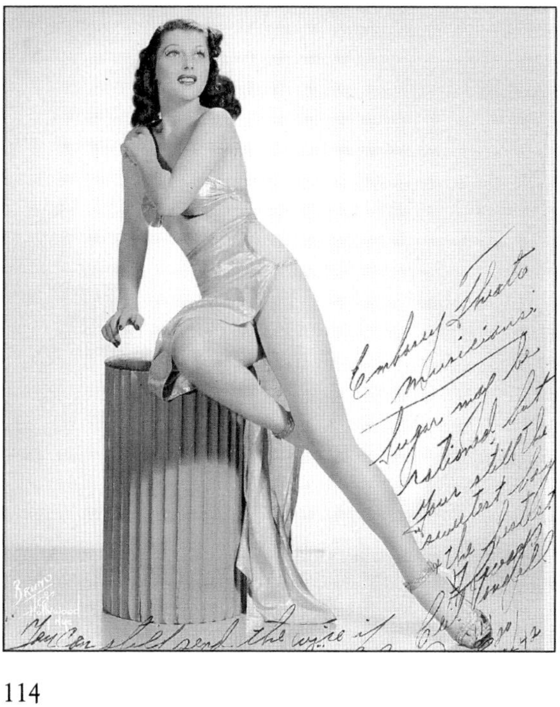

This November 1942 wartime message to the boys in the band was autographed by Ceil Vonzell, also known as Clare De Lune.

This photograph was taken backstage at the Embassy during the early 1940s. "Charlie" was the man who made the wisecracks during the show. He seems to enjoy his work.

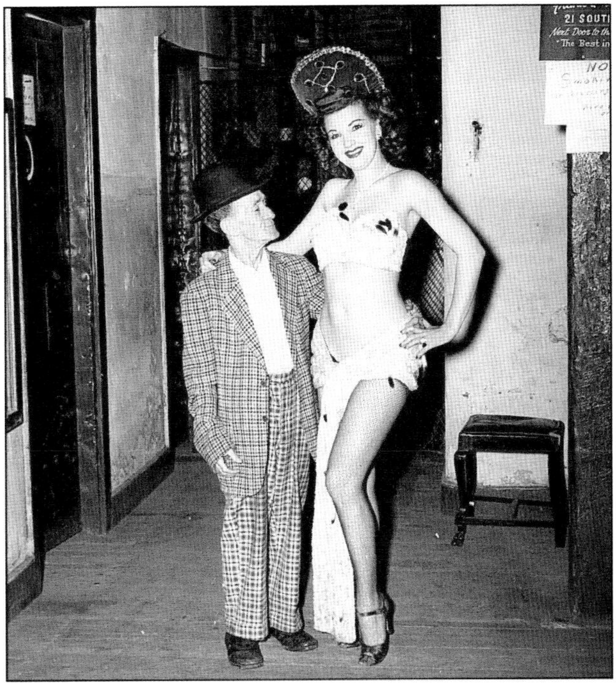

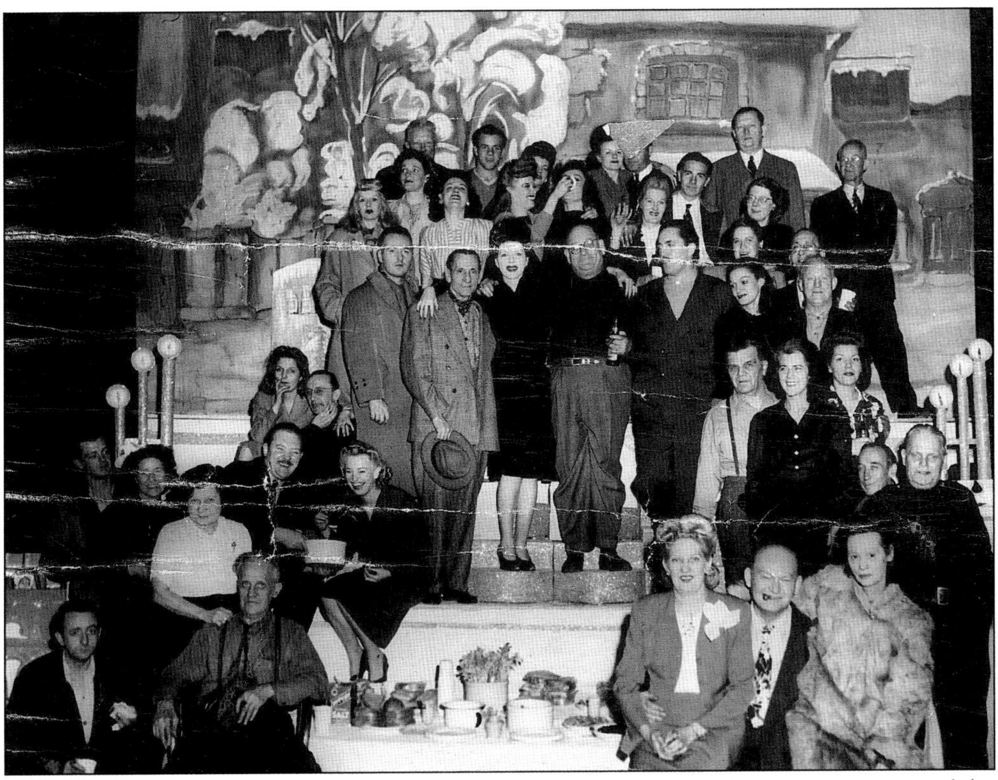

At the height of World War II, workers at the Embassy threw a backstage party. Most of the city's younger men were in the service. This tattered photograph was rescued from a property room before the theater was demolished to make way for the Rochester Convention Center.

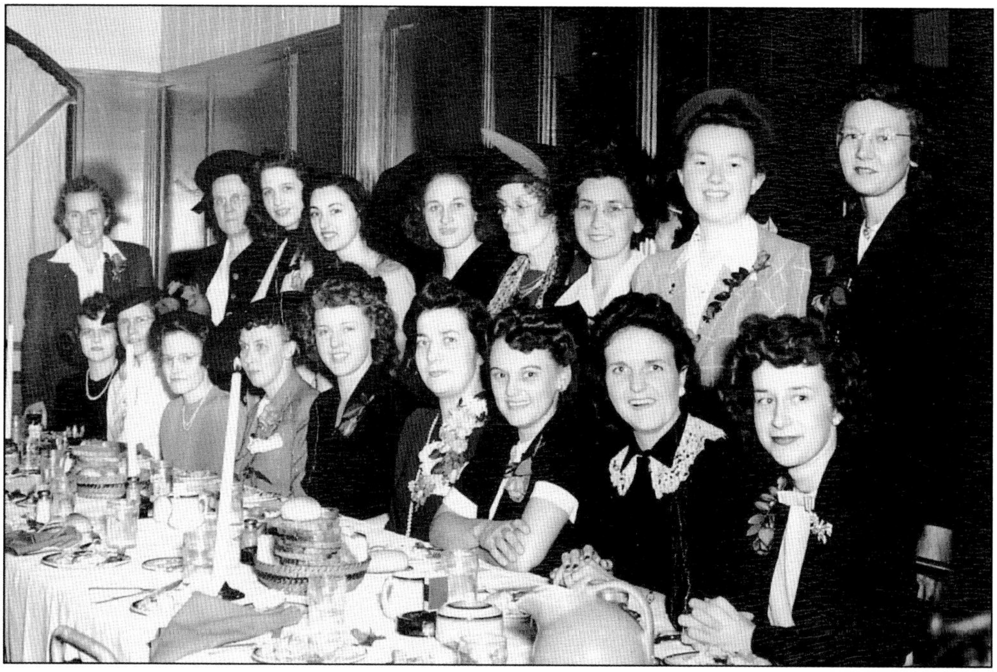

Rochester offered a number of fine dining places during the World War II years. This party was given for Jane Fitzgerald at the Eggleston Restaurant on November 4, 1943. The young women in the photograph were employed at the Rochester Manufacturing Company.

Our Prices are same as Ceiling Prices of April 4 to 10, 1943

The Eggleston

SPECIALS FOR TODAY—Friday, July 21, 1944

« **Ask For Our Old Fashioned Made With Lord Calvert** »

60c EXTRA FOR FULL COURSE DINNER

Celery — Olives — Radishes
Fruit Cocktail, Tomato Juice Cocktail or Soup du Jour
Chef's Salad, French Dressing
CHOICE
Vanilla, Chocolate Ice Cream — Jell-O with Whipped Cream
Sherbet — Pineapple or Chocolate Sundae — Pies or Pudding
Coffee, Milk or Tea

Appetizers

Fresh Jumbo Shrimp Cocktail .50 — Fruit Cocktail .35
Cherrystone Clams on Half Shell with Cocktail Sauce 40
Clam Stew, plain 45 — With Milk .50 — With Cream .60
Fresh Lobster Stew with Cream 1.00
Lobster Cocktail .. 1.00 — V-8 Juice Cocktail . .15 — Tomato Juice ..... .20
Radishes .... .15 — Marienated Herring 35 — Celery .... .25
Stuffed Olives .... .25 — Queen Olives ...... .20

Soup
Coney Island Clam Chowder — cup .15; plate .25
Hot Consomme .20 Clam Broth . .20 Jellied Consomme .. .20

Fish
Broiled Fresh Georgian Bay Whitefish Maitre d'Hotel . 90
*The Chef's Seafood Special Plate 90
*Fried Deep Sea Scallops, Tartar Sauce 85
*Fresh Caught Bullheads Sautè in Butter 75
*Stuffed Tomato with Lobster Salad 85

Entrees
Omelette with Rarebit Cheese 65
*Boiled Smoked Beef Tongue, Raisin Sauce 75
*Fresh Chicken Salad Plate .85
*Sliced Tenderloin of Beef Sautè Minute 1 40
*Chicken Cutlets with Tomato Sauce and Peas 60
*Assorted Cold Cuts with Chef's Salad 75
*Baked Meat Loaf with Noodles Au Gratin 65
*Roast Prime Ribs of Beef Au Jus 1 25

CHOICE OF TWO

Mashed, Parsley Boiled, Baked, Hash in Cream Potatoes or Potatato Salad
Fresh Spinach — Fresh Cut Asparagus
Cabbage Salad — Cottage Cheese

Puddings, Pies and Pastry

Apple, Raspberry or Cocoanut Cream Pies 20 — Vanilla Cream Pudding 15
Black Raspberry Shortcake .30
Raspberry Jell-O .... .15 — Orange Sherbet ... .15
Cafe Parfait ...... .30 — Chocolate Sundae .. .25 — Macaroons .... .20
Peach Melba ...... .35 — Pineapple Sundae .. .25 — Frozen Eclair .... .30
Macaroon Glace .... .30 — Ice Cream .... .15 — Chocolate Parfait .. .30

Fruits

Half Grapefruit ... .20 — Sliced Pineapple ... .20 — Figs in Syrup .... .25
Stewed Prunes ..... .20 — Grapefruit Supreme .25
Baked Apple ..... .20 — Bartlett Pears ..... .20 — Sliced Orange ..... .20
Iced Watermelon 25 — Honeydew Melon 30 — Ripe Canteloupe 25

Believe it or not, the 1944 menu for the Eggleston Restaurant, on South Clinton Avenue, advertises a full-course dinner for 60¢.

Almost everyone knew where Odenbach's was—on South Avenue just "two doors from Main Street." The popular German restaurant opened as the Hofbrau House in 1890.

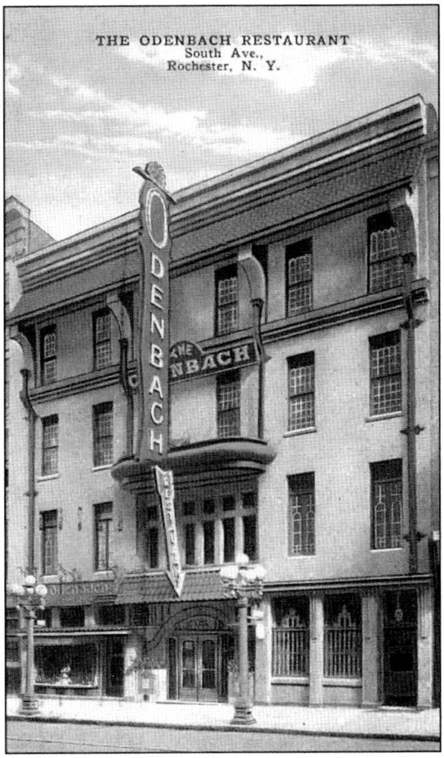

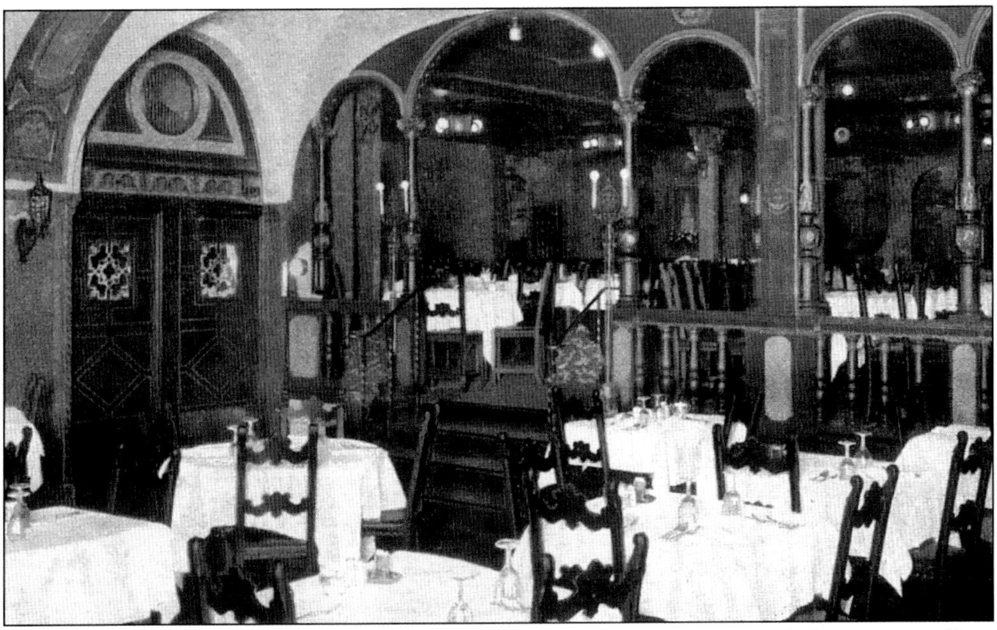

The Teutonic atmosphere of Odenbach's is apparent. The tempting German dishes were excellent (roast duckling with sauerkraut or apple sauce, 45¢), and the service was prompt. Dinner guests always enjoyed their meals while being treated to a wide variety of live entertainment. The restaurant closed on June 4, 1937.

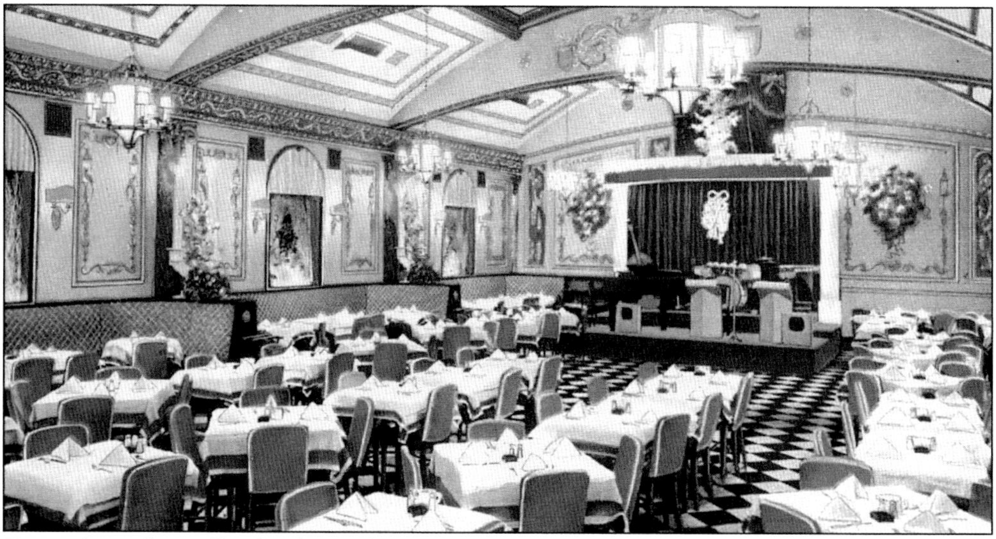

Once claimed to offer the finest dining between New York City and Chicago, Odenbach's Peacock Room was *the* place to go after the theater or for those special occasions when a gentleman truly wanted to impress his lady. In 1921, the Odenbach brothers gained ownership to the old Whitcomb Hotel, on the corner of East Main Street and South Clinton Avenue. In 1923, the Odenbach Company converted the lobby of the former hotel into the Peacock Room Restaurant. It soon became a mecca for "the young crowd seeking cabaret entertainment and dancing." Sadly, it closed after World War II. The contents of the famous restaurant were auctioned off in 1947.

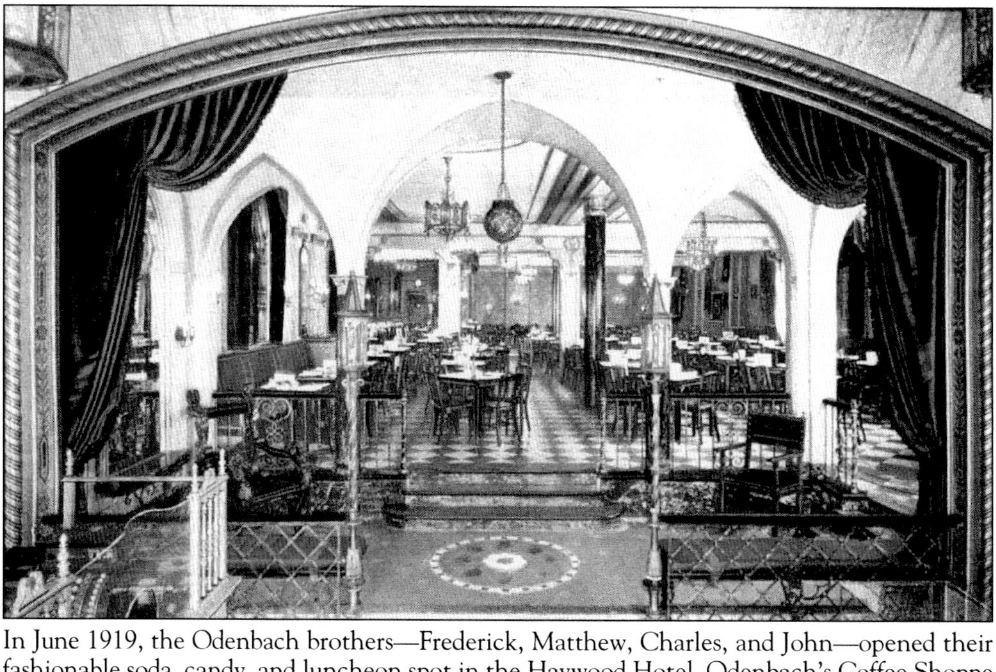

In June 1919, the Odenbach brothers—Frederick, Matthew, Charles, and John—opened their fashionable soda, candy, and luncheon spot in the Haywood Hotel. Odenbach's Coffee Shoppe featured Famous Coffee Shoppe Candies, holiday favorites with many Rochesterians. Located on South Avenue just south of the main entrance to the Hotel Haywood, Odenbach's Coffee Shoppe attracted shoppers at lunchtime and after-theater crowds during the evening.

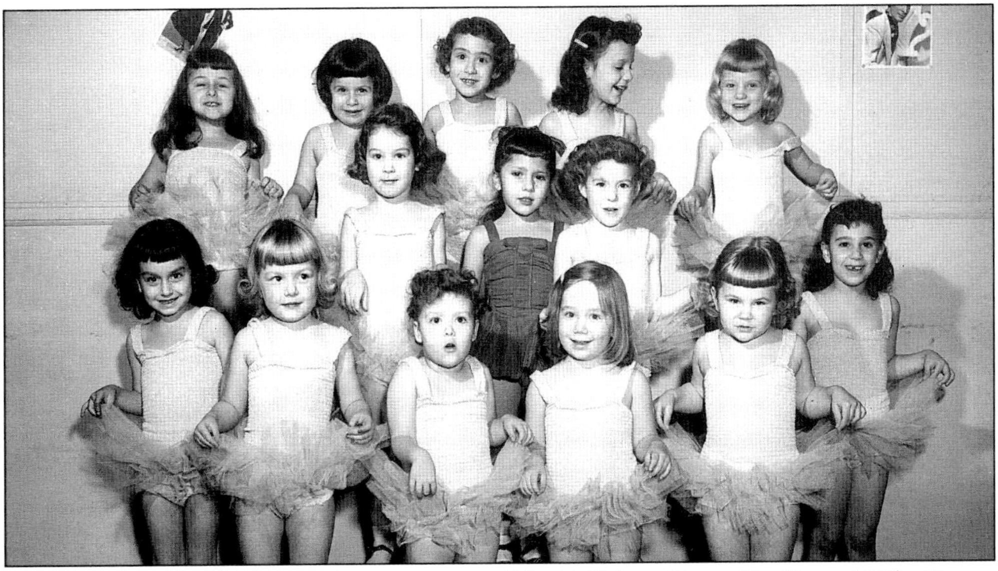

Rochester offered other forms of entertainment. The Val Mates Dance Studio, at 49 Elm Street, was a favorite place for Rochester families to send their young daughters to learn to dance. This 1940s photograph captures 14 kindergarten-aged dancers in their ballet tutus.

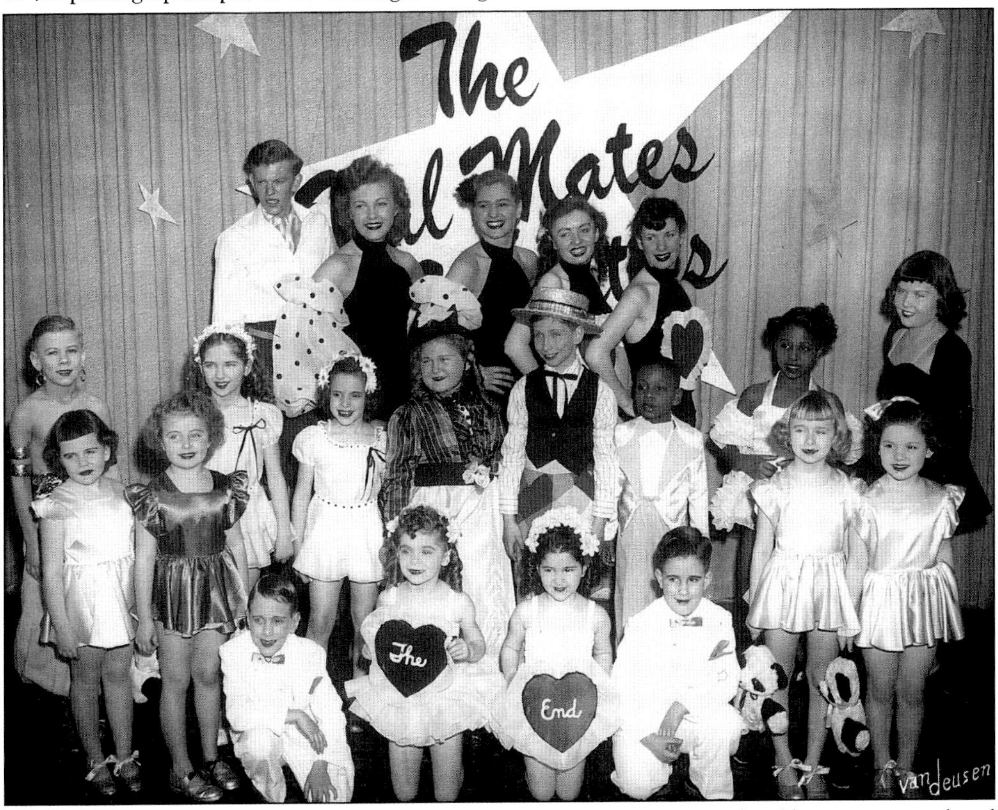

With glowing smiles, the costumed students of the Val Mates Dance School have just completed their formal dance recital in the 1950s. Today, these students could be mothers and fathers and even grandmothers and grandfathers.

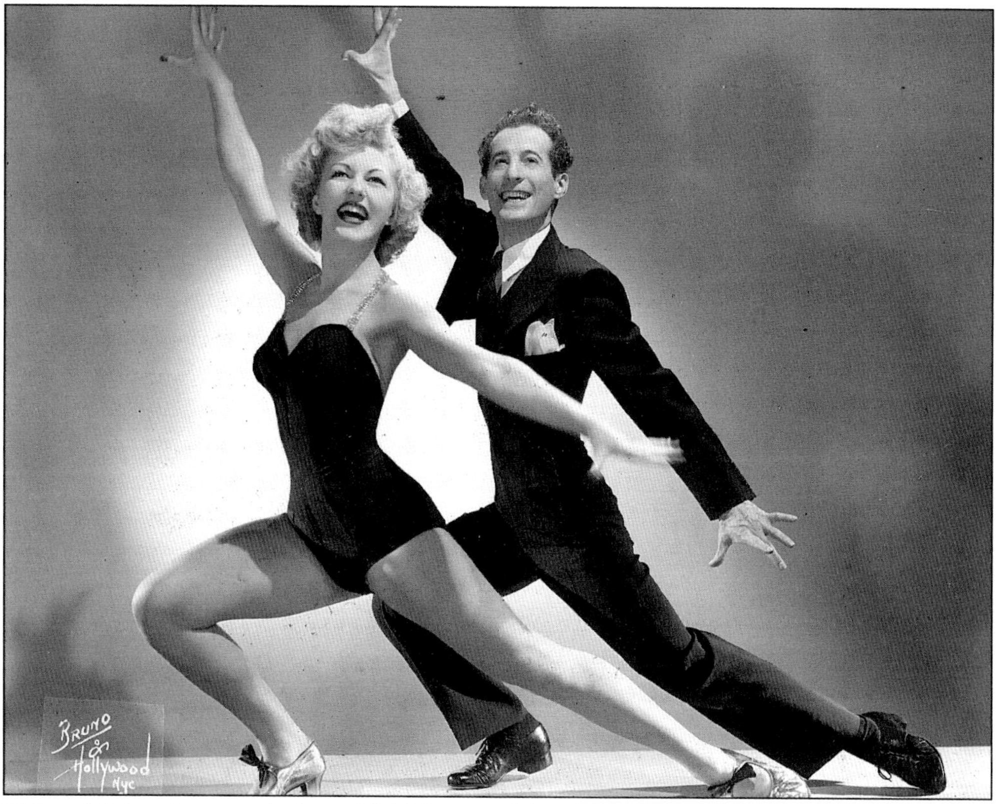

This publicity photograph shows Val Mates and his dancing partner Joan Grabell. The two performed in many night clubs in New York City as well as in other East Coast cities.

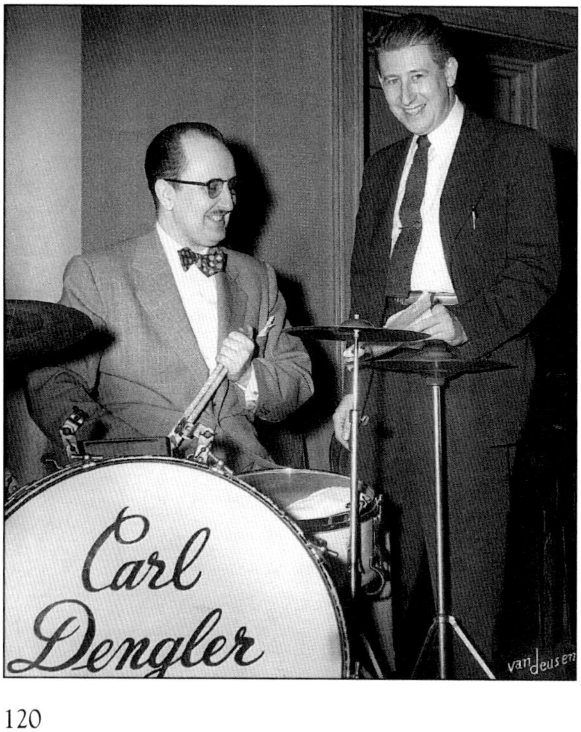

Carl Dengler is one of Rochester's strongest links to the 1930s-to-1940s era of great swing bands. In 1929, he debuted with the Madison Junior High orchestra on WHEC's *Buster Brown* radio program. Following years with other bands, he formed his own orchestra in 1935. His orchestra played for seven years at Odenbach's Peacock Room until it closed in 1947.

Eight

Pride in Rochester's Past

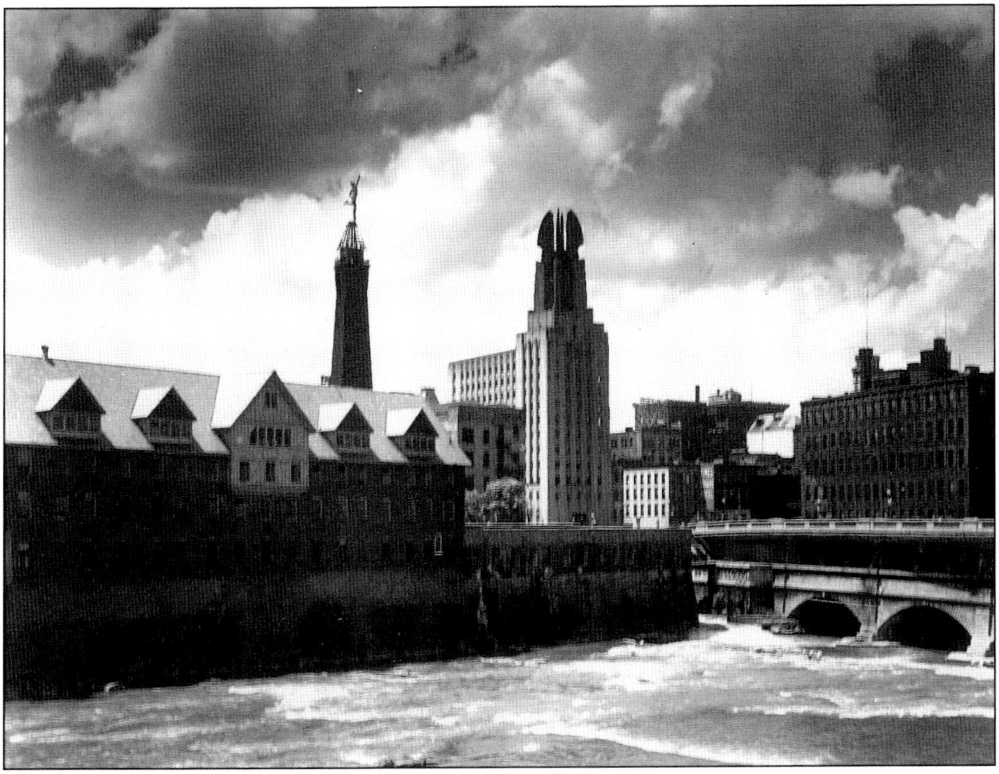

The statue of Mercury has been called Rochester's mascot. The statue graces the city's skyline, giving it charm and character. Not abstract art, Mercury is an honest-to-goodness classic motif, an icon, part of Rochester's civic pride. Perched atop the lofty old Peerless Tobacco factory smokestack for 70 years, the noble statue was viewed by countless thousands.

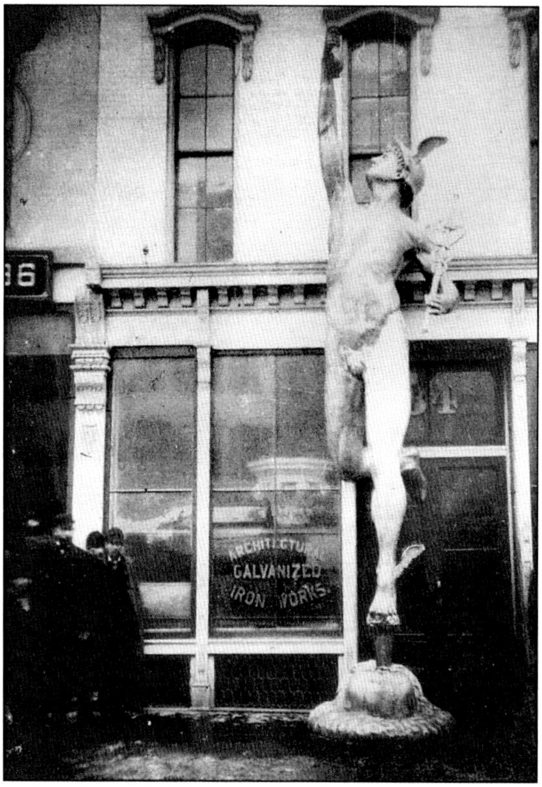

Mercury, fleet-footed messenger of the gods, symbolizes trade and the commercial vitality of Rochester. The statue's concept came from Laura Mitchell, wife of William Kimball of tobacco fame, to provide a classic aspect for her husband's factory smokestack. Her brother Guernsey S. Mitchell designed the 21-foot, 700-pound copper statue. The casting was prepared by the John Siddons Company of Rochester and was erected in January 1881. (Courtesy George J. Reynolds.)

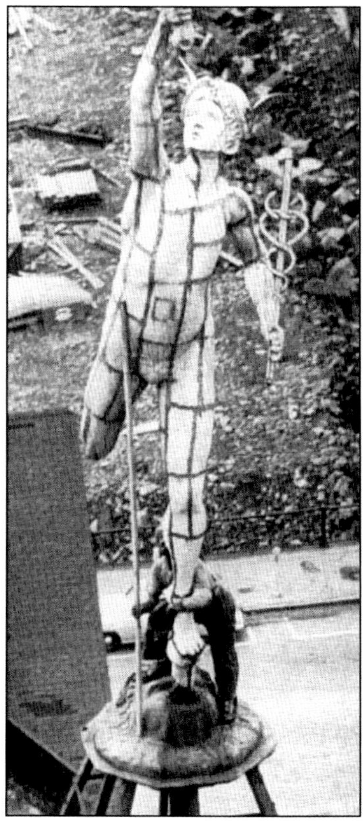

This 1951 view of Mercury reveals the castings that make up the statue after 70 years of exposure to the elements. The statue is being removed prior to the demolition of its smokestack perch. Although the copper has aged an antique green, Mercury is still in remarkably good shape. Only at this angle can one see that Mercury is set upon the head of Boreas, wild god of the North Wind.

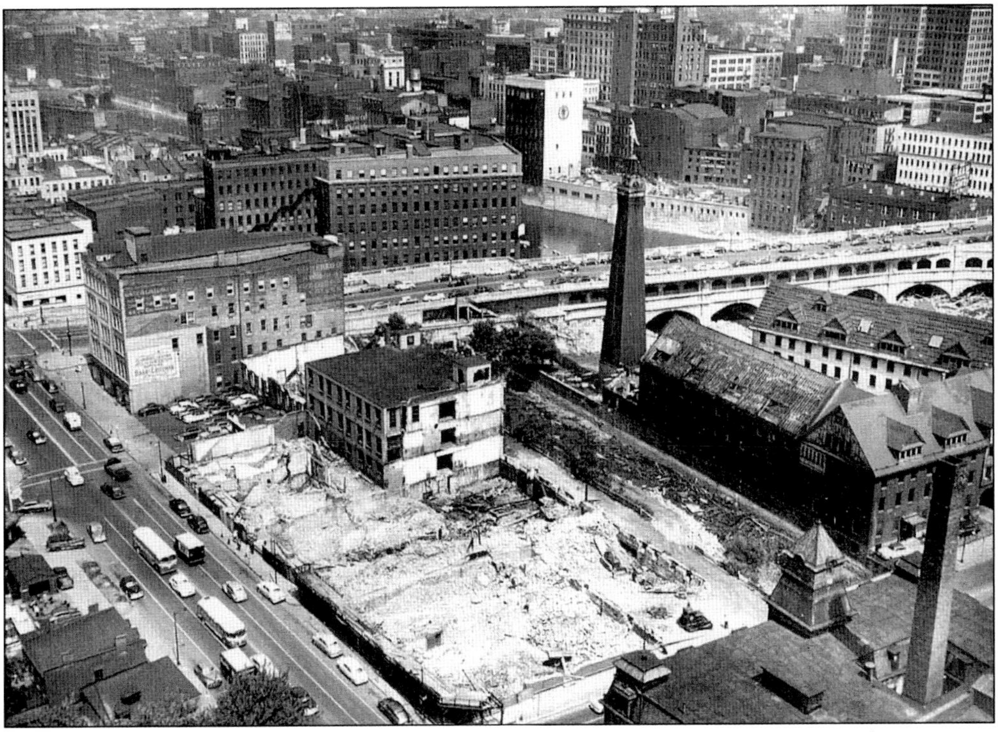

The city obtained possession of the Peerless-Cluet-Peabody Building in 1923, when George Eastman purchased the site. In 1951, the building (then known as the city hall annex) and surrounding ones were demolished to make room for construction of Rochester's War Memorial. In this view looking northeast, the jaunty statue and the former factory still stand. Broad Street Bridge is in the background. (Photograph S.P. Hines; courtesy George Brown.)

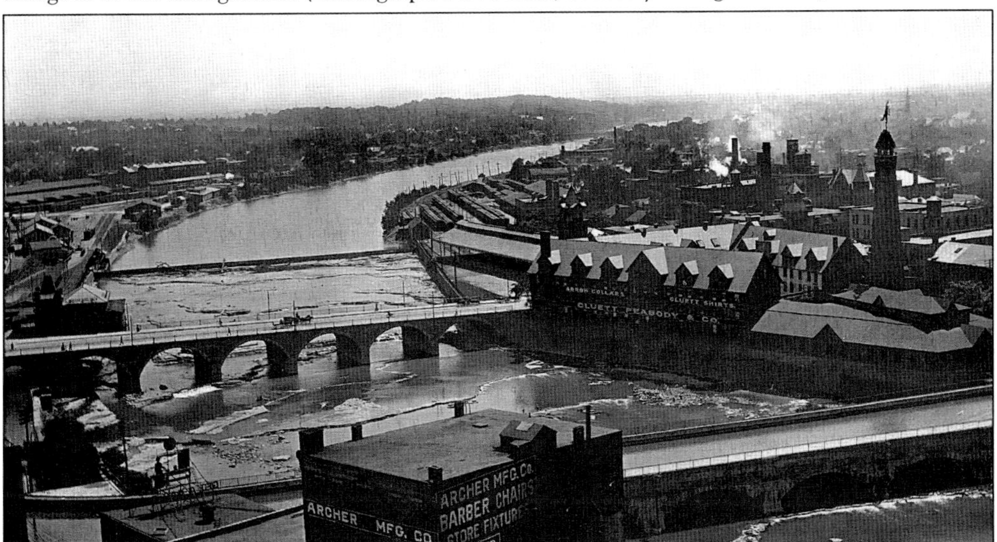

Taken from the Chamber of Commerce Building looking south, this photograph shows the Genesee River flowing past the Cluet-Peabody Company, seen at the right center. The shirt and collar manufacturers acquired the old Kimball tobacco company when it closed in 1905. The Erie Canal aqueduct is in the foreground.

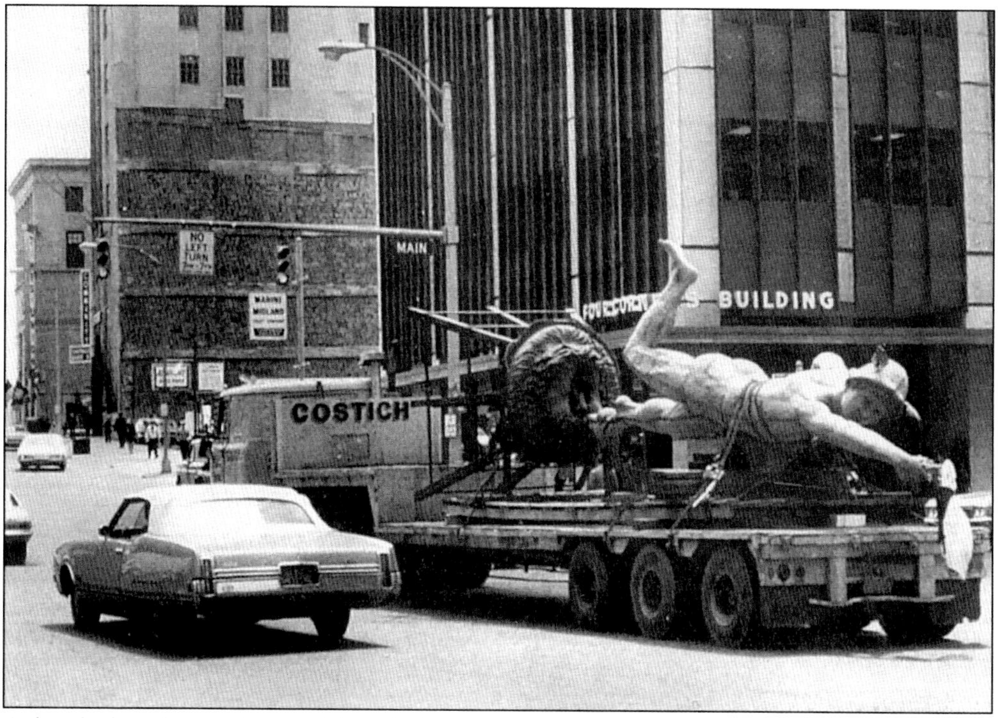

A low-bed trailer truck from Costich & Sons Movers trundles off the beloved Mercury to a municipal warehouse in Charlotte, where the noble statue was to languish for a quarter of a century.

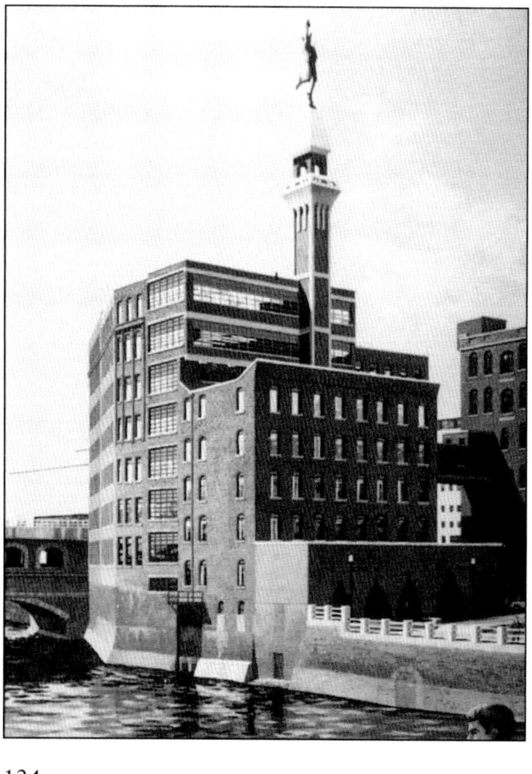

With Arch Merrill's persuasive campaign for the return of Mercury and the generous resources of the Lawyer's Co-operative Publishing Company, the city's "mascot" again arose in 1976, this time to be mounted some 163 feet above street level over the Aqueduct Building, atop the publishing firm's new 57-foot brick and concrete tower.

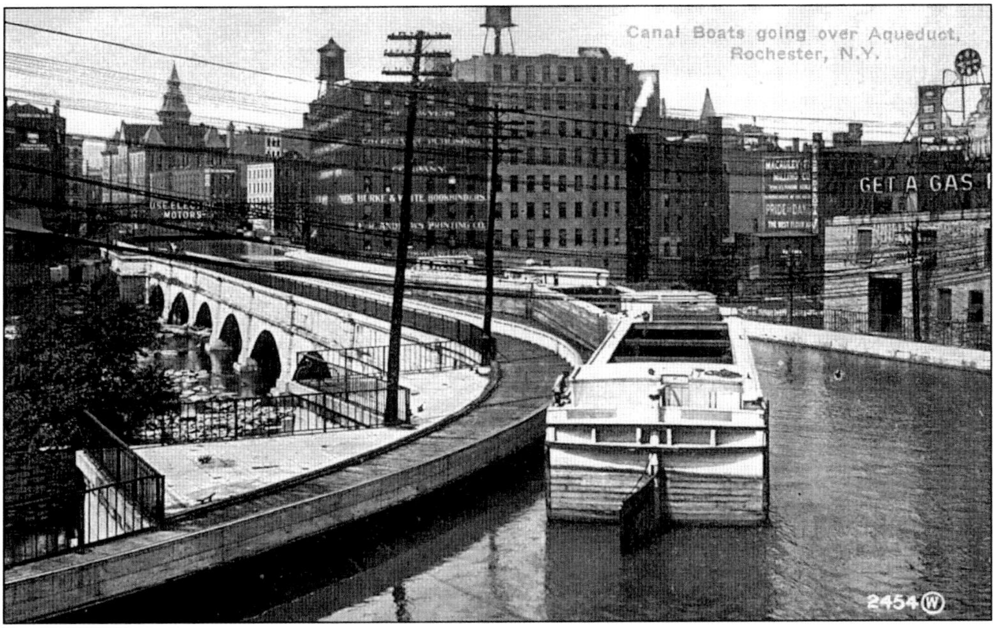

The longest aqueduct on the Erie Canal, this aqueduct was the only one built with a stone trough. When completed, it was considered a great engineering marvel of its day, one of which Rochester was justly proud. A freight boat navigates the tight bend onto Rochester's famous aqueduct. The 1912 photograph shows Lawyers Co-operative Publishing Company in the center, amid a maze of utility wires. City hall is visible on the horizon.

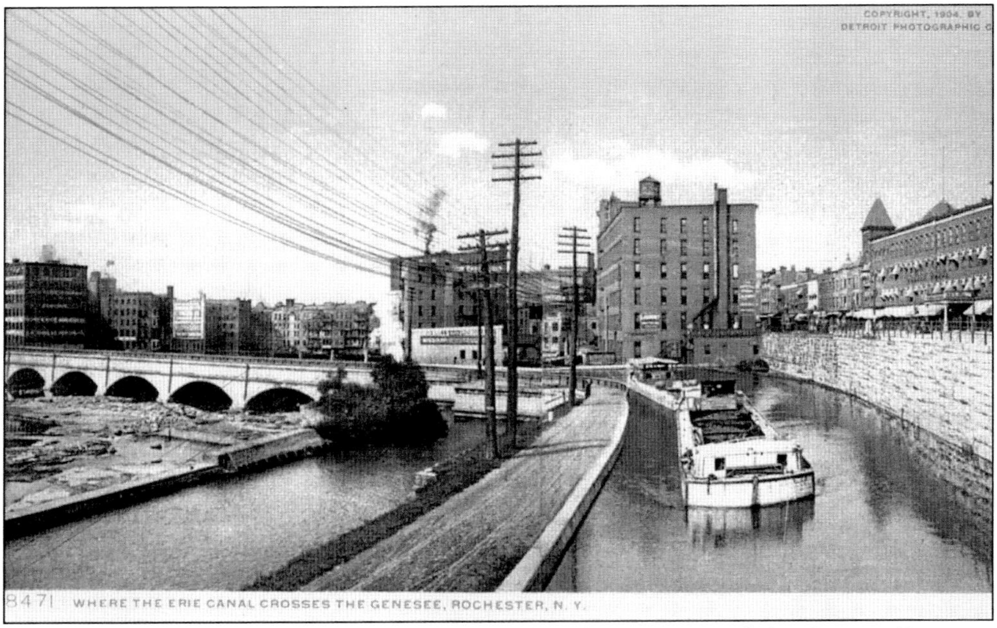

Seen in a view looking north in 1919, a freight boat has just crossed the Genesee River on the aqueduct. Constructed in 1824, the original Erie Canal aqueduct was built with blocks of Medina sandstone. A new structure of durable Onondaga limestone replaced the original in 1849. At the right is St. Paul Street.

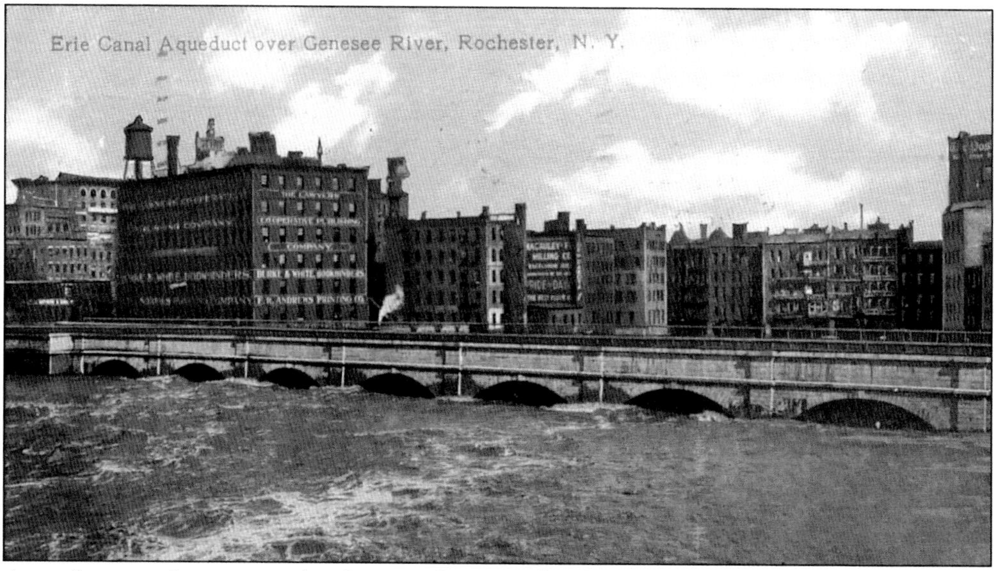

Annual spring thaws cause the Genesee River to flood, its waters hammering the aqueduct's limestone piers. However, this solid structure has steadfastly withstood the raging torrents with ease. Photographed in 1911, the swirling current has nearly covered the aqueduct's seven arches.

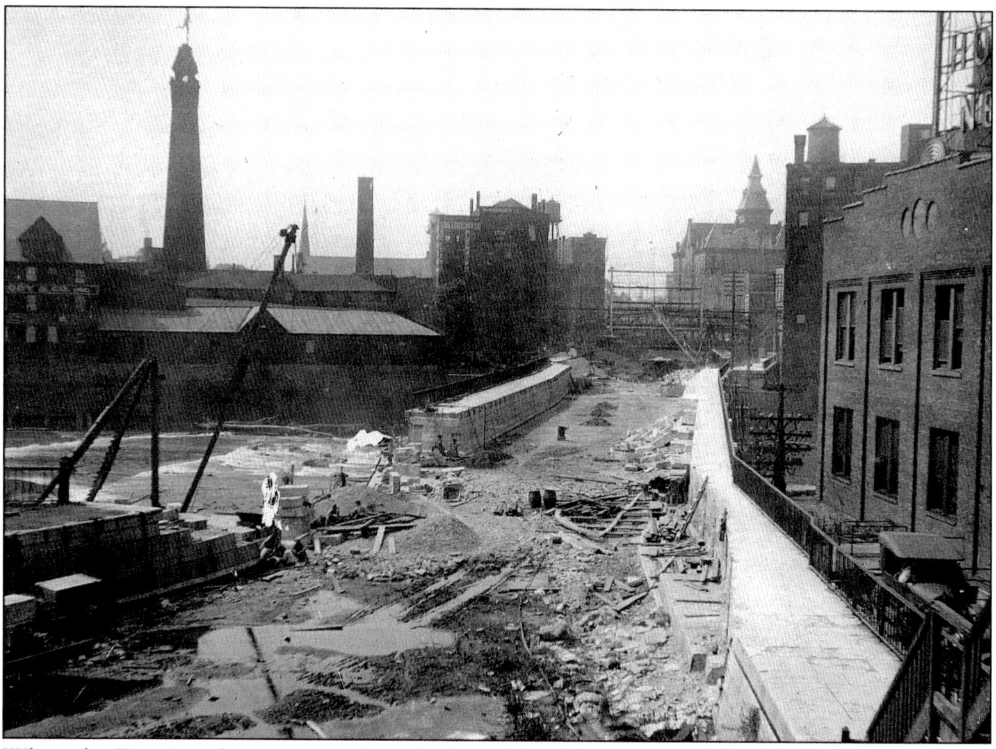

When the Erie Canal was rerouted south of Rochester in 1920, city fathers resolved to use the abandoned canal bed as the route for a new city subway. This photograph was taken in 1922 by W. Martin Jones, an amateur photographer. Looking west, it documents the work that was done on the aqueduct walls to expand them in order to make room for two subway rail beds.

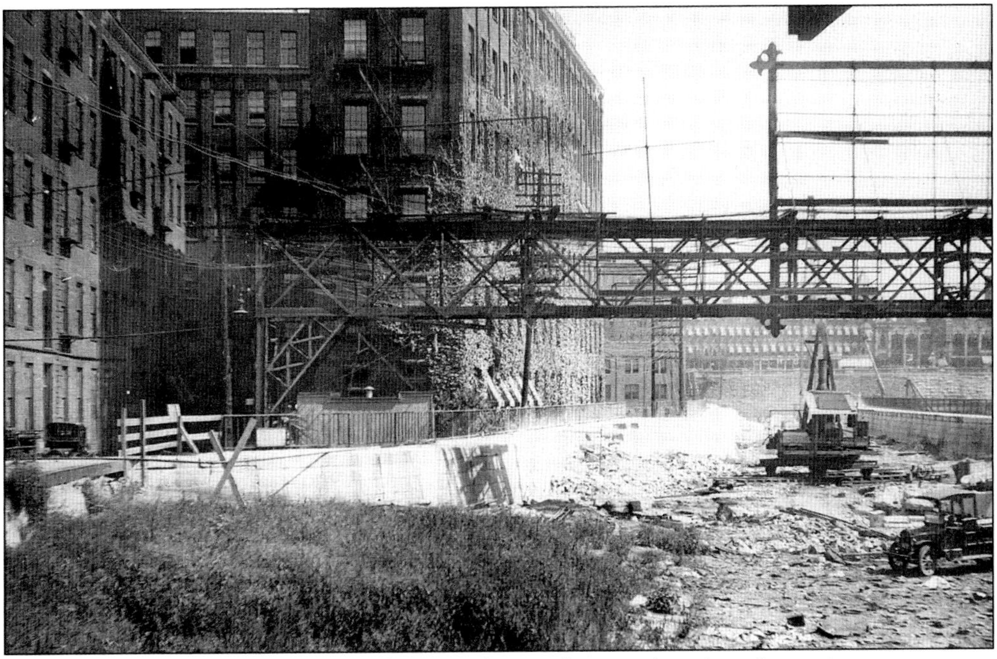

Looking east from Exchange Street, this view depicts the initial work in deepening a passageway to the aqueduct to accommodate both subway and rail cars. Lawyer's Co-operative Publishing Company is at the left.

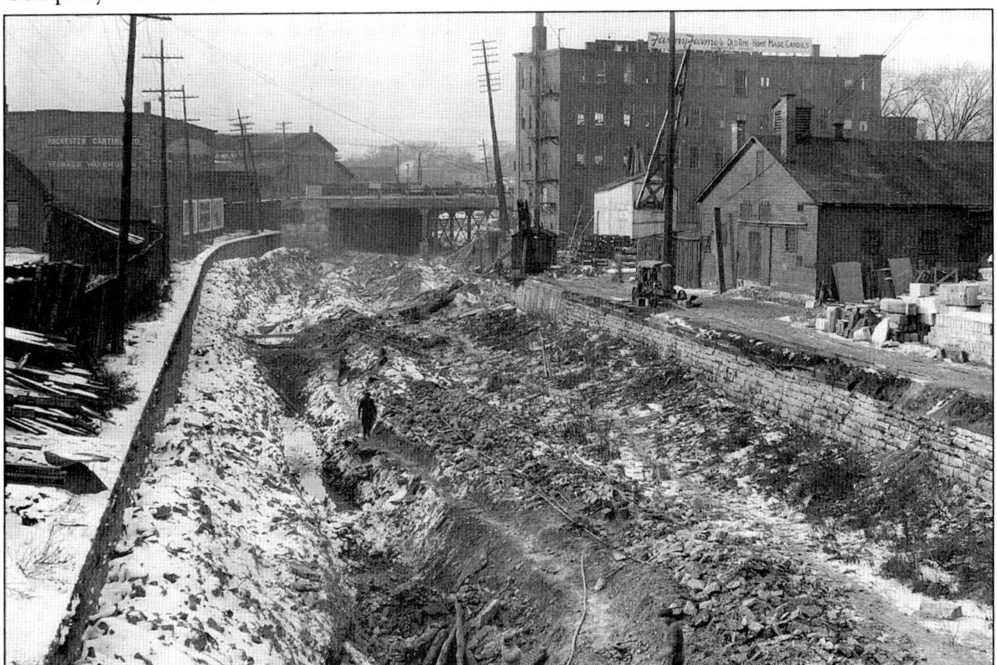

On the east side of the aqueduct, subway work progressed slowly. It was not until 1927 that the subway opened. To accomplish this, new walls were built, a drainage system was installed, tons of earth were moved, and rails were laid in position. At the left is the old stone warehouse on South Avenue. At the right is the Fanny Farmer candy factory.

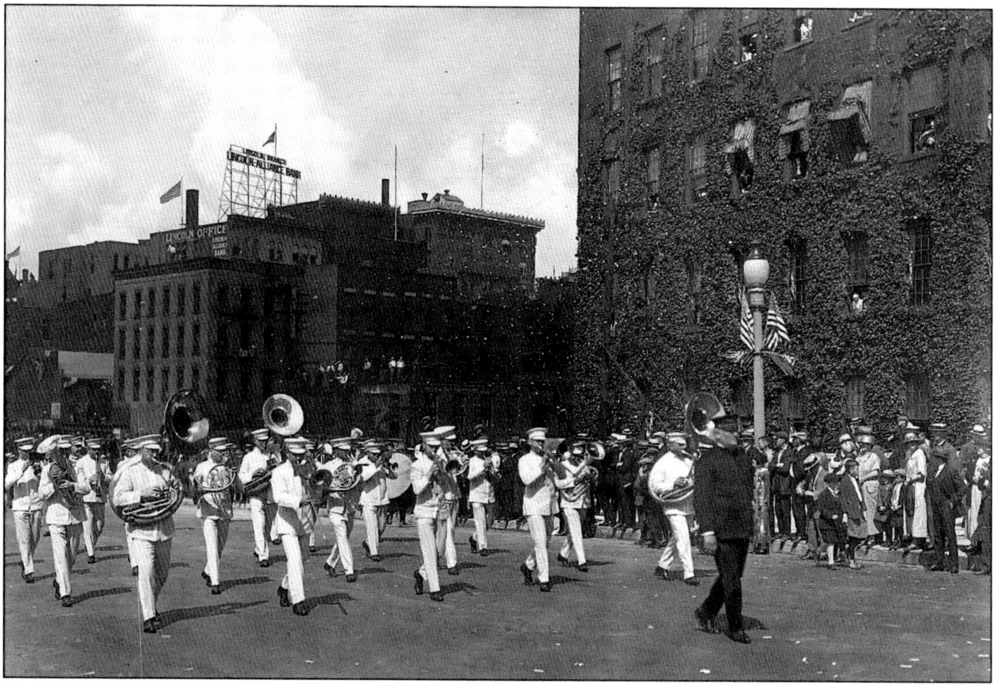

In order to bridge the aqueduct with an automobile route, it took "nearly 400 concrete columns and iron posts" to support the roadway. When completed, a parade and band concert were part of the Broad Street Opening Celebration, held on August 15, 1924.

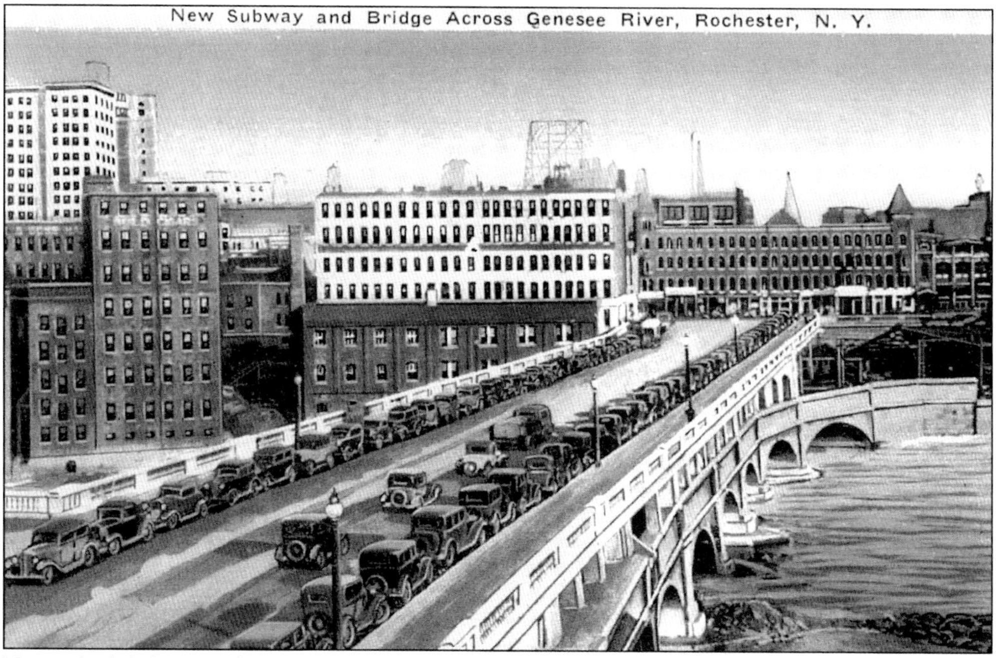

Not only did the aqueduct provide a path for the new subway, its bridging created a new access across the Genesee River. It serves as a parking area for more than 40 cars, as seen in this 1930s photograph. The Blue Bus terminal was at the Sullivan Building at South Avenue and Broad Street, on the left.